ARTHA

Meaning

FOUNDATIONS OF PHILOSOPHY IN INDIA

The series FOUNDATIONS OF PHILOSOPHY IN INDIA, initiated by the Centre for Philosophy and Foundations of Science, New Delhi, aims to make available a critical reassessment of the philosophical achievement of the classical Indian tradition in such a way that it contributes to the dialogue between civilizations of the new century. Although a wealth of literature is already available in translation, it exists in scattered form and is primarily oriented towards philological rather than philosophical concerns. The series will, uniquely in the history of scholarship in this area, focus on concepts and theories, rather than the conventional schools. The objective in each case will be to provide a rigorous and analytical examination of key arguments and doctrines in a manner that makes them available for contemporary engagement and reflection.

Although there is an interest worldwide in Indian philosophy, the absence of a corpus of texts which presents the contents of the tradition in a scholarly, well-researched yet accessible format, has long been a handicap. The FOUNDATIONS OF PHILOSOPHY IN INDIA series will, it is hoped, fill this gap in a systematic and comprehensive manner.

ARTHA

Meaning

Testimony and the Theory of Meaning in Indian Philosophical Analysis

Jonardon Ganeri

MOTILAL BANARSIDASS
PUBLISHERS PRIVATE LIMITED

OXFORD
UNIVERSITY PRESS

OXFORD
UNIVERSITY PRESS

Oxford University Press is a department of the University of Oxford.
It furthers the University's objective of excellence in research, scholarship,
and education by publishing worldwide. Oxford is a registered trademark of
Oxford University Press in the UK and in certain other countries

Published in India by
Oxford University Press
YMCA Library Building, 1 Jai Singh Road, New Delhi 110 001, India

First published 2006
Oxford India Paperbacks 2011
Third impression 2017

ISBN : 978-81-208-4122-2

Typeset in Nalandagaramond 10/12
at Le Studio Graphique, Gurgaon 122 001
Printed in India by Replika Press Pvt. Ltd.

Contents

Symbols

A	A set $\{A_1, A_2, \ldots, A_n\}$ of objects
A	The property A-hood, whose extension is A
/**A**/	The extension of **A**; i.e. the set A
$\mathbf{A} \leq \mathbf{B}$	The pervasion (*vyāpti*) relation between properties; defined as holding just in case $A \subseteq B$
A/x	The possession relation; defined as holding just in case $x \in A$
$\mathbf{A} \wedge \mathbf{B}$	The co-location relation between properties; defined as holding just in case $A \cap B \neq \varnothing$
$A \times \{\mathbf{A}\}$	The set of ordered pairs $\{\langle A_1, \mathbf{A}\rangle, \ldots, \langle A_n, \mathbf{A}\rangle\}$
$\{\mathbf{A}\}_=$	The set of properties co-extensive with **A**
Â	The individual essence (*tadvyaktitva*) of the object which, uniquely, is A
R	A relation; that is, a set of ordered pairs $\{R_{11}, \ldots, R_{ij}, \ldots, R_{nm}\}$
R	A relational abstract; a relational property such that /**R**/ = R
$R \vert B_j$	The class of things that stand in relation R to the object B_j; that is, the set $\{x: \langle x, B_j\rangle \in R\}$
$R \vert B$	The set of things that stand in relation R to some B; that is, the set $\{x: \langle x, y\rangle \in R; y \in B\}$
'A^i'	An inflected noun, having case ending i, where $1 \leq i \leq 7$
(S1)	'$A^6\,\mathbf{B}^1$' is true $\equiv A_i \in B$ ('$\equiv$' means 'if and only if')
(S2)	'$A^7\,B^6\,\mathbf{R}^1$' is true $\equiv \langle A_i, B_j\rangle \in R$
(S3)	'A^6 B–$\mathbf{R}^1$' is true $\equiv A_i \in R \vert B_j$, where 'B' is a proper name
(S4)	'A^6 B–$\mathbf{R}^1$' is true $\equiv A_i \in R \vert B$, where 'B' is a general term
(S5)	'$\mathbf{A}^3$ B–$\mathbf{R}^1$' is true $\equiv R \vert B \subseteq A$
$\mathcal{M}$	A meaning relation, holding between word-tokens and objects
$\mathcal{M}'$	A meaning relation, holding between word-tokens and object—mode pairs

$\mathscr{V}$	A content relation, holding between belief-tokens and objects
$\mathscr{V}'$	A content relation, holding between belief-tokens and object—mode pairs
'the* *F*'	A singular term referring to an object which is *F*
N	The property being-the-substratum-of-sounds, uniquely located in *ākāśa*
$\mathbf{S}^u$	The property being-the-speaker-of-utterance-*u*
$\mathbf{O}^u$	The property being-the-object-being-thought-of-by-the-speaker-of-utterance-*u*
$\mathbf{M}^u$	A property which is a qualifying mode thought of by the speaker of utterance *u*
$\underline{\mathbf{M}}^u$	The second-order property being-the-qualifying-mode-thought-of-by-the-speaker-of-utterance-*u*; that is, $\{\mathbf{M}^u\} = /\underline{\mathbf{M}}^u/$

Acknowledgements

I am grateful to Ranjit Nair, Director of the Centre for Philosophy and Foundations of Science, for his invitation to bring out a volume on the concept of meaning in the Centre's new series of volumes dealing with foundational concepts in Indian philosophical thought. The present work revises and updates my earlier treatment of the subject, published by Clarendon Press under the title *Semantic Powers*. That title hinted at the Sanskrit term *śakti*, a term used to denote the relationship between word and world. The new title mentions another technical term, *artha*, a rich term whose use in the context of philosophy of language is primarily in reference to the relata of the *śakti* relationship. The English term 'meaning' is, of course, ambigous in its use, extending to include both *śakti* and *artha*. This book deals with both of these concepts, and relates them, in particular, to the importance of testimony and the epistemology of meaning in the Indian discussion.

I would also like to thank Aparajita Basu at Oxford University Press India, with whom I have had the great pleasure of collaborating on a number of projects, of which this is only the latest. I have benefited too from reviews of *Semantic Powers* by Godabarishi Mishra, Stephen Phillips, Harold Coward, and Eivind Kahrs, whose thoughtful comments have been of considerable help in the preparation of this new text.

JONARDON GANERI

Introduction

Words have powers, as do the people who understand them. A word has the power to stand in for or take the place of a thing. Vibrations in the air, or ink marks on paper, manage somehow to act as substitutes for people and places, planets and atoms, thoughts and feelings. It is to this extraordinary function that the Sanskrit term for 'meaning' calls attention: *śakti*—the power or capacity of a word to stand for an object. People who understand words have powers as well; most remarkably, the capacity to acquire *knowledge* about people, places, planets, and so on, just by hearing noises or seeing marks. This too is a power, just as surely is the power to see or remember or reason. It is the power to receive knowledge from the testimony of others. It is not all that surprising that these two powers, the semantic power of a word and the epistemic power of a hearer or reader, should be connected; but it was the singular achievement of the Indian philosophers of language to analyse the nature of that connection in far greater depth than anyone had done before.

The study of language, indeed, occupies a position of immense significance in India's intellectual history. Many centuries before the emergence of organized philosophical schools, sophisticated linguistic techniques including rule-based grammars and quasi-empirical methods of investigation were being developed in order to explore the structure of the Sanskrit language. Pāṇini's fourth century BC grammar, which the linguist Leonard Bloomfield famously described as 'one of the greatest monuments of human intelligence' (1933: 11), proved an impressive model for later grammarians and philosophers of language. Those grammarians who followed him, notably Patañjali and Bhartṛhari, drew out questions of an explicitly philosophical and logical nature from Pāṇini's work.[1]

The Indian linguists were not, however, the only ones for whom the study of language was of pre-eminent importance. The proper interpretation of the Vedic canon, especially the meaning of injunctions and precepts involved in ritual practice, was of great significance within

Brahminical society. Mīmāṃsā, the science of Vedic hermeneutics, involved itself not only with questions about the consistency and coherence of the Vedic corpus, but engaged more widely in developing a philosophical account of language, the origins, and nature of meaning. Then there were the mainstream philosophical schools belonging to the Indian epistemological tradition: the Nyāya, Vaiśeṣika, Buddhist, and sceptical authors who operated within the conceptual boundaries of the *pramāṇa* methodology. For these philosophers too, language occupied a central place, this time because of the epistemological importance attributed to testimony. Concern with the communication of knowledge focused attention on the nature of understanding and interpreting another's speech, and the relation between meaning and truth. From this confluence of interest, the main themes later to emerge in Indian philosophy of language were debates over whether semantic properties are natural or conventional, extended discussion of the nature of the meaning relation and its proper relata, the issue of whether words as against sentences are the principal bearers of meaning, and more general explorations into linguistics and the epistemology of testimony.

In this book I will give attention to thinkers in the various grammatical and philosophical schools, but will concentrate primarily on the school of Nyāya, whose authors entered into an extraordinary rich and diverse discussion of the problem of meaning over a period of some fifteen centuries. Their ideas, I will argue, speak strongly to contemporary concerns in the philosophy of language. Two principal claims will inform the theory of meaning whose contours are to be developed. The first is that the central function of a word is to stand for an object, and hence that the meaning (*artha*) of a word is to be identified with the object for which it stands. The Indian literature in general exhibits from a very early stage a preference for a 'realist' or 'direct referential' approach to meaning (Chapters 1, 2). This is in marked contrast to the western literature, in which that approach has only recently become widely respectable.[2] Attention to the indexical nature of many expressions led Indian philosophers to draw a distinction between two notions of meaning: the reference of an expression on any occasion of its use (*artha* or *padārtha*), and a constant, unvarying meaning element, variously thought of as the 'basis' for the use (*pravṛtti-nimitta*) of the term, as the delimiter of its scope (*śakyatāvacchedaka*), or simply as what remains constant across contexts (*anugama*). One of the later Navya-Nyāya philosophers, Gadādhara Bhaṭṭācārya (fl. AD 1604–1709), was unusually sensitive to the problems ensuing from the realist theory, and this is one reason his work in semantics is of such significance. Uniquely in Indian literature, he considers the distinctive semantic properties of a great variety of referential constructions, including anaphoric pronouns, indexicals embedded within speech reports, and stipulatively introduced theoretical terms. The disciplines of philosophy of language and semantic theory should recognize him as one of its great historical figures.

Another idea to inform the Indian account is that a language is primarily a device for the reception of knowledge (Chapters 4, 5). The Indians developed an epistemology based upon the doctrine that epistemological agents are endowed with capacities or faculties for the acquisition of knowledge, the so-called *pramāṇas*. The perceptual and the inferential faculties are the paradigmatic examples. Just how such faculties are to be characterized is a difficult question, but it seems that they are processes whose non-defective or actual function is the production of true beliefs. Beliefs produced by such a process, in the absence of defeating conditions, carry epistemic warrant. The extension of this idea to language motivates a claim that to be linguistically competent is itself to be endowed with a faculty the exercise of which leads to the acquisition of knowledge, knowledge gleaned from the testimony of others. From its earliest time, the Indians study language as *essentially* a device for the reception of knowledge from others. We find this idea even in the *Nyāya-sūtra*, where it is said that 'speech is a didactic statement made by an authority'.[3] It is from this use that the word *pramāṇa* enters the English language in its Persian corruption *firman*, meaning 'an edict or order issued by an Oriental sovereign'.[4] In later Nyāya, the idea takes a rather different direction. The emphasis there is that the possibility of testimony constrains the form a theory of meaning must take. Gaṅgeśa, the founder of Navya-Nyāya, states that meaning is that relation between words and objects which is 'favourable' to the production of testimonial knowledge.[5] We decide what meaning is by describing what must be the case if language is to be a source of knowledge. This significantly complicates the identification of the 'meaning' (*artha* or *padārtha*) of a word with its reference alone, and leads to a reconceptualization of the old debate over whether 'meanings' are particulars on universals, contextually determined individuals or context-free generalities.

There is, indeed, a tension between the conception of language as primarily an instrument of knowing and the realist theory of meaning. The problem is that the epistemic warrant of a belief produced by the language faculty is not invariant under substitution of co-referring terms. It is not sufficient for the acquisition of testimonial knowledge that one gets the reference right. So the epistemological constraint on meaning necessitates a revision in the realist account. As we will see, each of the major thinkers attempts, in one way or another, to resolve this tension between the two central tenets in their theory of meaning.

One solution is to introduce 'modes of thought' (*viṣaya-tāvacchedaka*) into the theory of meaning. Briefly, the argument is that, if the possibility of testimony is central to the correct use of language, and more particularly, if correctly understanding an utterance typically consists in assenting to what is said, and the belief so formed is, subject to the satisfaction of certain external conditions, an item of knowledge, then the meaning of an expression must be identified with its contribution to the content of items of knowledge to which its utterance gives rise. Now, if the speaker utters the sentence '*Fa*', and the hearer, assenting to this utterance, forms the belief that *Fb*, where, as it happens, $a = b$, then, while the hearer has picked out the right object, the belief does not constitute knowledge. Testimonial beliefs are warranted only if the hearer identifies the object in a certain way, under a certain 'mode of thought'. So the meaning of an expression is not to be identified with its reference alone, but also with the way the reference is to be thought of (Chapter 6).

The introduction of modes into the theory of meaning raises many questions, about their nature and their role. The modes, I shall argue, satisfy one main condition for being Fregean senses: as adverbial modifiers of the thought-object relation, they are implicated in one's possession of discriminating knowledge of objects. The later Indian philosophers of language, indeed, construct a taxonomy of expressions based on what is involved in discriminating the reference of a term. Having introduced modes of thought into the theory of meaning, they are able to give a new account of two important kinds of term which earlier writers had little or no success in explaining: names (Chapter 8)and pronouns (Chapter 9). The material in this book need not be read in the order I have arranged it. A reader who wishes, first of all, to see what each of the various Indian schools or system has to say about 'meaning' might prefer to take the material in still another order. Discussion of the theory of meaning in a range of different schools is to be found throughout the book. In particular, the sections of the book correspond to schools roughly as follows: Grammarian theories of meaning (Vyāḍi, Vājapyāyana, Pāṇini, Patañjali, Bhartṛhari) §§ 1.3, 2.2, 2.3, 3.1; Mīmāṃsaka theories of meaning (Jaimini, Śabara, Kumārila) §§ 1.2, 4.2, 4.3, 8.2; Buddhist theories of meaning (Dinnāga, Śāntarakṣita, Kamalaśīla) §§ 2.2, 8.2; early Naiyāyika theories of meaning (Gautama, Uddyotakara, Jayanta, Udayana) §§ 1.4, 3.2, 6.3, 8.1; Navya-Naiyāyika theories of meaning

(Gaṅgeśa, Vardhamāna, Raghunātha, Jagadīśa, Gadādhara) Chapters 6, 7, §§ 8.3, 8.4, Chapter 9. Vedāntin theories of meaning (Śankarācārya, Rāmānuja) receive brief treatment in Chapter 6 and Chapter 8 notes.

It is my great privilege that this book is appearing in the series Foundations of Philosophy in India, coordinated by Ranjit Nair and published by Oxford University Press, India. The guiding conception of this important new series is 'to provide a rigorous and analytical examination of key arguments and doctrines in a manner that makes them available for contemporary engagement and reflection', its aim to 'make available a critical reassessment of the philosophical achievement of the classical Indian tradition in such a way that it contributes to the dialogue between civilizations'. This conception is one I wholeheartedly endorse, and I very much hope that the approach to the Indian literature on meaning I have taken in this book makes a contribution to the important ambition of the series.

Notes

[1] See, for example, Coward & Raja (1990), Houben (1995), and Scharfe (1961).

[2] J.S. Mill and Bertrand Russell are exceptions, but the majority of western philosophers of language argued that there must be an intermediate entity, be it an idea, concept, or Fregean *Sinn*, to which the notion of meaning attaches. Kripke, Putnam, Kaplan and others have revived the realist or 'direct reference' theory in recent times.

[3] *śabdam āptopadeśam* (NS 1.1.7).

[4] This meaning is from the O.E.D., s.v. firman.

[5] *śābdabodha-hetu-padārthopasthityanukūlaḥ pada-padārthayoḥ saṃbandhaḥ vṛttiḥ*. Gaṅgeśa (1901). The primary source for the Navya-Nyāya account of testimony is Jagadīśa, specifically the first five *kārikas* of his *Śabda-śakti-prakāśikā* (Jagadīśa 1934). A French translation of this section has been published by Kamaleswar Bhattacharya (1979), and there is an inadequate English translation in Vidyabhusana (1920: 470–6). Jagadīśa's arguments are considered by several contributors to the collection of Matilal & Chakrabarti (1994).

Part I

Meaning and Meanings

1

Artha

Meanings as Entities

1.1 The Realist Theory of Meaning

The realist theory of meaning states that the meaning of an expression is the external object for which it stands.[1] Some form of the realist theory has a good claim to be our pre-theoretical or 'folk' semantics, to capture an intuitive view about meaning. Its roots lie in a basic idea about the nature of symbols: that symbols are *stand-ins* for things symbolized (see the discussion in Kahrs 1998). In the Indian philosophical tradition, much speculation about the notion of meaning centred on, or better assumed, such a theory. This is particularly so in the work of the early grammarians, Mīmāṃsakas, Buddhists, and Naiyāyikas who belonged to the classical period of Indian philosophy, a period which ended in AD 900 or 1000. In this chapter, I will examine the arguments of these philosophers.

One main debate was not so much whether it is correct to identify meanings with external entities per se, but rather with what sort of entity they should be identified. The early Indian philosophers of language focused their attention on so-called 'general nominal terms' (*jātiśabda*), that is, nouns like '[a/the] cow', '[a/the] pot', and '[a/the] person', a group which corresponds with the class of non-complex descriptions in English.[2] The pivotal debate concerned the relative merits of two rival positions: 'meaning particularism' (*vyakti-śakti-vāda*) and 'meaning generalism' (*jāti-śakti-vāda*).[3] The first of these positions asserts that the meaning relatum of a nominal is a particular object, a doctrine which is very roughly comparable to the thesis that descriptions are referential or singular terms.[4] The other side, generalism, asserts that the meaning relatum of a nominal is a general feature or property. One way to understand that position is in comparison with Russell's theory that descriptions do not refer, but have the logical form of quantifier-predicate constructions, the basis for the comparison being that the extension or 'semantic value' of a predicate is a class.[5] Another way is to understand generalism as speaking in the first instance about the so-called 'generic' uses of nouns. We will examine these different construals of the doctrine in the next section.

I will separate out two distinct issues in this debate. Let us assume that descriptions do have an external correlate, a semantic value. The first issue concerns the nature of this entity: is it particular or general? Another way to put this, the question here is whether descriptions are referential or non-referential, for a term is 'referential' if its semantic value is a particular. The second issue concerns the defensibility of identifying the *meaning* of the term with its external correlate (its *artha*). That is what the realist theory of meanings asserts, independently of any resolution of the first question. Particularism is the doctrine that the meaning of a description is a particular, a doctrine which thus factors into the pairs of claims (i) that the realist theory of meaning is true, and (ii) descriptions are referential expressions. In this chapter, I will examine the arguments for and against a referentialist interpretation of descriptions. In the next chapter, I argue that Indian philosophers of language came to see that the referentialist interpretation is inconsistent with the realist theory of meaning, and I will examine the consequences of that realization.

We must first delineate more precisely the syntactic class with which we are concerned. A 'general term' or *jāti-śabda* is composed of a stem derived from a nominal base, to which is added an inflection indicating number, gender, and case. Thus, from the base *go* 'cow', one derives *gauḥ* = *gau* ± *ḥ* '[a/the] cow', *gāvaḥ* = *gau* ± *aḥ* '[some/the] cows', and so on. I have already remarked that this group of NPs corresponds to the class of non-composite descriptions. However, it is well known that classical Sanskrit only very rarely employs determiners, and it is therefore open as to whether the inflected nominal is to be thought of as corresponding to a definite or to an indefinite description (hence my use of bracketed determiners in the translation). Furthermore, whether definite or indefinite, it is also open as to whether the inflected noun is being used generically or non-generically.[6] There are thus four possible syntactic categories into which any given use of an inflected nominal might fall: (1) definite generics; (2) indefinite generics; (3) definite non-generics; and (4) indefinite non-generics. In fact, instances of all four uses can be found even within the examples our authors themselves discuss[7]:

(1) *gauḥ sāsnādimān* The cow has a dewlap, etc.

(2)	*gaur gāṃ janayati*	A cow produces a cow
	gaur na padā spraṣṭavyaḥ	A cow should not be kicked
(3)	*kauṇḍinyasya gauḥ*	The cow belongs to Kauṇḍinya (or Kauṇḍinya's cow)
	gaur niṣaṇṇaḥ	The cow is lying down
(4)	*gām ānaya*	Bring a cow
	vaidyāya gāṃ dadāti	He gives a cow to the physician

The lack of syntactic markers to distinguish these uses in Sanskrit makes for great potential confusion. Yet the distinctions matter crucially for a proper understanding of the arguments. For clearly one might be a referentialist about *definite* descriptions without being so about *indefinite* descriptions; likewise, one might be a referentialist about generic uses, but not about non-generic uses. It is particularly easy to be confused here about the status of meaning generalism, the thesis that the meaning relatum of a general term is a universal property. This thesis is naturally read as a proposal about the generic use of descriptions, that when used generically a description 'means' a genus. However, it is also read as a proposal about non-generically used descriptions, that *they* are not referential expressions. While we cannot expect the early authors always to escape confusion, we can, with care, disambiguate their claims and evaluate them accordingly.

As well as occurring as the subject in a sentence, an inflected nominal can also occur predicatively. Here too there need be no syntactic indication that the noun has a predicative role. The reason is that classical Sanskrit permits the construction of so-called 'nominal sentences', sentences in which two or more nouns stand in apposition without any verbal element, one being the subject, the other a non-verbal predicate. Such constructions are a feature of many Indo-European languages, but are rather rare in English. When they do occur, they are distinguished from sentences merely involving ellipsis of the verb in that their subject is typically enclitic: 'dark the Sun and Moon, and the Almanach de Gotha' (T.S. Eliot, cited in Coulson 1976: 47). Word order, though less important, is relevant in Sanskrit too, serving to distinguish a non-verbal predicate from an adjective qualifying the subject. The general rule is that the predicate takes final position:[8]

(5)	*ghaṭo nīlaḥ*	The pot is blue.
	nīlo ghaṭaḥ ...	The blue pot ... .
	svalpo ghaṭo nīlaḥ	The small pot is blue.

When the predicate is a substantive, however, this rule need not hold:

(6)	*ghaṭaḥ saḥ*	That is the pot.
	svalpaṃ sukhaṃ krodhaḥ	Anger is a small pleasure.

The terms we are interested in can occur, then, in both subject and predicate position. This raises the possibility that the two proposals for the semantics of these terms, particularism and generalism, are not rivals at all, but concern, respectively, the role of general terms as names and as predicates in a sentence. Fortunately, we can reject at least this possibility, for both parties to the debate are clear that they are discussing the role of a general term in subject position. Moreover, a 'two name + identity' theory of predication was widely endorsed, according to which both terms in a nominal sentence are used substantively, apposition between the inflections being the syntactic marker of an identity relation.

Throughout this book, I will use the following system of notation. I will extend the notation in various ways as we proceed. My aim will be to develop a notational system which accurately reflects the structure of the artificial Sanskrit employed by the Indian semanticists, while being reasonably in keeping with standard modern practice. Suppose that 'A' is a term belonging to the class of descriptive nominals. Then let A be the class $\{A_1, ..., A_i, ..., A_n\}$ of As. Here A_i is a member of A, where $1 \leq i \leq n$ and n is the cardinality of A. Furthermore, let '**A**' be the abstract term 'A-ness', and let **A** be the property A-ness. So A is the extension of **A** and A_i is one of its instances. Also, let 'A ...' be the predicate '... is an A'. So, if '/**A**/' denotes the extension of a property **A**, we have:

$A_i \in A = /\mathbf{A}/$. That is, each A_i is a member of the extension of the property **A**.

As we will see, the idiom of philosophical Sanskrit is intensional: it speaks of the property pothood being instantiated in a particular object where in English we would say simply that the object is a pot. My notation will help us to keep track of which concepts are genuinely intensional, and which are really extensional concepts in an intensional garb.[9]

1.2 Meanings as Generalities (jātiśaktivāda)

It was the celebrated grammarian Patañjali (*c.* 150 BC) who first discussed in detail the philosophical analysis of the meaning of descriptions:

> Now, what is the 'meaning' (*artha*) of a word? Is it a particular object (*dravya*), or is it a general feature (*ākṛti*)?[10]

An earlier etymologist Yāska had already divided the 'parts of speech' (*pada*) into four groups: nouns or names (*nāma*), verbs (*ākhyāta*), verbal affixes (*upasarga*), and particles or 'invariant words' (*nipāta*). Patañjali's question was about the meaning of the first of these groups, a group which in fact included proper names and pronouns, as well as descriptions. It seemed to the early grammarians that the linguistic significance of such words consists in their being associated with an entity of some kind. Yāska called this entity a *sattva* 'thing', and other grammarians used the term 'artha' in the sense of meaning-relatum or 'correlated entity'. They took for granted a realist, as opposed to ideational, theory of meaning: the meaning of an entity is the external object for which it stands, rather than an idea, concept or mental construct with which it is in some way associated.

What does Patañjali have in mind when he asks if the meaning of a description is a general feature? He elaborates the point by mentioning one of Pāṇini's grammatical rules, *P* 1.2.58, a rule which appears to link meaning generalism with the generic use of nominals. *P* 1.2.58 states that 'the plural is optionally used in the sense of the singular when designating a species (*jāti*)'. This rule permits one to replace a nominal in the singular with the same nominal in the plural, as in the replacement of '(A/The) young Brahmin is to be greeted by rising from one's seat' by 'Young Brahmins are to be greeted by rising from one's seat' (the example is Kātyāyana's). As Patañjali observes, if the nominal were construed as referring to a particular Brahmin, this rule would be invalid. The rule is valid, however, when the description has a generic sense, for something said about a kind can entail something about each of its members. A slightly different sort of example might be the replacement of singular with plural affix in the sentence 'Man is mortal', to produce 'Men are mortal'.

The pluralization rule *P* 1.2.58 is clearly applicable only when the description is being used in a generic sense. Patañjali claims that this rule shows that, at least when used in certain contexts, the meaning relatum of a generic nominal is a universal or class. It is clear that Patañjali's concern here is with the distinction between generic and non-generic uses of descriptions. His claim is that a description used generically refers to the genus. There is, however, a problem with this claim. For we must be careful to distinguish between *distributive* predicates, like '... is a mammal', which are true of each member of the kind individually, and, on the other hand, *collective* predicates, like '... is becoming extinct', which are true of the kind without being true of its members. The sentence 'The whale is facing extinction' does not entail that each individual whale is facing extinction, for only a species can become extinct. Now Patañjali's claim that descriptions used generically refer to the genus seems to be correct at best for sentences where the predicate is collective, for such sentences do seem to be singular predications of the genus. The problem is that it is only for sentences with distributive predicates that the pluralization rule is valid!

What might we say to this? Suppose that 'The A' is a generically used description, and that 'B' is a distributive predicate. Furthermore, suppose that we define a partial order '$\leq$' on the class of properties, such that:

(1) $\mathbf{A} \leq \mathbf{B}$ iff $A \subseteq B$.

The partial order '$\leq$' came to be known in the Indian literature as the 'pervasion' (*vyāpti*) relation. One property is pervaded by another iff the extension of the former is within the extension of the latter. Thus, although defined over properties, pervasion is really an extensional notion (see also §3.2). The truth-condition for generic descriptions with distributive predicates, on the generalist assumption that descriptions take properties as external correlates, must then be:

(2) 'The A is B' is true iff $\mathbf{A} \leq \mathbf{B}$.

Thus, the sentence 'The A is B' does not state a *singular* predication of a kind, but a *second-order* relation between properties. The truth-condition given here is equivalent to the more familiar truth-condition for sentences with universal subjects: $(\forall x: Ax)(Bx)$.[11] Thus, Patañjali's pluralization rule is indeed valid when the sentence has as its subject a generically used description and as its predicate a distributive predicate.

A rather different rule will pick out generic description sentences with collective predicates. What we need is a prohibition on the substitution of 'The F is G' by 'Some F is G'. For that substitution is permissible when the description is used non-generically, and also when it is used generically with a distributive predicate. It is only impermissible when the predicate is collective, as in the case of 'The whale is becoming extinct'. The correct result is obtained by taking the meaning of a generic description to be a property, and that of a collective predicate to be a property of properties. Let us denote the fact that an object, x, possesses a property $\mathbf{A}$, by '$\mathbf{A}/x$', where this is defined as: $\mathbf{A}/x$ iff $x \in A$. We therefore treat the concept of property possession as if it were equivalent to the extensional notion of set membership. Then, when a sentence is read as having a generic subject and collective predicate, its truth-condition has the form:

(3) 'The A is B' is true iff **B**/**A**.

Thus, 'The whale is becoming extinct' is true iff whale-hood is a extinction possessor. The upshot is that we can indeed give a satisfactory account of the generic uses of descriptions along the lines Patañjali proposes, provided we allow that the logical form of sentences with distributive predicates is different from those with collective predicates.

As for the non-generic uses of descriptions, Patañjali himself is a referentialist (see §1.3). So, for an account of the non-generic use within a generalist framework, we must look elsewhere. The generalist theory is that, for any inflected nominal 'A',

(G) 'A' means **A**.

This thesis is endorsed, most notably, by the Mimāṃsaka philosophers. They wanted to explain the universal application of Vedic injunctions. As Matilal notes, 'Vājapyāyana [a grammarian to whom Patañjali attributes the generalist theory] was, perhaps, more concerned with law-like statements and the Mīmāṃsā formulae of the Scripture. Hence, he stressed the quality aspect (the generic aspect) of meaning, thus creating the philosophical background for the development of the notion of universal' (1971: 107). The idea is not that Vedic injunctions are all universally quantified statements, though indeed some are. Their law-like status consists in their not mentioning any particular object. Kumārila (1903: 273) offers a down-to-earth example:[12]

> When no [particular] object is indicated, an order 'Bring [a] cow' is an instruction to bring any individual belonging to the species [cowhood]. It is not [an instruction to bring] a specific [cow] nor [to bring] all [cows]. If, however, a particular is [taken to be] the meaning-relatum (*abhidheya*), then since every [cow] is simultaneously 'meant' (*abhihita*), [the order] would be to bring [all of them] without remainder. Or else, one should bring just that one [particular] which is the meaning-relatum. However, from the fact that [the order commands that] he brings an unspecific [object] belonging to the species, it is ascertained that the meaning-relatum (*padārtha*) is a generality (*sāmānya*).

Kumārila here clearly takes the logical form of the injunction to be an existential quantification. The point, then, is that the Mīmāṃsā injunctions are quantified constructions, containing no reference to *particular* objects.

Kumārila, clearly, is concerned with non-generics used indefinitely, and not with the generic use of nominals. His argument is that we cannot take an indefinite description to refer to a particular, for this would give a sentence containing an indefinite the wrong truth-conditions. The sentence 'A cow has been bought', for example, is true just in case some arbitrary cow has been bought. It does not state that some definite cow, Śābaleya say, has been brought. Kumārila therefore proposes that the semantic value of 'a cow' here is the property cowhood. The sentence is true just in case cowhood is co-located with the property being-bought. The 'co-location' relation '$\wedge$' between two properties is defined in the obvious way, in terms of non-empty intersection:

(4) $A \wedge B$ iff $A \cap B \neq \emptyset$.

Kumārila's proposal is thus that:

(5) 'An A is B' is true iff $\mathbf{A} \wedge \mathbf{B}$,

where 'An A' is an indefinite and non-generic use of a description. This is equivalent to the more familiar truth-condition for indefinites, $(\exists x: Ax)(Bx)$. 'A cow is to be bought' is true iff the class of cows intersects the class of things to be bought.

It is in extending this thesis to the class of *definite* non-generic descriptions that the Mīmāṃsaka comes into conflict with referentialism. For the argument above has little force when the description is used to refer to some definite particular. As Gautama (*Nyāya-sūtra* 2.2.60) observes, a description enters into a range of linguistic constructions distinctive of singular terms. First, a description can be the correlative of a relative clause: 'the cow which is standing up ...'. Second, a description can encode the Patient of such transitive verbs as 'brings', 'gives away', 'grabs': 'bring the cow'. Third, it can be the Agent for such verbs as 'grows fat', 'becomes emaciated': 'the cow grows fat'. (For the semantic roles Agent, Patient, etc. see §3.1.) Fourth, it can be adjectivally qualified by other nouns, such as 'white': 'the white cow ...'. Finally, it can occur as the first member of compounds, such 'cow-welfare' (for compounds, see §3.2). Gautama alleges that, in all these cases, the sentence is 'about' some definite particular, the object described by the description, and not 'about' the genus.

Commands are particularly important, for they link what someone understands by a sentence with the sorts of action they ought to perform.[13] Consider the command 'Bring cow'. If the term 'cow' here is construed as a definite description ('the cow'), a singular term referring to some definite particular, Śābaleya say, then someone so commanded ought to fetch Śābaleya and no other thing. If, on the other hand, the term 'cow' is construed as an indefinite description ('a cow'), one who understands the utterance ought to fetch any object, provided only that that object is a cow.

Śabara and his followers reject this argument. They explain the definite uses of descriptions by appealing to a very general distinction between two kinds of referential mechanism, one literal (cf. *śakti*), the other 'deflected' or 'secondary' (cf. *ākṣepa, lakṣaṇā*). The distinction enables them to say that, even though the literal reference of a descriptive noun is a property, it can sometimes be used or understood derivatively, as referring to a particular object in the conversational context. Their thesis is that the use of a definite description to refer to a particular is a non-semantic feature of the role of descriptions in communication.

An ordinary example of the deflected or secondary use of a word is the role of the word 'staff' in the sentence 'Give food to the staffs!'. The word is understood here as referring to the Brahmins, because Brahmins always carry staffs. Another example is the role of the word 'Ganges' in the sentence 'The village is on the Ganges'. To make sense of this sentence, we cannot construe it as literally asserting that the village is (floating) on the Ganges; we must take one of the words as having a non-literal meaning. The Indian semanticists always say that we are to construe the word 'Ganges' as referring to its bank. The figure of speech these examples typify is metonymy. Gillon (1997: 141–2) offers some idiomatic examples of the figure in English: 'The Crown granted an amnesty to the rebels'; 'Have you read any Shakespeare?'; 'track shoes are forbidden'; and even 'The nail caused our flat tyre'.

In each case, a noun-phrase refers indirectly to something related to its literal referent. Two criteria govern the deflected construal of a term.[14] First, the literal reference must not fit in the context. That is to say, construing the words literally will not represent the speaker as saying something plausible or sensible. If the chairperson says 'The discussion now goes to the floor', it would be perverse to interpret this as a request for the floor to say something. A principle of interpretive charity necessitates a metonymic construal. Second, there must be a relation between the literal referent and the derived referent, between the semantic value and the metonymic value of the utterance. In the example of the Brahmin and his staff, this is the relation of contact: the word 'staff' indirectly refers to the Brahmin, for it is he who is holding the staff. Likewise, in the sentence 'The discussion now goes to the floor', the term 'the floor' is used to refer to those standing on the floor. In 'The nail caused our flat tyre', the term 'the nail' indirectly refers to a causal event which has the nail as a constituent, so here the relation is one of composition.

Deflected reference is a phenomenon in which a hearer construes a word as making a reference to an object other than the word's literal referent, and he does this by relying on there being a relation between the literal referent and the object in question. Moreover, he relies on the fact that the speaker knows of this relation, realises that the audience will see that she intends to make a non-literal reference, and construe her remark accordingly. The *speaker*'s use of the term is a special case of 'indirect reference', which is such that something is referred to indirectly just in case it is referred to by way of referring to something else (see Bach 1987: 68). This is a phenomenon whereby the conversational context, especially the manifest intentions of the speaker, enable a term to be understood as referring to an object other than its literal referent. The deflected construal of a term is a *hearer*-centric counterpart to such acts of 'speaker's reference' (cf. Kripke 1979; Geach 1980: 31); it is a linguistic mechanism in which the hearer relies on conversational maxims and contextual cues to construe the speaker as referring to a certain object other than the literal reference of the term used.

The Mīmāṃsaka thesis is that the mechanism of deflected reference explains the role of descriptions in sentences which are 'about' a definite object.[15] In contexts such as 'The cow is lying down' or 'The cow is standing up', when the hearer takes it that a particular cow is being spoken of, the term 'cow' should be interpreted as metonymically referring to an individual cow rather than the cow species. The relation in virtue of which a descriptive noun such as 'cow' is understood to be referring to an individual cow would thus be the relation being-the-substratum-of (*āśrayatā*): the description is construed as indirectly referring to something which possesses its semantic value, here taken to be a property. It follows that a sentence containing a non-generic description 'A' has the same truth-condition whether the description is definite or indefinite. The distinction between the definite and indefinite uses is a pragmatic one. Definite uses are those where the conversational context makes a certain definite object salient to both speaker and hearer. In such a context, the description is said to be used non-literally to refer to that particular. Definite descriptions indirectly refer to particulars via the property which is their literal meaning.

This is somewhat akin to the move typically made in modern literature, by those who wish to explain the referential use of definite descriptions from within a Russellian quantificational theory of descriptions (cf. Neale 1990, §3.4). There is however a difference in motivation. The Mīmāṃsā hermeneuticians want to find non-contextual, eternal truth-conditions for the Vedic sentences they analyse. It is for them a priori that the meaning of Vedic discourse does not depend on contingent circumstances, and hence that it can be discovered without resort to empirical enquiry. They seek to preserve the eternality of Vedic discourse by constructing a theory of meaning in which every sentence has context-invariant truth-conditions. When the sentence contained a nominal, it is analysed as involving an expression of generality, an existential or universal quantifier. Non-semantic features of the communicative situation explain the *use* of nouns to refer to particulars, and hence the relation between the Vedic injunctions and the actions to which they lead.

The seventeenth-century Nyāya philosopher Gadādhara (1927: 209–23) discusses the theory at some length. He distinguishes a number of different possible accounts of the relationship between the literal and the indirect meaning. The view presented above, that indirect reference is metonymic value, is that of the Bhāṭṭa Mīmāṃsaka. An objection to this account is that, if the relation between the semantic value and the metonymic value *has* to be one of substratumhood, then it is not after all determined by pragmatic contextual factors, and the distinction between literal and non-literal meaning threatens to collapse. Another view, endorsed by some Prābhākara Mīmāṃsakas, claims that the causal explanation of a hearer's ability to understand an utterance of a noun, and in doing so to think of a particular object, need attribute to the hearer knowledge only of the generalist meaning clause ⟨'A' means **A**⟩. This theory is called the theory of 'stooped meaning' (*kubja-śakti-vāda*; *kubja* = crooked, curved). Deshpande (1992: 142–3) explains: 'First a generic property is cognized from a word, but the cognition which comprehends the generic property also automatically comprehends the individual, because a generic property is ontologically inseparable from its locus, the individual.' The difference between this theory and the referentialist theory we shall discuss in §1.4 and §2.3, that knowledge of meaning is knowledge of a clause ⟨'A' refers to A-possessors⟩, seems, however, to be little more than terminological.

1.3 Meanings as Bare Particulars (*vyāktiśaktivāda*)

Referentialism is the doctrine that descriptions, at least in some of their uses, refer literally to particular objects. Patañjali apparently believed that non-generic uses of descriptions are referential. With remarkable philosophical insight, he sharpens the dispute about the meaning-relata of descriptions by linking it with an important and controversial syntactic rule taken from Pāṇini's grammar. While his discussion becomes somewhat technical, I believe that it contains an important argument for the referentialist thesis. What Patañjali tries to do is to give a syntactic criterion for a word to be a singular term, and to show that in some uses descriptions meet that criterion (1968: 79):

> Supposing that a general feature (*ākṛti*)[16] is the word-meaning, [Pāṇini] says 'the plural is optionally used in the sense of the singular when designating a species (*jāti*)' (P. 1.2.58). [But] supposing that a substance (*dravya*) is the word-meaning, he tackled (the grammatical notion of) 'one-remainder' (*ekaśeṣa*) with the rule: 'When there is the singular ending, only one of a series of repeated stems remains in use (*eka-śeṣaḥ*)' (P. 1.2.64).

This passage rewards careful attention. The idea is that questions about the meaning-relata (*artha*) of expressions are connected with questions about the validity of certain kinds of grammatical rule. For one way to make more precise the idea that the semantic role of a singular term consists in its referring to a particular is to note that there are patterns of inference which are valid *only* for singular terms and not, say, for quantifier expressions. Consider, for example, the inference from '$F(a)$' and '$G(a)$' to 'There is a thing which is both F and G'. This is valid if 'a' is taken to be a singular term, but not valid if it is taken to be an expression of some other type, say the quantifier 'something'. One cannot validly infer that some one thing is both F and G from the premises 'something is F' and 'something is G' (assuming that $F \neq G$). This is enough to show that the semantic role of a quantifier expression is not the same as that of a singular term, and it captures the thought that the function of a singular term is to introduce a particular object into the discourse, an object about which many different things can then be said. Patañjali apparently regards Pāṇini's rule *P* 1.2.64 as having a similar significance: anyone who takes the rule to be valid must be assigning to nominals the semantic role of a singular referring expression, and hence associating them with particulars as their meaning-relata. Let us, therefore, look at this rule in more detail.[17]

'One-remainder' (*ekaśeṣa*) is a grammatical rule in Pāṇini's system permitting the replacement of a series of repeated singularly inflected nominals by a single nominal taking a dual or plural inflection. In English, such substitutions are common when the repeated term is a pronoun: we are able to replace 'you and you' (pointing at two people) with 'you two', or 'my car is white and your car is white' with '(both) our cars are white'. Intuitively, the possibility of such substitutions is due to the fact that each of the repeated terms is taken to denote a distinct particular. Pāṇini asserts that the rule is applicable even to descriptions: thus from '(the) tree is green' and '(the) tree is green', we are licensed to derive '(the) two trees are green'. Using subscripts to distinguish different tokens of the same nominal, the rule can be seen as asserting that a certain inference schema is valid:

F_1 is G

F_2 is G

Two Fs are G.

Patañjali's claim is that this pattern of inference is valid only if the semantic role of the nominal 'F' here is referential, a term whose meaning-relatum or semantic value is a particular.

It might be thought that this is trivially so, because someone who takes the meaning relatum to be a property or class cannot even formulate the conclusion of the inference—it makes no sense to speak of *two* universals treehood. This line of argument, which is due, incidentally, to Śabara, is unsound because there are two distinct ways to analyse any atomic sentence. The sentence 'Socrates is wise', for example, could be regarded either as composed from a singular term 'Socrates' and a first level predicate '... is wise'. Alternatively, it could be regarded as predicating of '... is wise' or 'wisdom' the second level predicate '... is Socrates-instantiated'. Applying the second analysis to the sentence 'Two trees are green', the dual case-affix would be construed as an adverbial modifier of the co-location relation between two universals, tree-hood and green-ness. The sentence would be analysed, by one who takes the value of 'tree' to be the universal or class treehood, as stating that treehood is *doubly* co-located with tree-hood.

Patañjali's idea is that the generalist cannot permit the 'one-remainder' rule, not because its conclusion is ill-formed, but because the inference schema would be invalid. It simply does not follow from 'treehood is co-located with green-hood' and again 'treehood is co-located with green-hood' that 'treehood is doubly co-located with green-hood'. Translating into a quantificational language, the 'one-remainder' rule would, on the generalist hypothesis, be a special case of the following *invalid* inference schema:

$$(\exists x\colon Fx)(Gx)$$

$$(\exists y\colon Fy)(Gy)$$

$$(\exists x\colon Fx)(\exists y\colon Fy)(x \neq y \;\&\; Gx \;\&\; Gy).$$

If the 'one-remainder' rule is *valid*, it can only be because it is an instance of a quite different pattern of inference. Patañjali's proposal is that it exemplifies the following inference-schema:

$$Ga$$

$$Gb$$

$$(\exists x)(\exists y)(x \neq y \;\&\; Gx \;\&\; Gy).$$

Here each occurrence of the nominal 'tree' is treated like an individual constant, referring to a particular. Patañjali attributes this view to a certain earlier grammarian called Vyāḍi. We will return to Vyāḍi's theory in Chapter 2. It does not matter that this inference pattern is not *generally* valid, relying as it does on the hidden premise '$a \neq b$',[18] for there is no corresponding hidden premise whose addition would make valid the previous pattern. What is more important to observe here is that this proposal treats each occurrence of a nominal as a distinct individual constant or name, and as a result discerns no more common structure between two tokens of the same general term than there is between 'Rāma' and 'Sītā', or better, between the names of two distinct Rāmas. We will see later how this lacuna leads to an important argument against Vyāḍi's theory.

Patañjali's thesis is that the validity of the 'one-remainder' rule leads to the conclusion that the meaning relatum (*artha*) of a nominal is a particular. To put matters another way, the idea is that there is a general syntactic criterion for singular terms, a grammatical rule satisfied only by singular terms and not by quantifiers or other types of expression. The rule in its full generality states that one is permitted to substitute a series of repeated nominals in the singular with a single nominal in the plural.

Thus, instead of saying 'you and you and you and you', we can say 'you (four)'. Intuitively, this can only be because each occurrence of 'you' refers to a (distinct) particular person. Likewise, if, instead of saying 'Felix and Tabby are in the garden', we can say 'the two cats are in the garden', it is again because each occurrence of a proper name refers to a (distinct) particular animal. The general rule does seem to be valid for two recognized classes of singular terms: proper names and indexicals. The 'one remainder' rule covers another special case of this phenomenon, namely the case where we have repeated occurrences of the same *descriptive phrase.* So if descriptions conform to the rule, as 'one remainder' asserts that they do, then descriptions too are singular terms. Admittedly, it is not idiomatic in English to say 'the cat and the cat are in the garden', even if one has just two cats, but perhaps that is because the 'one remainder' rule not only *permits* us to say instead 'the two cats are in the garden', but *prescribes* that we do so.

What are we to make of Patañjali's criterion? We must distinguish between definite and indefinite uses of a description. A modern Russellian claims that a definite description is a quantifier-predicate construction and not a singular term; specifically that 'The A is B' is true iff there is a unique A and it is B. In virtue of the uniqueness clause, although the description does not refer to any particular, it does 'denote' one, where denotation is a semantic not a pragmatic notion. Now, in the sentence 'the cat and the cat are in the garden', neither occurrence of the phrase 'the cat' is a *complete* description—'neither' uniquely describes an individual. In general, the Russellian argues that when a description is incomplete, the context supplies extra descriptive material, material which completes (renders unique) the description.[19] In the present case, the completed descriptions might, for the sake of argument, be 'the wholly black cat belonging to JG' for the first occurrence of 'cat', and 'the wholly white cat belonging to JG' for the second occurrence. Then the sentence 'the cat and the cat are in the garden' is properly paraphrased as 'There is a unique wholly black cat belonging to JG and it is in the garden, and there is a unique wholly white cat belonging to JG and it is in the garden'. This indeed entails that there are two cats in the garden, validating the one-remainder rule, and it does so without a referentialist account of descriptions.

Notice that this defence is not available to the generalist, as I described their position. The generalist takes the truth-condition of any description sentence, whether definite or indefinite, to accord with the simple clause, 'A/The A is B' is true iff there is an A which is B. When the description is used in a definite sense, uniqueness is the result of pragmatic facts, rather than being built into the semantics, and we have already seen that the inference rule is invalid for simply quantified constructions. This shows too that Patañjali's criterion is defensible for indefinite descriptions: the inference from 'An A and an A is B' to 'Both As are B' is only valid if 'An A' is referential. The manoeuvre in the previous paragraph is unavailable here, since completion of a description is solely to do with the uniqueness clause, which is present in the Russellian analysis of definite descriptions, but absent in the Russellian analysis of indefinites.[20]

A number of recent writers have sought a criterion of precisely the sort for which Patañjali too was searching. Dummett (1981: 59–61) argues that it is possible to isolate a set of inference patterns which are individually necessary and jointly sufficient for an expression to be a singular term. It is, he argues, the existence of such a syntactic criterion for being a proper name that allows Frege to define an object as that which a proper name refers to. Dummett's proposal is that an expression '*a*' is a singular term iff the following inference patterns are valid:

(1) $$\frac{Fa}{(\exists x)(Fx)}$$

(2) $$\frac{Fa \quad Ga}{(\exists x)(Fx \,\&\, Gx)}$$

(3) $$\frac{\text{It is true of } a \text{ that } F(\text{it}) \text{ or } G(\text{it})}{Fa \vee Ga.}$$

It is clear, as Dummett points out, that these criteria suffice to discriminate between proper names and indefinite and plural descriptions, as well as the quantifier expressions 'something', 'nothing' and 'everything'. For example, one cannot validly infer from 'A tree fell down' and 'A tree is growing in the garden' to 'Something both fell down and is growing in the garden'. Our question, however, is whether they discriminate between genuine proper names and Russellian definite descriptions. Let us take '*a*' to be the description 'the tallest tree in Britain'. The first of Dummett's criteria fails to rule this out, for we may validly infer from 'The tallest tree in Britain is very old' to 'Something is very old'. Neither does the second criterion rule it out, for the validity of the inference from 'The tallest tree in Britain is very old' and 'The tallest tree in Britain is a conifer' to 'Something is both very old and a conifer' is a consequence of the uniqueness clause in Russell's theory of definite descriptions. Finally, the third criterion does not rule out definite descriptions either, since the inference from 'It is true of the tallest tree in Britain that it is very old or it is a conifer' to 'The tallest tree in Britain is very old or the tallest tree in Britain is a conifer' is easily seen to be valid when descriptions have a Russellian analysis. Thus, Dummett's criteria fail to discriminate between genuine proper names and attributively used definite descriptions.

Let us then consider again the argument which purports to show that Patañjali's criterion does not adequately delimit the class of singular terms, on the grounds that completed definite descriptions will also satisfy the criterion. This argument is in fact faulty. Recall that the inference was rendered valid when the Russellian completed the descriptions. This manoeuvre worked, however, only because the extra descriptive material had a special property: the predicate that completed the first occurrence of the incomplete description is true of no object for which the predicate that completes the second occurrence is true. In my example, the predicates were 'wholly black' and 'wholly white'. If this were not the case, then the very same object could be denoted by both completed descriptions, and the inference to a plural subject would be invalid. Yet, there is no a priori reason why the completing predicates must have this property. For the extra descriptive material is determined by the context of utterance of each description individually. Thus, the inference is claimed valid for Russellian descriptions on the grounds of an implicit premise for which there is no warrant. Patañjali's criterion appears to succeed where Dummett's failed, in distinguishing between genuine singular terms and Russellian definite descriptions.

1.4 Meanings as Qualitied Particulars (*viśiṣṭaśaktivāda*)

I now turn to the early Nyāya discussion of semantics, which sets the scene for the later, more sophisticated discussion in Navya-Nyāya. The point of departure is *Nyāya-sūtra* 2.2.66. Having reviewed and criticized the particularist and generalist theories of meaning, Gautama attempts a compromise. He states that the meaning of a word is a conjunction of a particular (*vyakti*), a 'form' (*ākṛti*), and a universal (*jāti*):

> [The term 'cow' does not mean a mere particular] because there is a lack of fixity (*avasthāna*) towards it (*NS* 2.2.61)
>
> [It does not mean a mere universal] because a universal is not manifested independently of a particular and a 'form' (*NS* 2.2.65)
>
> The meaning of a word is a particular-*cum*-form-*cum*-universal (*NS* 2.2.66)

Mention of a 'form' as distinct from a universal was apparently for the sake of the uses of a description like 'cow' to refer to clay or toy cows, things which have the shape or appearance of real cows. Since such uses are tangential to my discussion, I will ignore this element in the *Nyāya-sūtra* definition.[21] What does he have in mind when he says that a description cannot mean a mere particular due to the lack of fixity? Perhaps his point is that a 'fixed' description would have to behave like a proper name, attached to one and only one object. The description 'cow', however, whether indefinite or incompletely definite, can describe different particulars on different occasions of use.

The *Nyāya-sūtra* analysis of meaning is intriguing. According to his commentators, Gautama's intention in giving a conjunctive list of both the particular and the universal as the meaning is not that a nominal can take different meaning relata, sometimes a particular and sometimes a universal, in different uses. His view, rather, is that the meaning-relatum even of a referential use of a nominal is a pair of entities, a particular and a universal, or rather, a particular 'as qualitied by' (*viśiṣṭa*) a universal. The attempt here is to render referentialism compatible with the realist theory of meaning by introducing a complex structural entity as the meaning relatum (*artha*).

The early Nyāya philosophers, Uddyotakara (sixth century AD) and Jayanta (ninth century AD), construct a theory of meaning designed to make sense of this apparently strange claim. The central idea of this new theory is that the meaning of a descriptive noun is a propertied particular (*tadvān eva padārthaḥ* Jayanta 1936: 295). I quote Jayanta:

> The meaning of a word is a property-possessor (*tadvān*).
>
> [An objection is raised to this]: What is this thing called a '*tadvān*' ('that-possessor')? '*Tadvān*' literally means 'this has that' (*tad asyāsti*), so what is meant is that a particular is the owner of a property. But if it is the particular which is the designatum, then the infinity and discrepancy faults recur, [especially] since the property is not [considered by you to be] an undesignated indicator (*upalakṣaṇa*). And if both [particular and property] are designated, then the word has an excessive [semantic] burden.

> [Jayanta replies]: What is meant is this. The 'property-possessor' (*tadvān*) is not a particular individual, such as Śābaleya, which is indicated by the word 'this' [in 'this has that'], and it is not the collection of all the individual [cows, say] in the world. It is the substratum of a universal. The aforementioned particular Śābaleya is said to be the '*tadvān*' because it is the substratum of the universal [cowhood], and so neither infinity nor discrepancy are relevant [objections]. Nor do we admit that a word designates the qualificand [i.e. the particular] without designating the qualifier [i.e. the property]. Since [someone who understands the word] knows a relation [between it] and a property-substratum, [the word] just means a *tadvān*. So where is the word's excessive [semantic] burden? (1936: 295-6).

In this closely argued passage, Jayanta sets out all the main elements in the 'propertied particular' theory. Jayanta presents the theory as a response to a pair of classic arguments against the thesis that a description refers to a mere particular. These arguments, known as 'infinity' and 'discrepancy', I will examine in detail in Chapter 2. They represent a much more precise statement of the intuition behind Gautama's remark that there will be a lack of fixity. Briefly, the point is as follows. In treating every token utterance of a nominal as if it were a semantic primitive, particularism fails to notice a significant level of semantic structure, the common semantic element between any two utterances of the same nominal. Two tokens '$tree_1$' and '$tree_2$' of the same noun-type 'tree', used to refer to the objects $tree_1$ and $tree_2$, are analysed simply as unstructured names. Specification of the meaning of 'tree' would then be via an infinitely long list of token-object pairs, and since no speaker could know more than a finite part of this list, no one could be said to have full mastery of the term. Jayanta now shows us a way to recover the lost structure. An utterance of 'tree' should be thought of as having two elements: a variable element, expressed by a pronoun 'this'; and a qualifying, predicative component, '... has treehood', expressed by the possessive affix attached to the name of a property. In other words, the nominal 'tree' is analysed as having the underlying logical form 'this, having-treehood' or 'this, (which) is-a-tree'.[22] The pronoun ensures that the expression is token-reflexive, different utterances referring to different, demonstratively or anaphorically indicated objects. This object is what Jayanta calls the 'qualificand' (*viśeṣya*). However, the predicative component or 'qualifier' (*viśeṣaṇa*), '... has treehood', remains constant for any utterance. This fact, Jayanta suggests, is enough to diffuse the argument against particularism.

Nyāya particularism analyses descriptions as having a deep structure, in which a pronoun is combined with a predicate, the description 'a/the

A' being reparsed as 'that thing, which is A'. It is clear that descriptions are treated here as being referential, but there seems to be no distinction between definite and indefinite uses, and especially nothing specifying uniqueness. Let me denote the reparsed noun by '[that *x*: A*x*]'. Thus a sentence of the form 'A/The A is B' is reparsed as '[that *x*: A*x*][B*x*]'.

On the early Nyāya theory, a description both refers to a particular and predicates something of it. Under the influence of the realist theory of meaning, the early Nyāya try to find some single entity which will serve in a double capacity as the external correlate of the description. They speak of the 'propertied particular' or *tadvān* as if it were some new kind of entity, a sort of structured composite of a particular and a universal, a 'qualified' (*viśiṣṭa*) entity; and they specify the semantics of '[that *x*: A*x*]' by saying that

(PP) '[that *x*: A*x*]' means **A**-possessing-*x*.

The grammarian and Mīmāṃsā theorists, as meaning-realists, took meaning specifications to be extensional statements correlating words with objects; in other words, to give the meaning was just to give the reference. Jayanta tries to follow the same pattern, but in the property-possessor theory, this is a mistake. He clearly cannot take 'property-possessor'., the direct object in his meaning specification, as standing for a certain particular, Śābaleya say, for the meaning-clause would then collapse into a clause specifying the meaning relatum of a single token of the nominal. On the other hand, if this phrase is *mentioned*, then the meaning-clause becomes a mere restatement of the fact that 'A-hood-possessor' (A-*tvavān*) and 'A' are synonyms, which is a consequence of the fact that the abstraction and possession affixes are inverses of one another.[23] The equivocation between these two positions led the early Nyāya authors sometimes to speak as if a 'cow-hood-possessor' was a strange kind of entity, half-way between an individual and a universal! In fact, we find even in later Nyāya talk of 'complex objects' (*viśiṣṭa*), such as a cow-qualified-by-cowhood (see §6.2).

It is, I think, possible to reformulate the Nyāya position in a way which frees it from too close an allegiance with the realist theory of meaning. In fact, it is a familiar point that we cannot perspicuously give the meaning of many expressions by clauses of the realist form. For example, the meaning of the conjunctive particle 'and' cannot be stated by a schema of the form ⟨'&' means ...⟩.[24] Rather, we must give its meaning by specifying the truth-conditions of any sentence in which it occurs. Thus: for any pair of sentences P and Q, ⌜**P & Q**⌝ is true iff P is true and Q is true. In the same way, the meaning of '[that *x*: A*x*]' has to be given by stating the truth-conditions of sentences embedding it. '[That *x*: A*x*][B*x*]' asserts of some contextually salient object, that it is A and that it is B. Thus:

(1) '[That *x*: A*x*][B*x*]' is true iff $\exists x\ [x = \textit{that}\ \&\ Ax\ \&\ Bx]$

My suggested formulation resembles in certain respects Staal's (1988: 59, 83) proposal that general terms in Sanskrit be modelled by 'restricted variables'. The restricted variable **'$\alpha x(Fx)$'**, means '*x* such that $F(x)$'. In defence of the introduction of restricted variables, Staal says that

> restricted variables can be adopted whenever we want to represent a noun of which it cannot be said that it should be preceded by a definite or indefinite article—for instance, because there is no article at all, as in Latin or in Sanskrit. Restricted variables can also be used when the number of cases fulfilling a given condition is not known. For example, if $P(x, y)$ denotes '*x* is the father of *y*', αy **P(A, *y*)** may denote any of the sons of A. If there is only one son, this would be equivalent to αy **P(A, *y*),** 'the *y* such that P(A, *y*)' (1960a: 110).

The last sentence cannot stand: the mere fact that a variable is restricted by a predicate true of just one individual does not entail that it has the same role as Russell's iota operator. The reason is that the explicit statement of uniqueness in the latter is lacking in the former. It is also unclear whether Staal intends the restricted variables to be bound or free variables, and, consequently, whether he takes descriptions in Sanskrit to be referential or non-referential. They must be taken to occur freely if they are to model the property-possessor theory, for the Nyāya clearly think of descriptions as referential, and bound variables do not refer.

Even if the formulation of the propertied particular theory is revised so as to free it from the idiom of the realist theory of meaning, and we thereby avoid having to reify propertied particulars, there are difficulties with the early Nyāya position. The principal one is that, in giving the descriptive feature a predicative role, the early Nyāya account assigns to both 'The A is B' and 'The B is A' the same truth-condition. This is counter-intuitive, for we would expect there to be an asymmetry between the semantic role of F and G in sentences of this form, at least on the assumption that descriptions are referential. Roughly speaking, while the role of G is purely predicative, the role of F is individuative. In the light of the well-known arguments that objects are only singled out or identified under a sortal concept, we might say that its function is to help in setting up a subject for predication. As I will show in Chapter 6, this is just one place where the Navya-Nyāya theory of meaning for descriptive nouns is much superior to the earlier Nyāya theory or anything in the earlier philosophic literature.

The early Nyāya authors have a distinctive philosophical motivation for developing this theory of meaning. These Nyāya authors are in the first instance epistemologists. They study the means leading to knowledge and the criteria on the basis of which knowledge-claims are evaluated. As we will see in Part II, language is regarded as one such means, a cognitive process leading from the auditory perception of an utterance to a belief with a certain content. Hearers have the capacity to understand sentences, and to form beliefs, sometimes true, on the basis of what they hear. The purpose of a theory of meaning is seen to be to show what this capacity consists in, and it is therefore facts about understanding which determine the kinds of semantic property attributed to words. Uddyotakara hints at this approach when he remarks that 'the word "thing" (*sat*) is a meaningful expression; what does it mean? [The rule is that] that object *x* which is understood from [hearing] a word *y* is the meaning of *y*.'[25] The Nyāya authors are not driven, as were the Mīmāṃsā hermeneuticians, by the goal of validating Vedic discourse, but their epistemological project nevertheless made issues of understanding central for them. If a qualitied particular, rather than a bare particular, was taken to be the meaning-relatum (*artha*) of a noun, it has to be because someone who understands a sentence containing a noun not only thinks about the object which is its referent, but does so in a certain way or under a certain 'qualifier'. This idea, only hinted at in the early Nyāya, finds much fuller development in the work of the later Navya-Naiyāyikas.

Notes

[1] See, for example, Sainsbury (1979), who uses the phrase to label a position once adopted by Russell. The phrase 'meaning realism' is sometimes used to label positions in opposition to the sort of meaning scepticism developed by Kripke in (Kripe 1987), namely positions which assert that there are such things as meanings. While the Naiyāyikas obviously *are* realists about meaning in this sense, I am using the phrase to denote a much more specific doctrine about the nature of meanings, that they are external entities of some sort. The opposite of this would be something like 'meaning ideationism', the doctrine that meanings are ideas, mental representations, etc. What I am calling the realist theory of meaning is sometimes called the 'Fido'-Fido theory.

[2] I here follow the usual practice of the grammarians, who use the term 'general word' (*jātiśabda*) to denote any such common noun phrase, regardless of whether it is a natural kind term. Note too Vātsyāyana who, introducing the *Nyāya-sūtra* discussion of meaning (beginning with *NS* 2.2.59), asks for 'a critical examination having as its primary focus the nominal term (*nāma-pada*), a paradigmatic example of which is the word "cow"' (1936: 658).

[3] The traditional arguments put forward by the parties to this debate have been documented and discussed at some length in the recent literature. For example, Raja (1963), Matilal (1971), Deshpande (1990), and P. Scharf (1990).

[4] This thesis is particularly associated with Strawson and Donnellan, though neither would endorse the stronger claim that the meaning of a description consists entirely in its reference or in its having a reference.

[5] See Russell (1905) and Neale (1990). According to Russell's theory of descriptions, the sentence 'The *F* is *G*' has the underying form 'There is exactly one thing which is *F*, and it is *G*'. What corresponds to the nominal '*F*' in this analysis is a certain predicate, *F*, whose semantic value or reference is the class of *F*s. It is in this sense that the Russellian is a generalist.

[6] The word *jāti*, we may note, normally designates a universal or natural kind, and it has been a frequent practice to translate *jāti-śabda* by 'generic nominal'.

[7] Example 1 is frequently encountered; examples 2i, 3i and 4ii are from Vātsyāyana *NSB* 2.2.60; examples 2ii and 3ii are from Uddyotakara NSV 2.2.66; example 4i is from Kumārila.

[8] *śābdabodhe carama-nirddiṣṭa-padārthasyaiva vidheyatvāt*, Gadādhara, *Viṣayatāvāda*. See Bhattacharyya (1990: 180). Gadādhara later qualifes the rule, stating that it does not apply to compound terms (1990: 184).

[9] An analogous system of notation will be used when we come to introduce terms that are relational, for example, 'substratum', 'cause', and 'sibling'. The Indian semanticists indeed make widespread use of abstract relational terms, such as 'substratumhood', and 'causehood'. Suppose then that 'R' is a term belonging to the class of relational nominals. Then let R be the class $\{R_{11}, \ldots, R_{ij}, \ldots, R_{nm}\}$. Since the extension of a relation is a set of ordered pairs, there are sets A and B such that $R \subseteq A \times B$, and $R_{ij} = +A_i, B_j$, for some $A_i \in A$ and $B_j \in B$. Finally, we will let '**R**' be the abstract relational term '**R**-hood', and **R** be the 'relational abstract' (Ingalls 1951: 45) **R**-hood, so that R is the extension of **R**.

[10] *kiṃ punar ākṛtiḥ padārthaḥ, āhosvid dravyam*. Patañjali (1968: 78).

[11] I will use restricted quantifiers when I give truth-conditions in a quantificational language. These, I believe, mirror most closely the Sanskrit constructions. For a discussion of the use of restricted quantifiers, see Neale (1990).

[12] The example discussed by Śabara under *Mīmāṃsā-sūtra* 1.3.33 is the injunction 'One should build the falcon-altar'. For an analysis of this example, see Scharf (1990).

[13] Under *Mīmāṃsā-sūtra* 1.3.30. It seems that the idea is due to Kātyāyana. See P1.2.64, *vārttika* 47: 'Because, in the case of injunction-based actions, the particular is seized' (*codanāsu ca tasya [dravyasya] ārambhaṇāt*).

[14] Discussions of the rules governing metonymy have been extensively catalogued by Raja (1963: 229-73).

[15] For references in the *Mīmāṃsāsūtrabhāṣya*, see Deshpande (1992: 102, n.292; 98, n. 277). Deshpande suggests the view is traceable to another of Kātyāyana's *vārttikas*, *vārttika* 61 under P1.2.64: 'A word denotes the substratum metaphorically' (*adhikarana-gatiḥ sāhacaryāt.*). Compare Śabara: 'Words which denote a "form" indirectly designate the individual which is the metaphorical base of it' (*ākṛti-vacanaḥ śabdas tat-sahacaritāṃ vyaktiṃ lakṣayati*). Quoted by Deshpande (1992: 102).

[16] Patañjai's use of the term *ākṛti* 'form' is unclear, and has been the subject of some discussion. It seems that Patañjali sometimes meant by 'form' a universal, and sometimes a class. See Deshpande (1992), Tiwari (1993), and P. Scharf (1990).

[17] See also Matilal (1982*b*), (1971: 98–100), Hiriyanna (1938), Raja (1963: 75–8).

[18] If it were generally valid, one could derive from 'Borges and I', the title of a story by Jorge Luis Borges, the phrase 'We two'! Compare *P* 1.2.72, which permits one to derive under the *ekaśeṣa* rule 'Those two' from 'Devadatta and he'. That the 'one remainder' rule relies on a hidden premise was noted by Kātyāyana, who stated that it depends on the following principle: 'for each object a [distinct] name is used' (*pratyarthṃ śabdaniveśaḥ*). Modern writers have found the meaning of this principle somewhat obscure (cf. Matilal 1982: 123), but it may plausibly be interpreted as a statement of the hidden premise '$a \neq b$'.

[19] There are, however, many problems with the idea that incomplete descriptions can always be completed by context. See, for example, Neale (1990: 93–102) and Ramachandran (1993).

[20] It is interesting to note that something akin to the Russellian uniqueness clause is achieved by the Sanskrit particle *eva* 'only, alone'. The meaning of *eva* is said by the grammarians and Naiyāyikas to be 'exclusion from being connected to what is other' (*anyayoga-vyavaccheda*) (cf. *Nyāyakośa* s.v. *eva*). Thus 'only Rāma is strong enough' means that Rāma is strong enough and anyone other than Rāma is not strong enough. More formally: $Fa \,\&\, (y)\, (y \neq a \rightarrow \neg Fy)$, where '$F$' stands for 'is strong enough', and 'a' for Rāma. The second conjunct is a uniqueness clause in contraposed form. For further details see Ganeri (1999).

[21] For further discussion of the notion of *ākṛti* in early Nyāya, see Tiwari (1993) and Scharf (1990). The use of 'cow' to refer to clay cows is a *systematic*, and hence eliminable, ambiguity. Compare Geach: 'A systematic ambiguity, like the way that a common noun can be used to label either a thing of a given kind or a picture of such a thing, or again like the way that a word may be used to refer to that word itself, ... [is] removable by the use of special signs, e.g. the

modifying words "picture of a", or quotation marks' (1980: 172). Some later Naiyāyikas took the term '*ākṛti*' to denote the relation (*vaiśiṣṭya*) by which the universal qualifies the particular.

[22] The relative pronoun is just a place-holder in the open sentence '... is a tree'.

[23] The general maxim that NP-*tvavān* = NP has an exception, namely when NP is a numeral. Thus, we may say (at least in Sanskrit) 'The sky possesses two-hood', if it is one of a pair of objects under discussion, but not 'The sky is two'. See Ganeri (1996*b*; 2001) for a discussion of the Nyāya theory of the semantics of numerals.

[24] See also Sainsbury (1979: 17–20).

[25] *sad iti cāyam abhidhāna-śabdaḥ, kasyābhidheyaḥ? yo yasmāt pratīyate sa tasyārtha iti.* (Gautama 1936: 677).

2

Śakti

Meaning as a Relation

2.1 A Meaning Theory for Philosophical Sanskrit

The meaning relation is that relation which attaches meanings to terms. This is the 'power' (*śakti*) of words—to stand in for, and to stand in relation to, things. Let us denote this relation $\mathcal{M}$. Two questions will concern us in this chapter: which relation is $\mathcal{M}$, and what sort of knowledge about $\mathcal{M}$ is needed in order to understand the terms of a language? If the realist theory of meaning is correct, meanings are external entities of some sort. In that case, $\mathcal{M}$ will be what in model theoretic semantics is called an assignment function, a recursively specified function that assigns to each expression in the language a semantic value. However, if the meaning of a term is taken to be something more than its semantic value, then $\mathcal{M}$ will determine an assignment function without being identical to one. A recursive specification of $\mathcal{M}$ is what we will call a 'grammar' or a 'meaning theory' for the language.

We will see in later chapters that the Indian philosophers of language look for epistemological constraints on the form of meaning theories. One constraint is that someone who knows the meaning theory must be in a position to acquire empirical knowledge testimonially (see Part II). A different constraint is that a meaning theory must be knowable by someone with *finite* intellectual capacities. I will be concerned in this chapter specifically with the second of these constraints and, especially, with classical arguments against the realist theory of meaning which follow from it.

Indian philosophical texts use a regimented and slightly artificial Sanskrit. It is the meaning theory for this language that I shall try to construct in this section. Let us begin by noting that philosophical Sanskrit displays a much greater facility for abstract nominalization than a language like English. Systematic nominal abstraction is achieved by concatenating an abstraction suffix (usually '*-tā*' and '*-tva*' in Sanskrit, like '-hood', '-ness' or '-ty' in English) to the term. The use of the abstract is very much wider in Sanskrit than in English, and can be applied to almost any noun phrase, regardless of whether the ensuing abstract noun denotes a natural state or condition.

As we saw in the last chapter, a sentence comprising two nouns in apposition is well-formed in Sanskrit. A technique involving abstract nominalization is widely used to distinguish between the subject and predicate in a nominal sentence. The technique is to place the subject in the genitive and take the abstract of the predicate. Thus (1) is reparsed as (2), and (3) as (4):

(1)	*ghaṭo nīlaḥ*	The pot is blue
(2)	*ghaṭasya nīlatvam*	Of the pot, blueness
(3)	*brahma caturmukhaṃ*	Brahma has four faces
(4)	*brahmaṇaś caturmukhatā*	Of Brahma, fourfacedness

We get an English construction near to that of the Sanskrit in 'the fact of ϕ's being φ'.[1] The construction corresponds to Staal's transformation rule T1.[2]

It will be convenient to use numerical superscripts to indicate grammatical case. The Sanskrit grammarians themselves number rather than name the cases, to avoid confusing them with the thematic role on *kārakas* (cf. §3.1). So we will have:

1. nominative
2. accusative
3. instrumental
4. dative
5. ablative
6. genitive
7. locative.

The terms in our language will be of the form 'A^k', where *k*, the case index, is such that $1 \leq k \leq 7$. Sentences consist of two or more terms in apposition.[3] In keeping with our earlier practice of using bold type to indicate abstraction, (2) above would be written 'pot^6 **blue**^{1}'.

When the predicate of the nominal sentence is in an oblique case, the sentence is relational:

(5)	*ghaṭo*	*bhūtale*	
	pot^{1}	ground^{7}	
	'The pot is on the ground'		

It will also be relational if the subject is in apposition with a relational term, the second term of the relation being put in the genitive:

(6)	*daśaratho*	*rāmasya*	*pitā*
	Daśaratha^{1}	Rāma^{6}	father^{1}
	'Daśaratha is Rāma's father'		

(7)	*agnir*	*dhūmasya*	*kāraṇam*
	fire^{1}	smoke^{6}	cause^{1}
	'Fire is the cause of smoke'		

A relational sentence cannot without risk of confusion be straightforwardly transformed into a genitive + abstract, for both subjunct and adjunct would then take a genitive (for example, 'the fact of Daśaratha's being the father of Rāma').[4] Instead, in philosophical Sanskrit, the subjunct is placed in the locative. Thus (6) becomes:[5]

(8)	*daśarathe*	*rāmasya*	*pitṛtā*
	Daśaratha^{7}	Rāma^{6}	father-hood^{1}
	'Rāma's fatherhood is in Daśaratha'		

The typical form of a relational sentence in philosophical Sanskrit is thus '$A^{7}\ B^{6}\ \mathbf{R}^{1}$'. Other syntactic markers of the adjunct are also used.[6]

There is in fact a way of transforming relational sentences into the 'genitive + abstract' form. It depends on a syntactic construction whose use, like nominalization, is free in philosophical Sanskrit but rather heavily restricted in English. This is the formation of nominal compounds. The Sanskrit grammarians distinguish several types, of which the four most important are listed here, along with an English example and expansion of the compound form 'A–B':

dvandva (conjunctive)	'A and B'	'stop-go'
karmadhāraya (descriptive determinative)	'B which is A'	'house-boat'
tatpuruṣa (dependent determinative)	'B to/with/for/from/of A'	'sun-dance'
bahuvrīhi (exocentric)	'ϕ, whose B is A'	'hot-head'.

I will describe the semantics of these compound forms in §3.2. The possibility of forming an abstract compound nominal permits us to transform (6) into:

(9) *daśarathasya* *rāma-pitṛtā*
Daśaratha^6 Rāma-father-hood^1
'Of Daśaratha, Rāma-father-hood'

which might be rendered as 'the fact of Daśaratha's being a Rāma-father'.[7] Thus, when we allow nominal compounds into the artificial language, a relational sentence can be paraphrased by 'A^6 B–$\mathbf{R}^1$'. For the time being, we will restrict 'B' to the class of proper names.

Speaking of the abstract relation father-hood as being located in an object, Daśaratha naturally suggests a comparison between abstract relations and abstract properties. In fact, this comparison is used as the basis for the semantics. Let each token of a nominal 'A' be assigned an object $A_i \in A$. For example, to 'Daśaratha' is assigned Daśaratha, and to an occurrence of 'tree' is assigned some particular tree. The abstract nominal '**A**' ('A-hood') is assigned to a property **A** which has as its extension the set A. Likewise, the abstract relational term '**R**' ('R-hood') is assigned to an abstract relation **R** which has as its extension a relation R (that is, a set of ordered pairs). We now interpret the sentences in the artificial language as follows:

(S1) '$A^6\ \mathbf{B}^1$' is true $\equiv A_i \in B$.

(S2) '$A^7\ B^6\mathbf{R}^1$' is true $\equiv \langle A_i, B_j \rangle \in R$.

S1 gives the truth-conditions for sentences like (2) and (4), while S2 gives the truth-condition for (8). What about (9)? Given any relation, we can form a relational property by treating as constant the adjunct of the relation. For example, 'being a Rāma-father' is a relational property of Daśaratha. So let us denote by '$R|B_j$' the class of things that stand in relation R to the object B_j; that is, $\{x: \langle x, B_j \rangle \in R\}$. Then we can give the truth-condition for sentences like (8) as follows:

(S3) 'A^6 B–R^1' is true $\equiv A_i \in R|B_j$.

S3 closely mirrors S1, the clause for non-relational sentences. Indeed, if we introduce the identity relation I, then (S1) can be treated as a special case of (S3), since $\{x: \langle x, B_j \rangle \in I\} = B$. As one would expect, $A_i \in R|B_j$ just in case $\langle A_i, B_j \rangle \in R$, so S2 and S3 coincide in their assignment of truth-conditions.

Though in some ways natural, this semantics is clearly referentialist: we assign objects rather than classes to the terms. That seems plausible for proper names like 'Daśaratha', but is less so for descriptive nominals like 'the pot'. To which object ought we assign this term? It is the attempt to give a satisfactory account of the form of $\mathcal{M}$, given a referentialist reading of the descriptive nominals, what will be our main concern in the remainder of this chapter. One motivation is just that a referential treatment of nominals is assumed by the simple and natural semantics for the language whose syntax I have just described. The use of the locative and of abstract nominalization strongly encourages a referentialist semantics. Furthermore, this semantics does not assign the same entity to the non-abstract and abstract nominals, as would the generalist reading (the point is Jayanta's). Another motivation is that the Navya-Nyāya philosophers who developed and promoted the use of this language with great success adopted a referentialist treatment of its primitive terms. A final reason is that, even the attempt to treat descriptions referentially fails, the semantic theory developed will be of the right form for paradigmatically referential expressions, such as indexicals, demonstratives, and proper names. We will examine the application of the theory to such cases in Chapters 8 and 9. In the course of developing a referentialist semantics, we will have to introduce the Nyāya theory of quantification; this too is a reason for examining their discussion.

The above paraphrase of relational sentences is also used in the meta-language, when specifying the meaning relation $\mathcal{M}$ itself. The referentialist thesis is that:[8]

(R) 'The* pot' means the* pot.

Here, and from now on, I will use 'the*' to denote whatever determiner we need to supply to get an English noun phrase with the same sense as a Sanskrit descriptive noun understood referentially. (R) is paraphrased, following the pattern of (8), as:

(10) *ghaṭe ghaṭapadasya śaktir* — the meaning of the word-token 'pot' is in the* pot

A^7 'A'^{6} $\mathcal{M}^1$.

It follows that the meant entity (*śakya*) is the subjunct, and the word (*śakta*) is the adjunct, of the abstract meaning relation (*śakti*). In other words, $\mathcal{M}$ is the relation '... is meant by ....' (*śakyatā*), and not the relation '... means ....' (*śaktatā*).

By (S2), we derive a meaning clause for (10):

(11) $\text{`A}^{7}\ \text{`A'}^{6}\ \mathscr{M}^{1}\text{'}$ is true $\equiv \langle A_i, \text{`A'}_j \rangle \in \mathscr{M}$.

Now this statement must be read as concerning word-tokens rather than word-types: the referentialist reading cannot assign the word-type 'pot' to some one particular pot. Thus, if we follow the semantics given above, (R) states that some given token of the word 'pot' means some given object. Given that (R) only specifies the meaning of a single utterance, there must, it would seem, be a clause like (R) in the meaning theory for every single utterance of every nominal! The problems inherent in such a supposition[9] are what we now discuss, and their resolution, the introduction of quantification into the language.

2.2 The 'Infinity' and 'Discrepancy' Arguments

An early grammarian Vyāḍi (*c.* 400 BC) was the first to offer a referentialist semantics for descriptions. Criticism of his position was the catalyst to later advances in the theory of meaning. Vyāḍi's main work, allegedly called the *Saṃgraha*,[10] is no longer extant, and we know his views on meaning only as they are recorded by Patañjali. According to Patañjali, Vyāḍi believed that the meaning of a description consists *entirely* in its being related to an individual object. Vyāḍi's theory is the conjunction of referentialism with the realist theory of meaning.

The view is reminiscent of J. S. Mill's suggestion that names are like name-tags or labels tied to a particular object, where knowing the meaning of the name is completely characterized as knowledge of a bare association between the name and its bearer. Vyāḍi's theory in fact treats each token or utterance of a nominal as if it were a Millian proper name. Consider the meaning of the description 'A'. $\mathscr{M}$ assigns objects to the tokens of 'A'. Now, Vyāḍi's thesis entails that to understand 'A' is to know every individual token-object pairing; that is, to know $\mathscr{M}$ in extension. Understanding is represented by Vyāḍi as the knowledge of a list:

S understands 'A' iff S knows that $\langle A_1, \text{`A'}_1 \rangle \in \mathscr{M}$
& that $\langle A_2, \text{`A'}_2 \rangle \in \mathscr{M}$
& that $\langle A_3, \text{`A'}_3 \rangle \in \mathscr{M}$
& ...

Later philosophers of language were highly critical of Vyāḍi's position. Their criticism revolves around a powerful pair of arguments, called the 'infinity' (*ānantya*) and 'discrepancy' (*vyabhicāra*) arguments. These arguments are important, because they are based on conditions of adequacy for *any* theory of meaning. The arguments may have been implicit even in Patañjali's *Mahābhāṣya*,[11] but came to prominence in the fifth and sixth centuries AD in the works of the Buddhist Diṅnāga, the grammarian Bhartṛhari, and the Mīmāṃsaka Kumārila Bhaṭṭa.[12] Although the early Naiyāyika Uddyotakara tried sophistically to question their soundness, they seem to have been accepted by virtually all later philosophers, including both Mīmāṃsā and Navya-Nyāya authors. They are mentioned, for example, by Śāntarakṣita and Gaṅgeśa, by later grammarians such as Kauṇḍabhaṭṭa, and were discussed too by the poetician Mammaṭa and the commentators on his *Kāvya-prakāśa*.[13] Thus enormous weight was placed on these arguments over a period of many centuries.

Let us look in some detail at the infinity and discrepancy arguments. For the sake of clarity in formulating them, I will follow the description given much later by the Navya-Naiyāyika Jayadeva Miśra (*c.* AD 1470) author of the famous *Āloka*. He puts the arguments this way:

> Suppose we say that one can only understand [a nominal 'A'] if one knows the meaning relation [for every token of 'A' and its referent]. Then, given that one cannot know such a relation for *limitless* individuals, one would not understand [a token] whose particular meaning relation one does not know. If, on the other hand, we say that one can understand [a token] without knowing its particular meaning relation, then there will be a *discrepancy* between knowledge of meaning relations and understanding.[14]

The infinity objection states that the meaning of a descriptive noun like 'cow' cannot consist entirely in its being associated with individual cows, because the number of cows is limitless. The idea is that Vyāḍi's model fails to correctly represent our actual linguistic competence. The competence in question is the ability of someone who understands the word-type 'cow' to understand *any* token utterance of it. Vyāḍi's model represents the state of understanding an uttered word 'A' as knowing a discrete item of information, namely that 'A' is a tag for a particular object. Our linguistic competence is represented by this model as possession of arbitrarily many discrete items of information, or by an arbitrarily long conjunction of such items. The meaning of the word will then potentially be unknowable to any person with finite intellectual capacities. This contradicts a plausible constraint on theories of meaning, that meaning ascriptions should be knowable by the members of the linguistic community whose language they describe.

The second argument, discrepancy, anticipates a possible reply to the first. Let it be conceded that the competent user does not know arbitrarily many items of information of the form '*w* is a tag for *x*'. The new suggestion is that knowledge of a finite collection of such items is sufficient for general competence, that is, for the ability to understand a token utterance even when its referent is not part of this finite corpus. The objection to this proposal is that the hearer's ability to understand sentences containing tokens of the nominal outside the base set becomes a mere 'aberration'. On the current model, in which each utterance of a nominal is like a discrete proper name, there should be a distinct item of semantic knowledge for every such utterance. Thus, even if I know that $token_1$ of 'tree' refers to an object *x*, $token_2$ of 'tree' refers to the object *y*, and $token_3$ of 'tree' refers to the object *z*, I am in no position to understand a new utterance, $token_4$ of 'tree'. So Vyāḍi's model fails to represent hearers' actual linguistic competence by the knowledge to which it ascribes them. This runs up against a second constraint on theories of meaning, that meaning ascriptions should be something the knowledge which is sufficient, even if not necessary, for someone to understand the expressions they govern.

Taken together, the arguments are closely related to one of Kripke's (1982) criticisms of dispositional accounts of meaning. Kripke observed that dispositions are finite, but competences are infinite (cf. §4.3). And the Buddhist Kamalaśīla (1968: 343) likewise remarks that 'no "convention" (*samaya*) can obtain [between a word and] the limitless unobserved things which have ceased to be or are yet to appear. For this would involve an unwarranted extension (*atiprasaṅga*) [of our use of the term]'. Vyāḍi's theory characterizes the ability of the hearer to understand any utterance of a nominal as analogous to the ability of a person who is able to identify a Picasso, having memorized all Picasso's paintings. The contrast would be with someone who likewise has the ability to identify a Picasso, but whose ability to do so is grounded in a general knowledge of Picasso's style. The distinction is between knowing a function in extension and knowing an algorithm that computes the function. For example, to know the square function $f(x) = x^2$ in extension, one would have to memorise every pair $\langle 1, 1\rangle$, $\langle 2, 4\rangle$, $\langle 3, 9\rangle$, $\langle 4, 16\rangle$, etc. To know an algorithm for the square function is to know how to compute $f(x)$ given any value for *x*. Given that it *is* possible to know what the square function is, the claim that such knowledge must be knowledge in extension is plainly false.

Vyāḍi's theory insists that each token of a nominal is a semantic primitive, for which, in the semantic theory for a language containing that token, one must provide a distinct semantic clause. It claims, as Russell once did, that indexical terms are 'ambiguous proper names' (Russell 1912). The infinity and discrepancy arguments combine to present this account with a dilemma. Either there are infinitely many rules in the semantic theory, one for each possible utterance of the nominal 'A', or else there are not. If there are, then the semantic theory fails a constraint mentioned, for example, by Davidson, that if a language is *learnable* it must be finitely axiomatized (Davidson, 1984: 9). A semantic theory with an infinite number of rules may, to be sure, correctly describe the language in question, but it will not be a theory which can be learned, because it cannot be known by any creature with merely finite intellectual resources. Suppose instead we restrict the semantic theory to include only a finite number of rules, rules for the tokens '$tree_1$' to '$tree_n$' say. We now run into a second constraint on an adequate semantic theory, that it should specify the meaning of *every* sentence in the language, including novel or yet-to-be-uttered sentences (cf. Davidson, 1984: 56). The restricted theory, however, fails to give the meaning (or truth-condition) of any sentence '$tree_i$ is F', for $i > n$. This is the 'discrepancy' between a speaker's knowledge of the semantic rules and her understanding: knowledge of the restricted semantic theory is not sufficient for understanding the language.

The source of the problem lies in the theory's failure to discern any common semantic structure between different utterances of the same nominal. This point was made by Śabara, when he observed that it does not represent the element of commonality in the judgement 'This is (a) cow and this is (a) cow'. For Vyāḍi, the judgement is merely 'This is a_1; this is a_2', which is of the same form as 'This is Śābaleya; this is Bāhuleya'. In taking a nominal to be a radically ambiguous expression, Vyāḍi's theory misses what different tokens of the same nominal have in common.

The infinity and discrepancy arguments show that Vyāḍi's account of the meaning of referential expressions is inconsistent with the thesis that descriptions are referential. It is open, then, either to reject Vyāḍi's theory or to deny that descriptions are referential. The Buddhists, it seems, accept the Vyāḍi model as a correct analysis of the meaning of referential terms, and use the argument to infer that nominals do *not* refer. Their alternative theory of meaning, the so-called 'exclusion' (*apoha*) theory, is a non-referential theory of meaning for such expressions (see Ganeri 2001b, §4.5–6).[15] The Nyāya, however, maintain that descriptions *are* referring expressions, and use the arguments to show that Vyāḍi's account is false. Both agree on one thing. The infinity and discrepancy arguments emphasize a central problem for any theory of meaning: to show how, if at all, general linguistic competence is related to the possession of a finite body of knowledge.

2.3 Meaning as Grounds of Use

Vyāḍi's theory claims both too much and too little. It claims too little when it fails to discern any common semantic structure between two tokens of 'tree', namely that both are names of *trees*. It claims too much when it says that for someone to understand the description 'tree', they must know the referent of every utterance of that description. Knowledge of the meaning relation $\mathcal{M}$ in extension is neither necessary nor sufficient for understanding. What one does need to know is something about $\mathcal{M}$ which, in combination with non-semantic information about the context of a given utterance, puts one in a position to determine a relatum of $\mathcal{M}$. That would necessarily discern common semantic structure between different tokens of the same word type, if it is not to collapse into a mere listing of token-object pairs.

It was to the grammarian Kātyāyana that the early authors looked for a further insight. In his fifth aphorism under *Pāṇini-sūtra* 5.1.119, Kātyāyana suggests that each descriptive noun is associated with a 'quality' (*guṇa*), and it is on the basis of this association that it refers to particular substances. He says that

> The residence (*niveśa*) of a word in a [particular] substance is due to the presence of such a quality [of the substance] as is denoted by [the addition to the nominal base of the abstraction suffix] *-tva* or *-tal*.[16]

Kaiyaṭa notes that what Kātyāyana means by 'residence' is the application or use (*pravṛtti*) of a term to refer to a particular. The quality of which Kātyāyana speaks is the 'basis' or 'ground' (*pravṛtti-nimitta*) for this use: it is at least partly because of an object's possession of this quality that the term is used to refer to it. The quality associated with the descriptive noun 'A' is denoted by the abstract noun 'A-hood'.

The natural way to interpret Kātyāyana's slogan, that nominals apply to particulars due to the presence of a feature, is to read it as specifying a rule on the assignment of objects to utterance-tokens of the word.[17] The meaning relation $\mathcal{M}$ for the descriptive nominal 'A' has the following property: only As are the meanings of any token uses of 'A'. More formally:

(1) For all objects x, and all uses y of the nominal type 'A', x is meant by y only if x possesses the property **A**.

How are such quantified statements expressed in the regimented Sanskrit whose semantics we are examining? That language contains so far no expression of quantification. Yet it is a simple matter to extend it to introduce a certain sort of quantification. In particular, consider a sentence like:

(2) *daśarathasya* *vīra-pitṛtā*
Daśaratha^6 **hero-fathcr**^{1}
'Daśaratha is a hero's father'.

This is again a sentence of the form 'A^6 B–$\mathbf{R}^{1}$', but 'B' is now a descriptive noun rather than a proper name. We must therefore assign a semantic value to the compound 'hero-father'. Its semantic value is the class of objects which are the father of some hero or other. Earlier, we defined the set $R|B_j$ as $\{x: \langle x, B_j \rangle \in R\}$, the set of things that stand in relation R to the object B_j. Let us now extend this definition, to include the case where 'B' is itself a class. So define $R|B$ as the set $\{x: \langle x, y \rangle \in R; y \in B\}$, the set of things that stand in relation R to *some* B. Such sets are the semantic values of relational compounds. For example, the semantic value of 'hero-father' is the class $\{x: \langle x, y \rangle \in \text{Father}; y \in \text{Hero}\}$, where 'Father' denotes the fatherhood relation, and 'Hero' denotes the set of heroes. The meaning of 'hero-father' is the class comprising fathers of a hero.

In Navya-Nyāya, this operation is said to be that of *restricting* (cf. *nirūpaka*) a relation to a property, thereby forming a relational property. Now (2) asserts that such a relational property belongs to Daśaratha. Given our practice of interpreting property possession extensionally, we will therefore say that:

(S4) 'A^6 B–R^{1}' is true $\equiv A_i \in R|B$.

The sentence would be represented in restricted quantifier notation as saying that $[\exists y\colon By]\,[aRy]$.

If restriction introduces existential quantification over the adjunct position, a different operation, delimitation, introduces quantification into the subjunct position. A delimitor (*avacchedaka*) of the relational property whose extension is $R|B$, namely **R**-restricted-to-**B**, is defined as a property **A** such that $R|B \subseteq A$. To say, for example, that being a hero's father is delimited by the property being-a-king is to say that the class of kings is an upper bound on the class of fathers of a hero.[18] The quantity introduced by means of this operation is 'only': only a king is the father of a hero. In the restricted quantifier notation, this sentence states that [only x: Ax][$\exists y$: By][xRy].

The quantity 'only' translates to the more familiar (Aristotelian) quantity 'no': only a king is the father of a hero just in case no non-king is the father of a hero (see also Ganeri 1999; 2001b, §4.6). We thus have an equivalence of the form:

(3) $[\text{only } x\text{: A}x]\,[\exists y\text{: B}y][x\text{R}y] \equiv [\text{no } x\text{: }\neg\text{A}x][\exists y\text{: B}y][x\text{R}y]$.

This equivalence lies at the heart of the Nyāya use of double negation to express quantity, which has been noticed by Ingalls and others (Ingalls 1951: 60, Matilal 1968: 79). It is also the reason for the use of a double negation (*anyāpoha*) in Buddhist semantic theory.

To recapitulate: The construction of a quantified sentence begins with an abstract relational property, **R**, corresponding to the open sentence '... is an R to ...'. The relata of this relation are now bound in turn. The second term is bound by saying that **R** is 'restricted' (*nirūpita*) by a property **B**. The relational property **R**-restricted-to-**B** has as its extension the class R | B, the semantic value of the predicate '... is an R to some B'. This relational property is either located in an object or 'delimited' (*avacchinna*) by a second property A. The statement that **R**-restricted-to-**B** is delimited by **A** is equivalent to the statement that $R|B \subseteq A$. This is the truth-condition for the sentence 'only an A is an R to a B', the basic quantified form in the language of philosophical Sanskrit.

The syntax of our regimented language has to be extended to include sentences with quantified subject terms. One way is to introduce the particle *eva*, meaning 'only, alone'. This particle is treated explicitly as a logical term, one whose meaning is said to be 'exclusion from connection with what is other'.[19] Thus the sentence 'only As are B' means 'B is excluded from what is other than A', or in other words, 'no non-A is B'. So the equivalence (3) is taken as the definition of the quantifier. Other quantities are introduced by the insertion of further negations binding 'A' and 'B'.

Another technique involves abstracting the subject term and placing it in the instrumental case, thereby forming sentence like '$\mathbf{A}^3$ B–$\mathbf{R}^1$' (cf. Guha 1968: 301). It is difficult to find any natural rendition in English of this construction. A sentence like 'fire is the cause of smoke' gets paraphrased as 'smoke-cause-hood is by way of being-fire'. The truth-condition for such constructions is:

(S5) '$\mathbf{A}^3$ B–$\mathbf{R}^1$' is true $\equiv R|B \subseteq A$.

With this much quantificational apparatus, we can consider again Kātyāyana's claim about meaning as the grounds of use. The property of the meaning relation to which he draws attention is in fact well suited for expression by means of the above system of quantification. μ - every M is such that only As are meant by uses of 'A'. That is just to say that A is the delimitor of $\mathcal{M}$-every M as restricted to 'A' (as before, I will let 'A' be the word-type, that is, the class of its token uses). So the stipulation (1) about the meaning of 'A' is paraphrased in our language as:

(1*) $\mathcal{M}$|'A' $\subseteq$ A.

We shall make much use of meaning clauses in this form. (1*) states that the meaning of a token of 'A' is a member of the class of As. This property of is $\mathcal{M}$ represented in Figure 2.1.

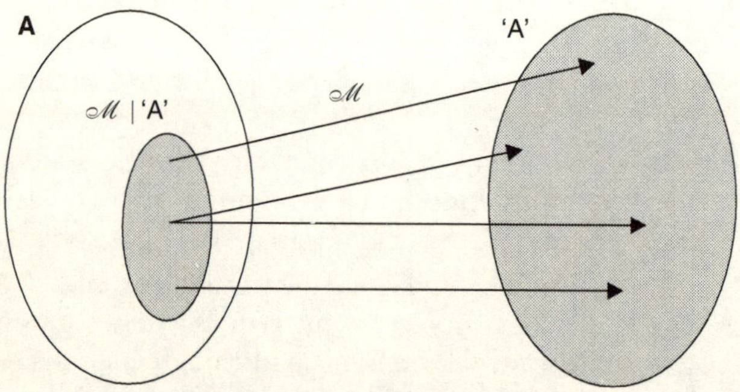

FIGURE 2.1 $\mathcal{M}$|'A' $\subseteq$ A.

The property A is the grounds of use, in the sense that it delimits the class of objects which are the meaning-relata of the term 'A'.

The idea is that knowledge of a single semantic fact, that only As are meant by tokens of 'A', combines with non-semantic knowledge about the context of use, to determine a meaning relatum (*artha*). Suppose that someone says 'Look in the garden. The* tree is in blossom'. On hearing an utterance of the description 'the* tree', the hearer knows, in virtue of her knowledge of meaning, that nothing but a tree is the semantic value. The context makes it clear *which* tree is the semantic value, namely, the tree in the garden. The speaker's referential intentions, acts of demonstration, prior linguistic information, or just the salience of one particular object, combine with such information about the appropriate class of object, to determine a reference.

We now have a new criterion of synonymy. Vyāḍi's theory of meaning stated that two terms are synonymous iff they have the same meaning relatum. The new criterion is that two words are synonymous iff they have the same 'ground'.[20] We might even say that the basis **A** is the meaning of the word *type* 'A', while some particular A is the meaning of any given *use* of 'A'.[21]

The relatum-basis distinction is partially akin to a distinction drawn in the recent literature. Strawson (1952: 188-9) puts the distinction in terms of what he calls 'meaning' and 'reference':

> For a singular referring expression to have a meaning, it suffices that it should be possible in suitable circumstances to use it to refer to some one thing, person, place, &c. Its meaning is the set of linguistic conventions governing its correct use so to refer. For the great majority of referring expressions, these conventions are such that a given expression may be used on different occasions to refer to different individual things, persons, places, &c.

In an earlier paper, he remarks that '[expressions capable of having a referring use] differ [from one another] in the degree of "descriptive meaning" they possess: by "descriptive meaning" I intend the conventional limitation to things of a certain general kind, or possessing certain general characteristics' (1950: 21). This idea seems to be very much what the Indian referentialists have in mind when, interpreting Kātyāyana's aphorism, they say that a property is the delimitor of a term's scope.

Strawson's idea finds more recent expression in the distinction between the 'content' of an expression and its 'character' or 'role'. The character of an expression is the general linguistic rule governing its use on any occasion; Kaplan (1989: 500–507) says that this is a function from contexts to contents. Thus, while the content of the word 'I', in any given context, is the person who utters the word in that context, its character is the rule ⟨'I' refers to the speaker⟩. I take it that the 'character' of a referentially used description will be something like ⟨ $\forall x$ ['The F' refers to x iff x is the most salient F in the conversational context]⟩. If so, a provisonal identification of the 'meaning relatum' with a content, and of the 'ground' with the property **F** specified by the character is possible In Part III, however, we will see some Indian thinkers moving in a different (possibly, more 'Fregean') direction.

Whether we speak in terms of the distinction between basis and relatum, or meaning and reference, or character and content, the substantive point is the same. In each case, there is an attempt to locate an invariant, constant element in the linguistic significance of a term, an element which delimits the term's semantic value. The later Indian philosophers of language made much use of this distinction. And its philosophical importance remains even if, like the Buddhists and Mīmāṃsakas, we do not accept the thesis that descriptions are referring terms.

Notes

[1] Cf. Speijer (1886: 181–2). As Speijer notes, the genitive in such constructions is subjective.

[2] Staal (1965: 176). The rule is also discussed by Matilal (1998: 28–30). Use of this and other related devices can blur the distinction between descriptions and sentences. Schayer (1933) comments that 'the distinction between "propositions" and "names" is made difficult not only by the nominal style of Indian languages but by the possibility of expressing every proposition by abstraction ... *śabdasya nityatvam* can easily be regarded as the "name" of an ideal object," "the eternality of a tone"; however, it can also be regarded as a "statement".' (I would like to thank Joerg Tuske for preparing translations of several of Schayer's articles.)

[3] The syntax of the language could be specified in terms of a set of simple phrase-structure rules: S → NP NP, NP → Nom Case, Nom → pot, ground, etc., Nom → Nom Abstract, Abstract → -hood, -ness, Case → 1, 2, ..., 7. The introduction of nominal compounds is via an extra rule NP → Nom Nom Case. We could easily add further rules for the sentential connectives.

[4] Note, however, that the former is a subjective genitive, the latter an objective genitive.

[5] Note how it is *not* said that Daśaratha's father-hood is in Rāma, which might be more in keeping with English idiom.

[6] Other syntactic markers of the adjunct are also employed: 'on the ground' becomes 'superstratum-*to*-ground' or 'groundy superstratum' [with the suffix -*īya*]. When the relation is causehood, the effect takes an accusative with the indeclinable particle *prati* 'towards': the causehood in fire is *towards* smoke. Thus—*agnau dhūmaṃ prati hetutvam* fire[7] smoke[2] towards causehood[1]. See Guha (1968: 298–9).

[7] This is Staal's transformational rule T4 (Staal 1965: 178).

[8] In Sanskrit, it is variously expressed as '*go-padaṃ gāṃ vakti*', '*go-padaṃ gāṃ brute*', '*go-padaṃ gor vācakam*', '*go-padena gaur ucyate*', '*go-padasya gaur vācyaḥ*', etc. See Gadādhara (1927: 6), and also Matilal (1982*a*: 67–8).

[9] Note that if generalism were true, the same problem would not arise. The form of $\mathcal{M}$ would simply be a function which assigns to each nominal type a property, and we would have: 'A^7 "A"^{6} $\mathcal{M}^1$ ' is true $\equiv \langle A, \text{"A"} \rangle \in \mathcal{M}$.

[10] See, however, Wujastyk (1993: xxv).

[11] Matilal claims this (1982: 74), but it is not clear to me that the comments under, for example, *P*1.2.64, would fully justify the attribution.

[12] For Diṅnāga, see Hayes (1988: 255). Vyāḍi's theory is discussed by Bhartṛhari in his Vākyapadīya, III.1.2, and in his *Mahābhāṣya-dīpikā*. For Kumārila's views, see *Tantravārttika* 1.3.33.

[13] Śāntarakṣita (1937: 466), Gaṅgeśa (1901: 557), Mammaṭa (1917: 32). For Kauṇḍabhaṭṭa, see Deshpande (1992).

[14] *yadi yatra śaktigrahas tatra śābdadhīs tad anantāsu vyaktiṣu śaktigrahābhāvāt agṛhītaśaktike śābdadhīr na syāt, yady anyatra śaktigraho 'nyatra śābdajñānaṃ tadā śaktidīḥ? śābdajñāne vyabhicāriṇīti.* In Gaṅgeśa (1901: 557–8).

[15] The *apoha* theory has been discussed by many authors. See especially Matilal (1986: 396–404), Hayes (1988), Katsura (1991), and Siderits (1991) and the articles in Matilal and Evans (1986). Roughly, the idea is that in applying a general term 'F' to an object *a*, we exclude that object from what is other than *F*. In other words, we assert the open sentence '$(\forall y)(\neg Fy \rightarrow y \neq a)$' which is logically equivalent to '*Fa*'. This is a clear treatment of general terms as predicates.

[16] *yasya guṇasya bhāvād dravye śabda-niveśas tadabhidhāne tvatalau.* (Patañjali, 1961: 83). *Pāṇini-sūtra* 5.1.119, which prescribes the use of the abstraction suffices, states that *-tva* and *-tal* designate the 'essence' or 'nature' (*bhāva*) of a thing. As Kaiyaṭa points out, however, the term '*bhāva*' in Kātyāyana's *vārttika* does not mean 'essence' but 'presence' (*vidyamānatva*). The *vārttika* should not be seen as committing Kātyāyana to a strong essentialism, in which anything capable of being referred to by a nominal expression has an essential attribute.

[17] The interpretation given to Kātyāyana's *vārttika* became a major question in the later classical phase of Indian philosophy (i.e. the fifth to seventh centuries AD). Nāgeśa explicitly notes that each of the three views about the meaning relatum (property, particular, and propertied particular) is consistent with some construal of the *vārttika*; see Patañjali (1962: 83). The generalist Mīṃāṃsakas understand the aphorism by taking the property, which is the 'ground for application' (*pravṛtti-nimitta*) of the noun, to be just its meaning relatum, and the 'use of the term to refer' to particulars to be an act of speakers' reference. The aphorism now reads: words indirectly refer to particulars via the property which is their literal referent. Compare Śabara: 'Words which denote a "form"

indirectly designate the individual which is the metaphorical base of it' (*ākṛti-vacanaḥ śabdas tat-sahacaritāṃ vyaktiṃ lakṣayati*). Quoted by Deshpande (1992: 102). The early Nyāya propose instead to read Kātyāyana's aphorism as asserting that the meaning is a qualitied particular: 'When we want to express just the located universal without its location, [the abstraction suffixes] *-tva* and *-tal* are used. As [Kātyāyana] said, '*-tva* and *-tal* [are used] to denote that quality due to the presence of which words are attached to substances.' This remark, that words are attached due to the presence of a quality, provides support for our view that what is denoted is the property-possessor' (Jayanta 1936: 297).

[18] The Nyāya philosophers sometimes also permit delimitors which are lower bounds and co-extensive bounds; they then specify which sort of delimitor they intend. See Matilal (1968: 76).

[19] I have discussed the semantics of the particle *eva* in Ganeri (1999).

[20] Compare: *śakyabheda eva śakter bhedaḥ*, and: *śakyatāvacchedakatā-bhedena śaktibhedaḥ*. See Gadādhara (1927: 85).

[21] Compare Fodor (1988: 99): 'Let's start with the most rudimentary sort of example: the case where a predicative expression ("horse", as it might be) is said of, or thought of, an object of predication (a horse, as it might be). Let the Crude Causal Theory of Content be the following: In such cases the symbol tokenings denote their causes, and the symbol types express the property whose instantiations reliably cause their tokenings. So, in the paradigm case, my utterance of "horse" says of a horse that it is one'.

Part II

Testimony and Meaning

3

Kāraka: Meanings in Composition

3.1 Semantic Role and Logical Form

An important feature of Pāṇinian grammatical theory is the distinction it draws between the superficial grammatical form of a sentence, and a deeper level of structure, known as the *kāraka* level. Later Nyāya and other philosophers of language attach great significance to this distinction, and develop Pāṇini's theory of *kāraka*s into an account of semantic structure. The description of an expression's semantic structure is called its '*vyutpatti*'.[1] Later philosophers also often use the term '*śābdabodha*' to denote the paraphrase of a sentence into a semantically perspicuous form.[2]

A *kāraka* is a semantic relation between the verb and a noun. Pāṇini isolated six such relations, namely[3]

1. *kartṛ* Agent
2. *karman* Patient
3. *karaṇa* Instrument
4. *sampradāna* Target
5. *apādāna* Donor
6. *adhikaraṇa* Place.

Consider the sentence

(1) In the kitchen, Rāma cooks rice for Sītā with firewood from the forest.

The verb in (1) denotes an event, viz. a cooking, and the denotation of each of the nouns stands in a semantic relation with that event. Thus, the event has an Agent—Rāma, a Patient—rice, an Instrument—firewood, a Donor—the forest, a Target—Sītā, and a Location—the kitchen.

The term *kāraka*, derived from the verb *kṛ* 'to do, make', literally means that which makes the event. The causal nature of the *kāraka*s is stressed by the early Naiyāyika Vātsyāyana, who points out that the labels Agent, Patient, Instrument, etc. do not describe the nominal denotata as such, but only *qua* their playing a certain causal role (Vātsyāyana, *Bhāṣya* under *Nyāyasūtra* 2.1.16; translation by Matilal, 1990: 43):

> [All] *kāraka* words apply through the incidence of some ground or other. In 'The tree stands [there]', the tree is the agent because it has 'independence' with regard to the matter of standing. In '[He] sees the tree', the tree is 'ardently desired' through the action of seeing [by the agent] and hence it is the object .... In '[He] sprinkles water for the tree', the tree is intended to be the 'beneficiary' of the action of sprinkling, and hence is the *saṃpradāna* 'beneficiary' or 'recipient' .... In this way it is neither the thing itself nor the action itself that is a *kāraka*. What then? *When a thing is a participant in an action or when it is endowed with a special functional activity* (kriyāviśeṣayukta*), it becomes a kāraka.*

A *kāraka* is clearly conceived of here as a specific causal role. It is now widely recognized that it would be a mistake to identify the *kāraka* categories with the purely grammatical cases, by which I mean the nominal declension groups. Sanskrit distinguishes eight such groups, named in western style grammars[4] as: nominative, accusative, instrumental, dative, ablative, genitive, locative, and vocative. Although, if one excludes the vocative and the genitive, which is a noun-noun relation, there is a superficial correspondence between *kāraka*s and declensional groups; it is clear from the above that the *kāraka*s are semantic and not syntactic relations.

The *kāraka*s closely resemble the participant roles or thematic roles of modern case grammar. For example, *kāraka*s remain constant under active-passive paraphrase. The Agent is encoded by a nominative marked noun in the active, and by an instrumental in the passive, while the Patient is encoded by an accusative in the active and a nominative in the passive:

(2) a.	Devadatta cooks rice	*devadattas* [NOM.]	*taṇḍulaṃ* [ACC.]	*pacati*
b.	Rice is cooked by Devadatta	*taṇḍulo* [NOM.]	*devadattena* [INS.]	*pacyate*

Nevertheless, there are difficulties with the identification of *kāraka*s as pure thematic roles, at least as they are treated in Pāṇinian grammar.

Pāṇini defines the Agent as that which is (causally) 'independent' (P1.4.54), the Patient as that which is 'most desired' by the Agent (P1.4.49), and the Place as the 'location' of the event (P1.4.5), understood to be the location either of the Agent or of the Patient. However, Pāṇini also states that the ground is the Place in (3a) but the Patient in (3b):

(3) a.	Devadatta sits on the ground	*devadatto* [NOM.]	*bhūmāv* [LOC.]	*āste*
b.	Devadatta sits on the ground	*devadatto* [NOM.]	*bhūmim* [ACC.]	*adhi* + *āste*

Certain verbs, notably *śī* (to lie down), *sthā* (to stay), and *ās* (to sit), are made transitive by the verbal prefix *adhi-*. If Pāṇini's *kāraka*s are pure thematic roles, then one ought to be able to discern a difference in semantic interpretation between (3a) and (3b); and yet, in both cases, the semantic role of 'ground' seems to be to denote the location. Pāṇini's response is to restrict his original definition of a Place by syntactic criteria, stating that when these three verbs are prefixed by *adhi-*, the location is not the Place but the Patient (P1.4.46). The extensions of 'Place' and 'Patient' are thus determined in part syntactically. Indeed, as Matilal notes (1990: 41–2), Pāṇini's rules governing the *kāraka*s fall into two general categories. There are six major rules that define the *kāraka*s in their primary meanings, and 'a number of additional rules which widened the scope of each category ... in terms of syntactic and other considerations'.[5]

Similar examples have been found problematical for English case grammars. Consider the following pair (Blake 1994: 75):

(4) a. John tapped the wall with his pipe

b. John tapped his pipe on the wall.

These two sentences describe the same state of affairs, and it is difficult to discern any difference in semantic interpretation. So we must either take the wall to be a Patient and the pipe to be an Instrument, as in (4a), and find some way to assign these roles in (4b), or else take the pipe to be a Patient and the wall to be a Place, as in (4b), and try to map these roles to (4a). Blake suggests that such examples might be understood by noting that 'encoding an entity as an object rather than as a non-core dependent often adds a sense of affectedness' (1994:75). In his example, it is respectively the wall or the pipe which is being affected by the action. The sense of affectedness, Blake suggests, is not something which will be represented at the semantic level, for it has to do with different perceptions of a single state of affairs.

The Navya-Nyāya authors make two innovations to Pāṇini's theory. First, they assign different semantic roles to the *kārakas*. The new semantic roles seem more robust under paraphrase than Pāṇini's original roles. Second, they use the *kārakas* as the basis for an analysis of logical form. In their discussion of the logical form of action statements, and the analysis of the notion of agency, they here anticipate some recent work in action theory.[6] As we will see, their theory allows a better solution for the problematic sentence pair (3).

We begin by defining a pair of causal relations. Let event A *instigate* event C just in case A and C occur, and there is a causal chain from A to C, a causal chain being a sequence of events each of which is caused by the adjacent prior member. So A instigates C if A is the first member of a causal chain to C. The Sanskrit term is *anukūla*, 'downhill from' or 'downstream from': C is downstream from A in the causal chain. A synonym is *prayojaka*, 'setting in motion', 'prompting' (*Nyāya-kośa*, s.v. *anukūla*). Some later effect in the causal chain is called the 'fruition', 'final effect' or 'culmination' (*phala*) of the chain.[7]

Second, let event *B* be a *functioning* for event *C* just in case *B* and *C* occur, and *B* is a member of a causal chain from some prior event to *C*. The Sanskrit term is *vyāpāra*, 'operation', 'occupation' or 'function'. The 'occupation' of a moving arrow is its flying through the air in order to hit a target. The definition of functioning events emphasizes their role as intermediaries: x is a functioning for y iff having itself been caused, x is a cause of y (*Nyāya-kośa* s.v. *vyāpāra*). Functionings are intermediary events in the causal chain which begins with an instigator and ends in a final effect. Functionings, as we will see, are closely related to Instruments.

The Navya-Naiyāyikas propose that the Agent of an event is one who performs an action (*kṛti*) which instigates the event.[8] That is, Agent $(e, N) \leftrightarrow \exists a$ [action (a, N) & instigates (a, e)]. An action is also described as an effort, attempt, or trying (*prayatna*). Trying to Φ is not Φ-ing: causal chains can be broken, attempts can fail. Neither is trying to Φ the same as willing or desiring to Φ; rather, it is what is immediately instigated by the willing or desiring.[9]

The Patient of an event is the 'home' of the final effect instigated by the event. That is, Patient $(e, N) \leftrightarrow \exists f$ [home (f, N) & culminates (f, e)].[10] A 'home' is a location, but not necessarily a spatio-temporal region. The final effect is often a change in the state of the Patient, in which case the 'home' of the final effect is the Patient itself. The final effect might also be the relocation of the Patient, in which case the 'home' of the final effect is the final location of the Patient.

The Place of an event is its location. As before, this is typically either the location of the Agent of the event, or the location of the Patient of the event.

The role these notions play may be seen in the analysis of (2). A typical analysis is given in the *Nyāya-kośa* (s.v. *dhātu*):

> The meaning of the sentence 'Devadatta cooks rice' is: Devadatta, qualified by being single, is the possessor of an attempt which instigates a functioning which instigates a softening resident in rice. [This paraphrase] has, as its chief qualificand, the meaning of the nominative-marked word. The meaning of the sentence 'Rice is cooked by Devadatta' is: rice, qualified by being single, is the locus of that softening which is caused by that functioning which is caused by that trying which inheres in Devadatta.

An initial paraphrase of (2a) is (5):

(5) Cooking (*e*) & Agent (*e*, Devadatta) & Patient (*e*, rice).

Now, an Agent of an event is one whose action instigates the event. So, substituting in (5):

(6) Cooking (*e*) & $\exists a$ [action (*a*, Devadatta) & instigates (*a*, *e*)] & Patient (*e*, rice).

The Patient of an event is the 'home' of the final effect instigated by the event. The final effect of cooking the rice is the rice's being cooked. We might distinguish these two events by means of subscripts, cooking_T and cooking_I, indicating that one derives from a transitive verb, and the other from a corresponding intransitive (cf. Pietroski 1998: 85). The cooking_I is the culmination of the cooking_T. The Nyāya prefer to describe the first as the active cooking (*pāka*) of the rice, and the second as the rice's being softened (*viklitti*). Both are in fact regarded as denotata of the verbal root, the first being called the 'doing' (*kriyā*), while the second is its fruition (*phala*) or culmination. Thus:

(7) $\exists f$ [softening (*f*) & culminates (*f*, *e*) & home (*f*, rice)] & $\exists a$ [action (*a*, Devadatta) & instigates (*a*, *e*)].

Notice that, since the cooking event *e* is instigated by Devadatta's action *a*, and itself instigates the rice's being softened *f*, it is a 'functioning' event, an intermediary in the causal chain.

In (7) we quantify over two events, the instigator and the final effect, but not over the functioning event. According to Davidson, we ought to do so. Thus, consider the difference between 'Brutus killed Caesar', which describes a single act, and 'Brutus kissed Caesar', which does not (there may have been several such kissings). We do not want to say that these differ in logical form, and so 'when we were tempted into thinking [that an action] sentence describes a single event we were misled: it does not describe any event at all. But if [it] is true, then there is an event that makes it true' (Davidson 1980: 117). That is to say, we should construe 'Brutus kissed Caesar' as saying that there is at least one kissing, by Brutus, of Caesar. Davidson's thesis that action sentences quantify over the main event place is widely accepted, and I too will assume that he is right. Revising the Nyāya analysis accordingly, the claim is that the logical form of action sentences typically involves a quantification over *three* event places. If $A\ \Phi_T s\ P$, then $\exists a \exists e \exists f$ [action (a, A) & instigates (a, e) & $\Phi_1(f)$ & culminates (f, e) & home (f, P)].

It is clear that the passive form (2b) is given exactly the same paraphrase in the above passage, the only difference being in the order of the conjuncts.[11] The analysis, moreover, explains why inferences of the following form are valid: $A\ V_T$ —, so — V_I. Such inferences are valid because, if P is $\Phi_1$ed, then $\exists f\ [\Phi_1(f)$ & home $(f, P)]$. The analysis also promises to shed light on the problematic case (3). Having drawn a distinction between the culminating and the functioning events, we must likewise distinguish their locations. In this analysis, the location of the culminating event is encoded as a Patient, while the location of the functioning event is encoded as a Place. So paraphrases of (3a) and (3b) are:

(8) a. $\exists e$ [Agent $(e$, Devadatta) & sitting$_T$ (e) & location $(e$, the ground)].

b. $\exists e$ [Agent $(e$, Devadatta) & $\exists f$ [sitting$_I$ (f) & culminates (f, e) & home $(f$, the ground)].

Perhaps we can capture the sense by saying that, in the first case, Devadatta is described as *on-sitting* the ground, while in the second case, he is described as *seated* on the ground. (3a) concerns the location of a functioning, an intermediary event, Devadatta's 'occupation' as being one of sitting. (3b) describes the location of the final effect, Devadatta's being seated. The peculiarity in transitive verbs of sitting, lying or staying is that the location of both events is (and, perhaps, must be) the same spatio-temporal region, and this is what gives rise to the puzzle. However, an analysis which distinguishes the two events is able to draw a semantic distinction even where no physical difference exists.[12]

The same feature of the analysis—quantification over multiple event positions—has a bearing on one of the classic puzzles in action theory (cf. Pietroski 1998: 82–4). Booth pulls the trigger of his pistol, thereby shooting Lincoln, who dies the next day. In killing Lincoln, of how many actions is Booth the agent? Many would share Davidson's intuition that Booth's pulling the trigger is his shooting Lincoln and is also his killing Lincoln, albeit under different descriptions. And yet his pulling of the trigger *cannot* be the same event as his shooting Lincoln, if (9) is true:

(9) Booth pulled the trigger with his finger but shot Lincoln with his pistol.

Likewise, Booth's killing Lincoln cannot be the same event as Lincoln's being killed, if (10) is true:

(10) Booth killed Lincoln on 13 April 1865 but Lincoln was killed on 14 April 1865.

In each case, there is an adjunct ('with his finger', 'on 13 April 1865') true of one event but not the other. The puzzle in (9) is resolved once we see that, even though the pulling and the shooting are distinct events, Booth is the Agent of both events in virtue of one and the same action. Thus, the logical form of (9) is

(9*) $\exists e_1 \exists e_2 \exists a$ {action(a, Booth) & [Patient(e_1, the trigger) & Instrument (e_1, his finger) & instigates (a, e_1)] & [Patient (e_2, Lincoln) & Instrument (e_2, the pistol) & instigates (a, e_2)] }.

The puzzle in (10) is resolved when we see that the description 'Booth's killing Lincoln' is ambiguous. It could be taken as denoting either:

(i) $\exists ! e$ [killing$_T$ (e) & Patient (e, Lincoln) & Agent (e, Booth)], or

(ii) $\exists ! f \exists e$ [killing$_I$ (f) & culminates (f, e) & home (f, Lincoln) & Agent (e, Booth)].

A killing$_T$ is a 'functioning', an intermediary event instigated by Booth's action and having its final effect in Lincoln's death. A killing$_I$ is the final effect of a killing$_T$. So (10) is true on the first reading, but false on the second.[13]

The three remaining thematic roles distinguished by the Indians are Instrument, Target, and Donor. The Target of an event is that which is desired by the Agent to be the recipient of the final effect caused by the event.[14] A 'recipient' (*bhāgin*) is one who receives a share or portion, though there is no implication that what is received is desirable (so the more common translation, 'Beneficiary', is misleading). This thematic role, unlike any of the others so far encountered, depends on the instantiation of another thematic role, namely, an Agent. We might represent the element of 'role anaphora' by quantifying over Agents. So let us formalize the analysis in this way: Target (*e*, *N*) $\leftrightarrow \exists f \exists K$ [Agent (*e*, *K*) & desired-recipient (*f*, *K*, *N*) & culminates (*f*, *e*)]. (11b) now gives the logical form of (11a):

(11) a. Devadatta gives milk to the Brahmin

b. $\exists e \exists f$ [Agent (*e*, Devadatta) & Patient (*e*, milk) & desired-recipient (*f*, Devadatta, the Brahmin) & culminates (*f*, *e*)].

The Donor of an event is the location of a displacement caused by the event, but not its Place.[15] Technically, a 'displacement' (*vibhāga*) is said to be located at both loci. Devadatta's falling causes his displacement from the tree, and since the Place of the falling is the location of Devadatta, the Donor is the tree. In this example, the object displaced is the Agent, and, since the Place of the event is the location of the Agent, the Donor will be the location from which the Agent is displaced. The displaced object need not be the Agent, however. In 'Devadatta drops his pencil from the tree', it is the Patient which is displaced. Say that an event e displaces *N* from *m* iff *e* causes *N*'s being at a location other than *m*. Then we can formalize the analysis: Donor (*e*, *l*) $\leftrightarrow \exists N \exists m$ [Place (*e*, *m*) & $m \neq l$ & displaces (*e*, *N*, *l*)]. Thus, (12b) is the paraphrase of (12a):

(12) a. Devadatta falls from the tree

b. $\exists e$ [Agent (*e*, Devadatta) & falling (*e*) & $\exists m$ (Place (*e*, *m*) & $m \neq$ {the tree & displaces (*e*, Devadatta, the tree)}].

The Nyāya analysis of an Instrument is the most problematic of all the *kārakas*. The notion of an Instrument is of paramount importance in Indian epistemology, since a 'means of knowing' (*pramāṇa*) is technically the Instrument of a knowing-event (*pramā*) (see §5.1). Pāṇini defines an Instrument as the cause *par excellence* of the effect (*asādhāraṇa-kāraṇa*, P1.4.42). This led one group of Naiyāyikas into regarding an Instrument as the penultimate cause of the final effect, that which causes the final effect without there being any intermediary.[16] This group is perhaps more interested in etiology than semantic theory, for an Instrument thus defined cannot be the object, such as a finger or a pistol, mentioned in a 'with *I*' adjunct. So another group of Naiyāyikas, whom we shall follow, say that the Instrument of an event is a cause which has a functioning that is excluded from non-connection with the final effect of the event.[17] Two clarifications are needed here. First, given that objects and not events are Instruments, we need to be able to speak of an object as having a functioning, or of a functioning as being a functioning of an object: the functioning of the arrow as it flies though the air; the functioning of Devadatta as he falls to the ground. Indeed, it seems implicit in the notion of a functioning event that there is an object whose functioning the event is.[18] Let us say that an event *e* is a functioning of *A* iff *e* is a functioning and *A* is a constituent of *e*. What is meant by saying that the Instrument of an event is a cause which has a functioning is that the event *is* a functioning of the Instrument.

Second, what does it mean to speak of a cause which is excluded from non-connection with the effect? The phrase is borrowed from the Nyāya analysis of the quantifier 'alone' (*eva*). The sentence '*A* is *B* alone' is said to mean that *A*s are excluded from non-connection with *B*s. In other words, all *A*s are *B*.[19] The reference, then, is to the law-like generalization: all functionings have a final effect. In terms of our analysis, what this requires is that whenever there is a quantification over functioning events (*e*), there must be a quantification over final effects (*f*). So the Instrument of an event is an object *A* such that *e* is a functioning of *A* and there is an event *f* which is the final effect of *e*. That is, Instrument $(e, A) \leftrightarrow$ functioning (e, A) & $\exists f$ [culminates (f, e)]. (13b) is the paraphrase of (13a):

(13) a. Devadatta cuts the tree with an axe

b. $\exists e$ [Agent (*e*, Devadatta) & Patient (*e*, the tree) & cutting$_T$ (*f*) & functioning (*e*, the axe)].

If the sentence has a noun whose role is to encode the Patient, the second clause in the definition of an Instrument will be redundant. However, we may permit sentences with elided direct objects, like 'Devadatta eats$_T$ with his fingers', whose logical form is $\exists e \exists f$ [Agent (*e*, Devadatta) & eating$_I$ (*f*) & functioning (*e*, fingers) & culminates (*f*, *e*)].

Let me conclude by attempting a paraphrase for the sentence with which we began:

(1) In the kitchen, Rāma cooks rice for Sītā with firewood from the forest.

The complete paraphrase of this sentence now runs as follows.

(1*) $\exists a \exists e \exists f$ [action (*a*, Rāma) & instigates (*a*, *e*) & cooked_{I} (*f*) & culminates (*f*, *e*) & home (*f*, rice) & desired-recipient (*f*, Rāma, Sītā) & functioning (*e*, firewood) & location (*e*, the kitchen) & displaces (*e*, firewood, the forest) & the kitchen $\neq$ the forest].

3.2 Compounds and Complex Descriptions

Udayana (*c.* AD 1050) is an important transitional figure in the history of Indian philosophy. He wrote commentaries within both the Vaiśeṣika and the Nyāya systems, and sought to find a common theoretical framework within which the two traditions could be combined. The centrepiece of this new framework was a study of the semantics of nominal expressions, and the related issue of realism about universals. There is little trace in his writings of the earlier Nyāya 'propertied particular' theory of meaning. Instead, we find him beginning to investigate the consequences of the separation of meaning and reference along the lines described in §2.3.

For each descriptive noun, there is an axiom in the meaning theory of the form: only As are meant by tokens of 'A'. Formulated as a property of the meaning relation, this states that:

(1) $\mathcal{M} | \text{'}\mathbf{A}\text{'} \subseteq \mathbf{A}.$

Knowledge of such an axiom constitutes the semantic factor in the determination of the meaning relatum of an utterance, the non-semantic factor being knowledge of salient information about the context.

Udayana, however, draws a distinction. He distinguishes between a class of simple, unanalysable descriptive nominals, which he calls *naimittikī* terms, and a class of logically complex descriptive nominals, called the *aupādhikī* terms. Belonging to the second category are both compound terms, like 'white-cow', and 'kingsman' and also terms which, though morphologically simple, have an underlying complexity. Examples are 'beast' (*paśu*), which means something like 'hairy animal with a long tail', 'cook', which means 'person who does the cooking', 'weed', meaning 'uncultivated garden plant', and 'chair', meaning 'item of furniture for sitting on'. Such terms are said to refer to the instances of a complex or 'synthetic' property (*upādhi*).

The group of 'simple' descriptions are correlated with a real property, either a universal (*jāti*) or a trope (*guṇa*), to the instances of which utterances of the term refer. Udayana offers a celebrated sixfold characterization of the distinction between a genuine universal and a synthetic property, to which we shall return later. His characterization strongly suggests that he takes the simple terms to be natural kind terms.[20] One of his conditions, for example, is that the extensions of two genuine universals cannot overlap partially: either one is a subset of the other, or else they are completely distinct. This condition closely resembles the 'genus-species' relationship characteristic of natural kinds. Thus Udayana's 'simple' nominals comprise primarily natural kind terms like 'cow', as well as colour terms like 'red' and a number of other trope terms.

Udayana asserts that the ground-for-use, which delimits the scope of a term, is, in the first case, a natural kind, and in the other, a synthetic property. His idea is that, when the description is logically complex, the restriction on the meaning relation is non-homophonic. Let us suppose that 'B–A' is the complex description 'A-which-is-B' (a 'descriptive determinative' or *karmadhāraya* compound; cf. §2.1). Then the meaning clause for this description will be:

(2) $\mathscr{M}|\text{`B–A'} \subseteq \text{A} \cap \text{B}.$

This meaning clause states, for example, that only a pot which is also blue is the meaning relatum of 'blue-pot'. It would be no difficult matter to formulate a composition rule under which such a clause follows from the axioms for 'A' and 'B'. The form of the meaning clause will be similar even if the description is not syntactically a compound. Thus, we give the term 'beast' a non-homophonic clause: ⟨only a hairy animal with a long tail is the meaning relatum of 'beast'⟩.

Analogous meaning clauses for the other sorts of compound can be formulated. Suppose 'B–A' is the 'conjunctive' (*dvandva*) compound 'A-and-B'. Then the meaning clause will be:

(3) $\mathscr{M}|\text{`B–A'} \subseteq \text{A} \cup \text{B}.$

Thus, if one says 'The men and women are dancing', the descriptive compound 'men-and-women' refers only to those things which are either a man or woman.

Dependent determinative (*tatpuruṣa*) compounds are based on an oblique case relation between the elements. Thus 'children's-book' is based on a dative: a book for children, while 'glass-house' is based on an ablative: a house made from glass. In general, if '$B–A^{l}$' is an inflected dependent determinative compound, it can be transformed into '$B^{k} A^{l}$', for some $k \neq l$ (if $k = l$, the compound is descriptive determinative). An oblique case relationship between two nouns is the syntactic mark of that there is some relation between As and Bs. Thus the phrase 'book for children' denotes things belonging the class of books which are written for children. So let R be the relation indicated by the oblique case relationship, and let R | B be the class of things which are R to some B. Then the meaning clause for 'B–A' is:

(4) $\mathcal{M}|\text{'B} - \text{A'} \subseteq \text{R}|\text{B} \cap \text{A}.$

Notice that we can derive the clause for descriptive determinatives as a special case by introducing the identity relation I, this because B = I|B. The property of $\mathcal{M}$ described by (4) is represented in Figure 4.2.

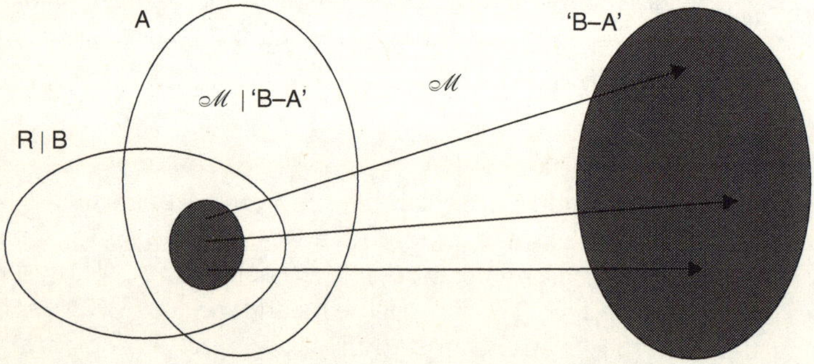

Figure 3.1 $\mathcal{M}$ for a *tatpuruṣa* compound

The fourth main type of compound distinguished by the Sanskrit grammarians is that of the 'exocentric' (*bahuvrīhi*). These compounds differ from the three other types in being adjectival: when the compound 'hot-head' is construed as exocentric, it does not mean a hot head, but rather someone whose head is hot. Thus, the reference of an exocentric is an object which itself stands in an oblique relationship with the second member of the compound. Clearly, for any exocentric compound there is always a corresponding descriptive determinative or dependent determinative. Thus, if 'B – A' is an exocentric, it refers to something to/with/for/from/of whom the A is B, or to something to/with/for/from/of whom the A is to/with/for/from/of B. In the first case, the meaning clause is:

(5) $\mathcal{M}$ |'B–A' $\subseteq$ R|(B $\cap$ A).

The example 'hot-head' is of this sort, R being the relation being-the-owner-of. What this clause states is that only a member of the class of things which are owners of a head which is hot is meant by utterances of 'hot-head'. If the exocentric is of the second sort, derived from a dependent determinative, the meaning clause is:

(6) $\mathcal{M}$ |'B–A' $\subseteq$ R_1|(R_2|B $\cap$ A).

Once again, if we allow R_2 to be the identity relation, this clause can be taken to be the general form covering both sorts of exocentric. If we allow R_1 to be the identity relation as well, this same clause will also include dependent and determinative descriptives.

This shows how the meaning of compound or logically complex descriptions is specified within the semantic framework we are developing. Udayana relies on such clauses in his account of empty descriptions, descriptions which lack a meaning relatum. There is, of course, no problem with descriptions *some* of whose tokens fail to refer: the statement that only As are meant by tokens of 'A' does not entail that every token of 'A' has a meaning relatum.[21] The problem is with a description *none* of whose tokens refer. For the Nyāya insist that the properties which delimit the reference of the primitive terms in their language are 'exampled' (*prasiddha*). That is, they insist that, if 'A' is a primitive term, then

(7) $\mathcal{M}$ |'A' $\neq \varnothing$. [Non-Vacuity]

Matilal calls this the 'implicit Nyāya semantic principle' (1971: 138). It is open, of course, for the Nyāya to make stipulations about what are to be the semantic primitives in their language. The claim is substantive only when the primitive-nonprimitive distinction is equated with another, that between natural kind terms and terms for synthetic kinds. Read as a claim about natural kind terms, (7) at first looks implausible: why must natural kind terms have a reference? However, it receives some support from Putnam's work on natural kind terms. For if it is correct, as he claims, that a natural kind term acquires a meaning through ostension of exemplars of the kind, there must be exemplars in order for the term to be meaningful. I will discuss the Nyāya account of natural kind terms in §6.3.

There are, nevertheless, meaningful descriptions which fail ever to refer. Udayana's pleasant examples are 'the* rabbit's horn' and 'the* turtle's hair'. The important feature of these examples is that they are both complex descriptions. The above method of formulating a meaning clause for complex descriptions is therefore straightforwardly applicable. Both descriptions are dependent determinative compounds based on a possessive (genitive) case relation. Thus, 'the* rabbit's horn' stands for 'the* horn possessed by a rabbit'. The possessive case is alleged to stand for the relation of 'location', construed in the rather wide sense in which properties are located in objects and bodily parts are located on animals. So let B be the class of rabbits, H be the class of horns, and L be the relation '... is located on ...'. Then, the meaning clause for 'rabbit's horn' is, by (8):

(8) $\mathcal{M}|\text{'B–H'} \subseteq \text{L}|\text{B} \cap \text{H},$

where L | B is the set of things located in a rabbit. This states that only a thing which is both a horn and which is located on a rabbit is a meaning relatum of the term 'rabbit's horn'. Translated into the notation of the predicate calculus, we have that the meaning of the term is given by a clause of the form:

(9) $\forall x[\text{Meant}\ (x, \text{'the rabbit's horn'}) \rightarrow (\text{H}x\ \&\ \exists y\ (\text{B}y\ \&\ x\text{L}y))]$

The point to note is that this clause specifies the condition for something to be the reference of the term, even if nothing *in fact* meets that condition. It therefore shows how a *referential* expression can be meaningful even if it fails ever to refer. The same strategy would work for empty names like 'Pegasus'. If we want to accommodate the notion that this name has meaning but no reference, we ought not try to construct a clause in the usual 'realist' form ⟨'Pegasus' refers to Pegasus⟩, in which the name is correlated with an external entity, since by hypothesis there is no such entity. Rather, we should have a clause like ⟨ $\forall x$ ['Pegasus' refers to x iff x is a horse & x is winged] ⟩, which states what condition any entity would have to meet if it is to be the referent.

This shows that the existence of meaningful but empty descriptions does not force us to abandon the claim that descriptions are referential. Indeed, semantic theories for descriptions along the lines suggested by Udayana have been constructed (see Burge 1974 and Evans 1982: 53). In particular, there is no reason to endorse Russell's argument that the existence of such descriptions entails that descriptions have a Russellian paraphrase. I stress this because a number of authors have claimed that Udayana's remarks on reference failure anticipate Russell's in this matter.[22] Notice, however, that for Udayana no statement containing an empty description is either true or false; no such statement is knowledge-apt. It is in the context of this discussion of empty terms that Udayana remarks that 'the limit to the capacity of speech is as a means of knowing. If this limit is overstepped, there will be only disorder' (1986: 190). He goes on to say that if someone were to ask of the non-existent person named 'Devadatta' whether he has or does not have some feature, it would make no difference if we reply in the affirmative or in the negative.

Udayana, as remarked before, goes further when he identifies the class of semantically primitive terms with the natural kind terms and trope terms. This is not a trivial thesis. Why should we not analyse 'cow' as 'animal with dewlap', or 'red' as 'colour with the greatest wavelength'? A possible reply lies in Udayana's discussion of the notion of a definition (*lakṣaṇa*). He argues that one role of definitions is in the discrimination (*vyāvṛtti*) of the thing to be defined from things not covered by the definition. By a 'definition' what is meant here is any true equivalence. For example, the following are both 'definitions' of a cow: $\forall x$ [x is a cow iff x possesses cow-hood]; and $\forall x$ [x is a cow iff x has a dewlap]. Similarly, Udayana observes that in the Vaiśeṣika system, a number of different definitions of 'substance' have been given. Since the property of being a substance is, for the Vaiśeṣika, a real universal, one definition is just: $\forall x$ [x is a substance iff x possesses substance-hood]. But other definitions are given, such as: $\forall x$ [x is a substance iff x possesses qualities], or $\forall x$ [x is a substance iff x is an inherent cause]. This highlights the distinction between definition and analysis. The purpose of a definition is simply to supply a second description with the same extension as the first, there being no implication that the new description is an analysis of the original one. In this sense of definition, even the simples in Udayana's system can be defined. Udayana's use of the term 'definition' is the same as Russell's: 'It is clear that if you define "red" as "The colour with the greatest wavelength", you are not giving the actual meaning of the word at all; you are simply giving a true description' (1956: 194).

Udayana would therefore want to say that the sentence '$\forall x$ [x is a cow iff x possesses dewlap]' is just a definition, whereas the sentence '$\forall x$ [x is a beast iff x is a hairy animal with a long tail]' is an analysis of the term 'beast', one which reveals its hidden logical complexity. But how do we decide which extensional identity sentences are definitions, and which are analyses? Udayana offers a series of six criteria (known as the *jāti-bādhakas*—'impediments to being a universal') to distinguish universals, the meanings of the primitive terms in his system, from the rest. The six impediments are (cf. Matilal 1971: 73-7; K. Chakrabarti 1975; Potter 1977: 136–7):

(i) 'non-plurality'—a universal must be plurally instantiated;
(ii) 'equipollence' (*tulyatva*)—two co-extensive properties cannot both be universals;
(iii) 'cross-connection' (*saṃkara*)—two universals must not partially overlap;
(iv) 'regress'—a property like universal-hood cannot itself be a universal, on pain of infinite regress (universal-hood-hood, etc.);
(v) a property like differentia-hood cannot be a universal, for by definition the basic differentia (*viśeṣa*) share no common universal property; and
(vi) a property like inherence-hood cannot be a universal, since it does not inhere in its loci.

Of these six, the last three are there to maintain the internal consistency of the Vaiśeṣika ontological system. The first impediment debars singly-instanced properties such as space-hood from the status of genuine natural kind. This is perhaps motivated by the thought that the very nature of a universal consists in its grounding judgements of the form '*x* is of the same kind as *y*', which presuppose that there are at least two entities belonging to that kind.

The second condition states that, if **A** and **B** are distinct universal properties, then A $\neq$ B. Note that this does not entail that universals are extensionally individuated, but only that no two universals can have the same extension. As for the third impediment, it states that if **A** and **B** are distinct universal properties, then either A $\subseteq$ B or A $\supseteq$ B or A $\cap$ B = $\varnothing$. These conditions entail that universals are ordered hierarchically. Jointly, they state that:

if **A** and **B** are two universals, then

(i) if A = B, then **A** = **B**
(ii) if A $\subset$ B, then **A** is under **B** in the hierarchy
(iii) if B $\subset$ A, then **B** is under **A** in the hierarchy
(iv) if A $\cap$ B = $\varnothing$, then **A** and **B** belong to distinct branches of the hierarchy.

Udayana's thesis is that universals are arranged in a hierarchy: given two universals, either they are related as genus and species, all instances of one being instances of the other, or else they are completely disjoint, having no instance in common. The demand that universals be organized hierarchically shows that the paradigm of a universal is a biological species, where this structure tends to be exhibited.

Do Udayana's criteria succeed in distinguishing universals from synthetic properties? Unfortunately, it does not seem true that hierarchical structure is sufficient for a group of properties to be 'natural'. Nelson Goodman, in his 'new riddle of induction' (1954: 74), shows that there can be inter-definable pairs of properties, one pair 'natural', the other not. He defines the non-natural pair of colour term ('grue', 'bleen') in terms of the natural pair ('blue', 'green'):

> *x* is grue iff *x* is green if examined before time *t* and blue otherwise.
>
> *x* is bleen iff *x* is blue if examined before time *t* and green otherwise.

Udayana would like 'blue' and 'green' to be primitive terms, and 'grue' and 'bleen' to be complex non-primitive terms. But, as Goodman shows, we can just as well define 'blue' and 'green' in terms of 'grue' and 'bleen':

> *x* is green iff *x* is grue if examined before time *t* and bleen otherwise.
>
> *x* is blue iff *x* is bleen iff examined before time *t* and grue otherwise.

Udayana's claim that only natural properties are organized hierarchically is therefore false, as both pairs, in this example, meet the criteria. More generally, no set of extensional criteria can distinguish between a universal and a co-extensive synthetic property: *that* distinction is an intensional one. Udayana, rather in the spirit of the logical atomist, wants the primitive terms in his semantic theory to correspond with the basic entities in his ontology, and tries to ensure the correspondence by having a semantic criterion for something to be a basic entity. That, perhaps, was the wrong way to go; it would have been better to claim that there just is a set of natural properties, and that a natural kind term is one which is used to refer to the instances of a natural property.

Notes

[1] Gadādhara's short text, the *Vyutpattivāda*, is an authoritative work on the topic, usually read along with the *Śaktivāda*. It has been translated by Bhatta (1990).

[2] The term '*śābdabodha*' suffers from an ambiguity—it denotes both the belief-episode which is the output of the language-process, and also the content (*viṣayatā*) of this belief-episode. It is usually clear from the context which of these two senses is intended. On this notion of paraphrase, see Cardona (1975, esp. pp. 260, 273).

[3] An older translation of the terms is: Agent, Object, Instrument, Destination, Source, Locus. However, the translation of *karman* as 'Object' obscures the distinction between *kāraka*s and purely syntactic cases. My translations are influenced by the meanings the terms are given by the Naiyāyikas.

[4] The Sanskrit grammarians do not refer to the cases by the names 'nominative', 'accusative', and so on, but simply by numbers. I will use the western case-names for convenience, though doing so runs the danger that it is liable to blur the distinction between cases and *kāraka*s.

[5] This formulation seems preferable to that of Kiparsky and Staal (1969). They argue that *kāraka*s are 'underlying relations of deep structure', belonging to a level *intermediate* between the level of semantic relations and the level of surface structure. Kiparsky and Staal concede, however, that the interrelations between the semantic and deep structure levels are many-many, as are the interrelations between the levels of deep structure and surface structure. It is difficult then to see what justifies the description of the *kāraka* level as 'intermediary'.

[6] The Nyāya account shares many features with the proposals of Pietroski (1998), in particular, his analysis of Agency, use of thematic roles, and view of actions as tryings (though not his appeal to complex events).

[7] In some theories of action, the notions of instigation and culmination are defined non-interdefinably, e.g. Pietroski (1998). For this reason I retain both terms. The Nyāya makes use of a rich causal idiom, and it is possible that the difference is marked, for example, in nuances in the meanings of '*anukūla*' and '*prayojaka*'.

[8] The Sanskrit equation is: *kartā* = *kriyā-anukūla-kṛti-mān.* Gaṅgeśa (1901: 831); *Nyāya-kośa,* s.v. *kartā.*

[9] Cf. *pravṛtti-sākṣād-anukūlatvam icchāyāḥ lakṣaṇam.* The analysis of Agency must be extended if we are to allow for non-volitional Agents. See Cardona (1974: 252 - 3), Matilal (1990: 44), and Sen's introduction to Raghunātha (1979: xiv). Raghunātha notes that a two-event analysis cannot always apply. For example, in 'Devadatta sleeps', the Agent is performing no action, and the verbal suffix (which is normally taken to denote the action), denotes simply the substratumhood relation between the Agent Devadatta and the sleeping event.

[10] The Sanskrit equation is: *karman* = *kriyā-janya-phala-śālī* (*Nyāya-kośa,* s.v. *karman*).

[11] Navya-Nyāya reparses the sentences into a subject-predicate form. The basic sentential form in this language comprises a 'qualifier' (*prakāra*), a 'qualificand' (*viśeṣya*), and a relation (*saṃbandha*). That is, basic sentences

have the form 'aRb'. In Matilal's standard (1968) symbolisation, this is written '*Q* (*a*, *b*, *r*)', 'Q' being a blanket 'qualification' connector somewhat akin to Strawson's predicative assignment function 'ass (*x*, y)'. When thus paraphrased, the active paraphrase has Devadatta as its qualificand, while the passive has the rice as its qualificand. For this reason, the active and passive versions are sometimes still regarded as having distinct logical forms by the Nyāya logicians.

[12] A similar point exposes a flaw in Nāgārjuna's 'grammatical' argument against motion (cf. Ganeri 2001b, §2.6). Nāgārjuna argues that the supposition that the sentence 'the traveller traverses the [place] being-traversed' implicates *two* motion-events—one denoted by the finite verb and one serving to individuate the position where the motion takes place—entails, absurdly, that there must be two Agents of motion. That conclusion does not, however, follow; for the correct paraphrase of the sentence is $\exists e \exists f$ [Agent (*e*, the traveller) & being-traversed$_I$ (*f*) & culminates (*f*, *e*) & home (*f*, the place being traversed)]. Notice that there is a single Agent of the functioning and culminating events, whether or not they are identical.

[13] See Pietroski (1998: 84). Pietroski's solution makes rather more use of the idea that 'shooting' and 'pulling' are sortals true of complex events. I do not find much trace of the idea of a complex event in the Indian literature, although there is a hint in Bhartṛhari (*Vākyapadīya* III.7.18).

[14] The Sanskrit equation is: *saṃpradānaḥ = kriyā-janya-phala-bhāgitayā kartur icchā-viṣayaḥ. Nyāya-kośa*, s.v. *saṃpradāna.*

[15] The Sanskrit equation is: *apādānaḥ = kriyānāśrayatve sati tajjanya-vibhāgāśrayaḥ. Nyāya-kośa*, s.v. *apādānaḥ.*

[16] That is, *phalopadhāyakaṃ kāraṇam. Nyāya-kośa*, s.v. *karaṇa*; cf. Matilal (1985*b*: 373).

[17] The Sanskrit equation is: *karaṇam = phalāyogavyavacchinna-vyāpāravat kāraṇam. Nyāya-kośa*, s.v. *karaṇam*; cf. Matilal (1985*b*: 375).

[18] Gadādhara claims that an Instrument is also dependent on the functioning an Agent (*kartṛ-vyāpārādhinatve'pi vyāpāravat kāraṇaṃ karaṇaṃ*). I will ignore this complication here.

[19] See Ganeri (1999).

[20] See Matilal (1986,: 424, fn. 55).

[21] It is less clear whether we should insist that each token is unambiguous. This is to insist that $\mathscr{M}^{-1}$ is a function. Matilal (1968: 25), for instance, translates *śakti* as 'functional relation'. Deshpande (1992: 53) is more explicit: '... this can safely be rendered by the term "signification function".... It could also be regarded as a function in the terminology of modern logic. The proposition "*x* signifies *y*" could be regarded as a diadic function of the form *F*(*x*, *y*), with *x* and *y* as variables.' However, one might think that every token of an ambiguous term itself has a plurality of semantic values. That, indeed, is what distinguishes an ambiguous term from an indexical one. See §9.1.

[22] Notably Matilal (1971: 123–45) and (1985: 77–85). Matilal's reading of Udayana is followed by Shaw (1974). A. Chakrabarti (1985) gives a more Strawsonian reading to Udayana, one with which I am in greater agreement, but comments that 'there is no rule which can fix the referential links between distinct, vacuous singular terms and discriminable non-existents simply because one end of the link is always missing' (p. 330). This does not seem to follow.

4

Śābdabodha
Meaning and the Structure of Understanding

4.1 Testimony Principles and Communication

What is the essence of language? The Indian reply to this question is entrenched in their conception of the philosophical enterprise. As epistemologists and advocates of the so-called *pramāṇa* theory, their leading interest is in the epistemological agent, and in the faculties or capacities in virtue of which one secures a corpus of warranted true beliefs. The primary function of a language, they claim, is as an Instrument for the acquisition of knowledge. Matilal (1990: 4–5) observes that:

> [W]hat we call the philosophy of language in India has always formed a part of the classical philosophers' general epistemological inquiry, part of the *pramāṇa-śāstra*, the theory of 'evidence' for belief, or knowledge.

An Instrument of knowing is an epistemic capacity, process or technique which, when functioning normally in appropriate circumstances and in the absence of defeating conditions, produces true beliefs as final events (see §3.1 for this notion of Instrument).[1] Perception is the paradigm: what makes the perceptual faculty an Instrument of knowing is that it is a causal process leading from the object to a true belief when there are no visual or cognitive defects, the lighting is adequate, and so on. The thesis that *language* is an Instrument of knowing is, therefore, a claim that someone who understands a language thereby possesses an *epistemic* capacity, one which in a range of conditions results in knowledge. We might call this the 'epistemological conception' of language. It is a conception which sees testimony as essential to the nature and function of a language.

The epistemological conception gives the notion of what it is to *understand* a language in a central role. Each hearer has a 'language faculty', analogous to their perceptual or inferential faculties, which grounds the ability of a linguistically competent hearer to move from the auditory perception of certain string of uninterpreted sounds to the formation of beliefs with specifiable contents. A competent hearer can hear some string of noises and come to believe that the speaker asked whether it is raining, or said that the moon goes round the earth. This capacity is what constitutes the hearer's ability to understand utterances of sentences in the language. A theory of understanding, then, is a theory of language-processing.[2] On hearing a speaker S's utterance of the sentence 'Rāma is cooking rice', the hearer H forms a belief involving the proposition that Rāma is cooking rice. This might be the belief that S *said* that Rāma is cooking rice, if S's utterance is taken to be an assertion, or that S *asked* whether Rāma is cooking rice, if S's utterance is taken to be a question, or that S *ordered* that Rāma is to cook rice, if S's utterance is taken to be a command, and so on. That is to say, the output of the language faculty is a belief that a certain proposition has been uttered by the speaker with a certain assertoric force.

It is a key claim in Nyāya philosophy of language that, for a basic category of utterances, the output of the language faculty is a pure belief in the proposition expressed. The salient category is of statements sincerely asserted by an honest and competent speaker. To put matters another way, the claim is that, under certain conditions, the proper understanding of an utterance involves the *direct assent* by the hearer to the speaker's utterance.[3] Thus, understanding an utterance of 'Rāma is cooking rice', made sincerely by a competent speaker, consists in the hearer's direct assent to the proposition that Rāma is cooking rice. Understanding issues sometimes in a belief not *about* what the speaker said but *in* what was said.

Beliefs formed by direct assent are apt to be instances of testimonial knowledge. The utterance must, of course, be true, and whatever further conditions are necessary for knowledge must obtain. We will look at what those conditions might be later. The Naiyāyika give the technical term *śābdabodha* or 'linguistically derived thought-episode' to an item of knowledge formed by direct assent to some speaker's utterance. This is where the epistemological conception of language comes in. For what the Nyāya thesis amounts to is that for a basic sort of utterance, understanding consists in the tokening of a belief which is apt to be an item of knowledge.[4] The language faculty is a sui generis epistemic faculty, reducible neither to perception, nor inference, nor to some combination of those two. The question for the Naiyāyika is: what properties must the language faculty have if it is to be a source of knowledge? Their anti-reductionist claim was not universally accepted; indeed it was strongly contested by Vaiśeṣika, Buddhist, and other thinkers. I will here, however, attempt an assessment of the viability of this approach to language.

Notice that there is no mention in the above of communication between speaker and hearer, of the intentions of the speaker, or the hearer's recognition of them. A rather different but more familiar conception of the relationship between language and testimony claims that communication is essentially the *transmission* of knowledge from speaker to hearer. Such a conception is found in Evans (1982: 310–20) and more especially McDowell (1980). We might, following Strawson (1971), classify theories of meaning under two headings: communication-intention theories and theories of formal semantics. The communication-intention theorist believes that we must account for the concept of meaning in terms of the possession by speakers of audience-directed intentions, specifically intentions to get the audience to think that the speaker has a certain belief. The formal semanticist, on the other hand, believes that the concept of meaning is to be given in terms of a formal theory specifying truth-conditions or informational content, the way the sentence represents the world as being. McDowell criticizes Strawson's classification, in part for taking the speaker's communicative intention to be to inform the hearer about his own beliefs, rather than simply about some state of affairs: 'The primary point of making assertions is not to instil into others beliefs about one's own beliefs, but to inform others—to let them know—about the subject matter of one's assertions' (1980: 127). Thus emended, a communication-intention theorist would say that communication between speaker and hearer takes place when the hearer recognizes the speaker's intention to communicate that *p*, takes that intention as a reason for believing that *p*, and thereby comes to believe that *p*. If 'communicates that *p*' has a success grammar, so that 'S communicates that *p*' entails that *p*, then the hearer's belief will often also be knowledge.[5]

McDowell contends that this mutual *awareness of intentions* is a characteristic of human communication. Transparency of communicative intention is what distinguishes human communication from the more primitive sort of information-transmission exhibited in such animal communication as bird-squawk:

> A bird might instinctively emit a characteristic sort of squawk on seeing a predator; other birds might acquire, on hearing such a squawk,

> a propensity towards behaviour appropriate to the proximity of a predator ... [which] is no less appropriately thought of as possession of information than is the state which standardly results from perceiving a predator (1980: 129).

While bird-squawk does involve the transmission of information, it lacks the 'overtness of intention' which characterizes communication between humans. The communication-intention theorist (from whom McDowell himself departs company at this point) takes the notion of communication, now characterized in terms of a mutual awareness of intentions to transmit knowledge, as the basis for a reductive analysis of the concept of meaning.[6]

A Naiyāyika reply to McDowell is to deny that the acquisition of knowledge by testimony necessarily involves anything like the *recognition of the speaker's intentions.* McDowell himself distinguishes two levels in the application of the concept of communication: the level at which the information stated by the utterance is transmitted, and the level which concerns shared information about the speaker's intentions. He claims that both sorts of information are transmitted whenever a speech act is understood: 'When a properly executed speech act is understood, such [second level] information is always transmitted—not only in informative assertions but also in assertions by which information is not transmitted and in speech acts which are not assertoric at all' (p. 131). But while it is certainly correct that, in communication, information about the speaker's intentions is always *available* to the hearer, for her intentions have in some sense been made public by the performance of her speech act, it does not follow that both sorts of information must always be transmitted. McDowell's second level is information which is necessarily available to the hearer, but does not describe information which is necessarily transmitted in communication. We need no more than this for it to remain the case that it is the hearer's capacity to acquire information about the speaker's intentions (and hence the possibility of withdrawing assent, and so on) that distinguishes human from animal communication.[7]

The Nyāya thesis, that understanding typically consists in direct, non-inferential, assent, is in sharp contrast to the inferentialist assumption implicit in McDowell's position: that assenting to another's utterance is never direct, but always depends on the hearer's awareness of the speaker's intentions, or of the speech act performed by the speaker. The Nyāya deny that it is the case that one assents to the proposition expressed only if one believes that the speaker has asserted it, and asserted it with certain intentions of the right sort. It is this claim that grounds the Nyāya anti-reductionist approach to testimony and distinguishes it from the approach of the communication-intention theorist.

Let us say that a hearer directly assents to an utterance σ and thereby believes that *p* iff her language faculty leads her non-inferentially to believe that *p* on hearing a speaker utters σ. The thesis that we normally directly assent to the credible assertions of others is what is sometimes labelled in the literature on testimony the 'Principle of Trust' or the 'Principle of Credulity'. Sometimes[8] it is argued that the principle is more than a contingent fact about the language faculty; in particular, the principle is defended by appealing to Davidson's work on radical interpretation, to argue that *any* interpretation of another's speech presupposes direct assent to at least some of what they say. However, we need not rely on any such argument here. The claim we are interested in is that for a basic category of utterances, direct assent is sufficient for understanding, and that a language-processing model of understanding shows how understanding an utterance could consist in directly assenting to it.

The idea that understanding an utterance could consist in directly assenting to it might be resisted on a number of grounds. One may feel that understanding an utterance cannot be the same as believing it, since it is clearly possible to understand what someone says without believing them. This is true, but it is no argument against the Nyāya claim. For the Nyāya thesis is that the familiar language-processing model of understanding has to be *supplemented* with an account of the conditions under which direct assent occurs. When those conditions do not obtain, understanding the utterance consists in coming to believe that the speaker said, asked, commanded, etc. a certain proposition. This first argument against the Nyāya thesis mistakes it for a much stronger one: that *all* understanding consists in direct assent.

A second argument makes the same mistake. This is the argument that, if understanding consists in direct assent, and direct assent consists in knowing, then it is impossible to understand a false assertion (cf. Mohanty 1992: 253). The Nyāya thesis, however, is only that understanding consists in direct assent *in certain conditions*, and direct assent constitutes knowledge *in certain conditions*. When those conditions do not obtain, the hearer either does not directly assent, or directly assents but does not know (see also §4.3).

Arguments against the direct assent account, therefore, have to claim that one *never* understands an utterance by directly assenting to it.

Perhaps the strongest such argument is based on the 'autonomy' of the understander. The idea is that any understander is free to assent to, or withhold assent from, the proposition expressed, so assent must involve an act of judgement with respect to a proposition antecedently presented. This line of thought, however, can come to seem like an over-intellectualization of the process by which we understand language. It claims that the conditions for direct assent must be recognized by the hearer as obtaining. It is fairly widely accepted that the analogous claim about testimonial knowledge is wrong: it is not necessary for the acquisition of testimonial knowledge that the hearer is reflectively aware of the speaker's epistemic credibility (cf. Audi 1998: 132–3). What is necessary is that the language faculty is surrounded by a set of complementary dispositional capacities which detect the failure of those conditions to obtain, or the obtaining of defeating conditions. The hearer has to be able, unconsciously or with the help of background beliefs, to detect cues that the speaker is lying, or is incompetent: cues like blushing, and fidgeting. So the counterfactual claim, that if the speaker were not sincere and competent, the hearer would come to be aware of it, can be true even if, in the normal situation in which the speaker is sincere and competent, the hearer has no reflective awareness that they are. The hearer remains autonomous in the sense that they will *withhold* assent if defeating conditions obtain, and will *withdraw* assent if they are later discovered to have obtained.

According to Frege's theory of understanding, understanding consists in 'entertaining' a thought-content, in advance of judging it to be true. Here, 'entertains ...' is a special sort of commitment-free propositional attitude. Can we criticize the Nyāya account on the grounds that it has no room for such a notion?[9] It is not enough simply to point to a lacuna in the Nyāya list of propositional attitudes.[10] The argument has to be that no account of understanding can give a central role to direct assent, that is, that entertaining a thought-content is *essential* to understanding any utterance. The language-processing model of understanding casts doubt on the need for such states in an explanation of understanding, but let us consider the matter further. One argument is that the capacity to entertain a proposition is possessed by anyone who can understand the playful use of language, in drama, fiction, and so on, when directly to assent would be entirely to miss the point. Now, since these playful uses of language depend for their existence on the more basic use to make assertions, questions, and so on, the argument is presumably a transcendental one: the basic use be such-and-such, if a playful use is to be possible. If this is to be an argument against the Nyāya theory, we need to be given a further argument, one which demonstrates that the direct assent theory cannot explain the playful use of language. While I have no theory of fictional discourse to offer, I can see no reason in principle why an explanation of fictional language could not be given within the parameters of a theory which claims that certain basic uses of language demand direct assent.[11]

A different argument for the introduction of such states might rest on the so-called belief-independence of informational states: being in certain sorts of informational state is independent of whether one believes one is in one (see Chakrabarti 1994: 122), and so those states are commitment-free in the same way as is the attitude of 'entertaining'. However, no fact about the independence of informational states from the realm of belief and judgement can ground a distinction within that realm.

A final argument is suggested by Dummett (1978: 130–1) on behalf of Frege:

> For a sentence to be able to be used to convey information, it must be possible to understand it in advance of knowing it to be true. Frege considers, specifically, an identity-statement, that is one of the form '*a* is the same as *b*', and argues that if, in order to understand the statement, the hearer is required to know the reference of the terms '*a*' and '*b*', then, if it is true, he must, if he understands it, already know that it is true; hence, on this supposition, such a statement could convey no information.

The force of the argument seems to be this. Anyone who understands the sentence '*a* is the same as *a*' knows that it is true *independently* of any further conditions obtaining or failing to obtain. However, someone who understands the sentence '*a* is the same as *b*' only knows that it is true if certain further conditions obtain. It is only by assuming that those further conditions concern the hearer's reflective states that one would be led to suppose that the distinction between understanding and knowing is a distinction between entertaining a proposition and knowing it to be true. Directly assenting to an utterance is, after all, a paradigmatic case of receiving information.[12]

Indian philosophers, and the Naiyāyikas in particular, spend much time trying to spell out just what further conditions turn direct assent into testimonial knowledge. For the time being, let us simply say that the utterance is *assent-worthy* if these further conditions are met. We have already remarked that an epistemic faculty, even if functioning non-defectively, produces warranted beliefs only if the external circumstances are suitable. A person with properly functioning eyesight will acquire warranted perceptual beliefs only if the lighting is strong enough, there are no mirrors or 'tricks of light', and so on. The assent-worthiness of an utterance is, likewise, part of what makes the external circumstances suitable for the properly functioning language faculty to produce warranted beliefs. The externalistically inclined Nyāya maintains that, just as there is no demand for a perceiver to have evidence as to the suitability of the lighting in advance of forming genuinely warranted perceptual beliefs, so too there can be no demand that an understander recognizes evidence that the utterance is assent-worthy in advance of forming genuinely warranted testimonial beliefs. Assent-worthiness consists, therefore, in the absence of defeating conditions. We might formulate the Nyāya analysis of testimonial knowledge as follows: H testimonially knows that *p* on hearing S's utterance σ iff (i) H directly assents to σ, (ii) σ is true, and (iii) there are no defeating conditions. I will develop the analysis in Chapter 2.

Let T be the following schema, the 'testimony schema' (in which 'S' denotes the speaker and 'H' the hearer):

(T) if S tells H that *p*, and H understands S's utterance and thereby accepts it as true, then H comes to know that *p*.

The problem of the relation between understanding and belief, and consequent issues about the reduction of testimony to inference, are finessed in this schema. The Naiyāyikas, as we have seen, claim that understanding sometimes *consists* in assent; the reductionist claim would be that one first understands the utterance, and only then infers it to be true in conjunction with other premises. Both, however, can agree with the form in which T is phrased. Let us now call a 'testimony principle' a statement of the form:

$T \rightarrow X$, or $X \rightarrow T$.

In principles of the first sort, X is a necessary condition for testimony; in principles of the second sort, X is a sufficient condition. A theory of testimony is a completion of '$T \leftrightarrow \phi$', for some set of conditions ϕ. An important testimony principle involving a sufficient condition is the so-called Transmission Principle. Here is Evans' version (Evans 1982: 310–11):

> If the speaker S has knowledge of *x* to the effect that it is *F*, and in consequence utters a sentence in which he refers to *x*, and says of it that it is *F*, and if his audience A hears and understands the utterance,

> and accepts it as true (and there are no defeating conditions), then A himself thereby comes to know of x that it is F.

Another version is given by Peacocke (1987: 149), from whom I take the label[13]

> If x knows that p and tells y that p and y understand x's utterance and come thereby to believe that p, then y comes to know that p.

The Transmission Principle is a testimony principle of the form:

> S knows that p[14] $\rightarrow$ T

The Transmission Principle and its converse ('T $\rightarrow$ S knows that p'), sustain the communication-theoretic approach to the epistemology of testimony. The claim that communication is essentially a mode of knowledge transmission takes the Transmission Principle as having a constitutive role in communication. Observe an important feature of the converse form of the Transmission Principle: it makes testimony *epistemically dependent* on other sources of knowledge. That is, testimony becomes a means for the transmission of knowledge from one person to another, but cannot be a source of knowledge in its own right.[15] The Nyāya attitude towards these Transmission Principles reveals a second aspect in which their perspective on testimony differs from the approach of a knowledge-communication theorist. For although I will argue in Chapter 5 that they do need to accept the Transmission Principle to deal with certain Gettier-style cases, it remains a striking fact about the Nyāya discussion how slight and decentralized a role the Transmission Principle plays. Testimony is not thought of in terms of the transmission of knowledge from speaker to hearer, but solely in terms of the functioning of the hearer's language faculty.[16]

The Nyāya, in fact, are much more preoccupied by the search for principles which are necessary for testimony rather than ones which are sufficient. Their interest is what must be the case, given that testimony is possible. A trivial testimony principle is what we might call facticity:

> T $\rightarrow p$.

The entire account of assent-worthiness, comprising an account of the physical, syntactic, and semantic properties of the utterance, the qualities of the speaker, such as trustworthiness, reliability, and sincerity, and the nature of the speech-act performed, is a search for the completion of the further principle:

> T $\rightarrow$ S's utterance is φ.

If the possibility of testimony is to constrain the theory of meaning, then what we must consider is whether there are any meaning-theoretic testimony principles.[17] In particular, we will consider principles relating to the internalized grammars and structural properties of the language faculties of the speaker and hearer, and the relation between the two. As an example of the sort of principle I have in mind, consider this:

T $\rightarrow$ the language faculties of S and H are extensionally equivalent.

Two language faculties are extensionally equivalent just in case they agree in their assignments of belief-contents to utterances. It is very likely that testimony would be impossible between a speaker and hearer who did not share this property. Suppose S utters the sentence 'snow is white', expressing thereby his belief that snow is white, and that H, on hearing this utterance and assenting to it, forms the belief that grass is green. H does not, here, come to know that grass is green. His belief, though true, is true by chance. Whichever epistemological theory one endorses, one must exclude knowledge by luck; the *pramāṇa* theorist does so by an appeal to the truth-following properties of the belief-forming process. In any case, the beliefs formed by this hearer do not qualify as knowledge.

This simple case exemplifies a general pattern of argument. The Nyāya philosophers of language, as we will see, reason that unless the meaning theories tacitly known by the speaker and hearer have certain properties, the belief the hearer forms on directly assenting to the speaker's utterance will not constitute knowledge. Later thinkers use this pattern of argument to motivate the introduction of modes of thought into the theory of meaning (see Part III). I will discuss in §5.3 a rather different application of the argument, designed to defend the existence of public conventions on word meaning. Before that, I need to say much more about the language faculty, the notion of an 'internalized grammar', and the Nyāya analysis of meaning.

4.2 Idiolect Meaning

The leading idea behind the Nyāya theory of meaning is that a hearer's language faculty determines a function from sentences to belief contents, and that this function is a meaning function. As Matilal remarks: 'To describe the content of a *śābdabodha* may be said to be equivalent to describing the "meaning" of the utterance' (1985: 408).[18] The hearer's language processing mechanism will generate an output belief-event from any given input sentence. The 'meaning' of a sentence in this hearer's idiolect precisely is the content so assigned to it. I will call this notion of meaning, 'I-meaning'—idiolect, individual or internal meaning.[19] We should not, pace Matilal (1990: 54), think of this as a sort of 'hearer's meaning', on a par with the Gricean notion of speaker's meaning. For idiolect meaning is not analysable in terms of the *intentions* of the hearer.

A sophisticated analysis of the notion of idiolect meaning is to be found in the opening sections of Gadādhara's *Śaktivāda*. He gives two definitions, one for 'meaning-relation' and one for 'word-meaning':

> The 'meaning relation' is [the relation] of a word to its meaning (*artha*). [It is of two types:] literal (*saṅketa*) and deflected (*lakṣaṇā*). Exactly that which is conveyed from the word through the meaning-relation is called the 'word-meaning'.[20]

Gadādhara's explication of the notion of word-meaning here is terse, and requires supplementation from his commentators. One point can be set aside, however, at the start. Gadādhara draws our attention to the fact that the term 'meaning' has a plurality of different uses, and that we must distinguish between the notion of literal meaning and the phenomenon of pragmatic or derivative meaning. We have discussed this distinction in §1.2. Instances of derivative meaning occur when the hearer, in order to make sense of the speaker's assertion, attaches a non-literal meaning to his or her words. Such an interpretative practice clearly can exist *only if* words have a literal meaning, and thus is not fundamental to the articulation of the notion of meaning.

Notice, however, there is an appearance of circularity in Gadādhara's two definitions, for the notion of a meaning-relation is defined in terms of the notion of a meaning-entity, but the notion of a meaning-entity is itself defined in terms of the notion of a meaning-relation. Of course, there is no harm in this if all Gadādhara is doing is labelling the terms of a relation, as we say that the parenthood relation relates parents to children, and a parent is someone who stands in the parenthood relation to some child. Genuine circularity threatens, however, if the definitions are understood as giving analyses of the terms defined.

In fact, there is no circularity, for the two notions are analysed as follows. The word-meaning-relation is that relation which is conducive (*anukūla*) to the production of items of testimonial knowledge (*śābdabodha*), by determining the content of a hearer's thought formed by directly assenting to an utterance of any sentence containing the word.[21] Hearers are disposed, in virtue of having a language faculty, to form beliefs with a certain content on hearing sentences containing a certain word. The induced mapping of words to belief-content constituents is the meaning relation for that hearer that is, the relation μ of Chapter 2 is now grounded in the idea of idiolect meaning. The 'meaning' of a word is that constituent which is part of the content of any belief produced by hearing an utterance of a sentence containing that word *due to the meaning relation.*[22] Why is the meaning relation mentioned here? It is because hearers can have a variety of irrelevant dispositions to respond to spoken words by forming beliefs. Imagine someone who hears a word and is reminded for one reason or other of an object, such as the person who on hearing the word 'pot' thinks of space, where the pot is located, or, on hearing the word 'tea' thinks of cucumber sandwiches. We want to say that the idiolect meaning of a word for a hearer is the object she is disposed to think of on hearing the word, but only in virtue of those dispositions which are grounded in the hearer's language faculty. The language faculty is a specific capacity or 'module', one which sustains a particular belief-forming disposition.

The Nyāya theory endorses the doctrine that hearers have tacit knowledge of a theory of meaning for the language they understand; the hearer's belief-forming dispositions are said to be grounded in the hearer's knowledge of word meanings. The substance of this claim, however, is only that, since states of tacit knowledge are themselves dispositional, ascribing tacit knowledge to the hearer does little more than redescribe a belief-forming disposition based on her having a language faculty. A hearer who is disposed to move from an auditory perception of the utterance 'The pot is blue' to a belief that the pot is blue, can be said in some way to represent internally the information encoded in the meaning clause (the term 'pot' stands for a pot),[23] and to draw upon that information in coming to understand utterances of sentences containing the word 'pot'.[24]

Gadādhara's definitions are therefore equivalent to the following definition of idiolect meaning for a particular hearer:

(I) A word *w* I-means an object *x* for a hearer A iff A's language faculty is such that A is disposed to form a belief about *x* on hearing the utterance of any sentence having *w* as a constituent.

The meaning of a word for a hearer is the entity with which it is correlated by her language faculty. There is a reversal here in the usual order of explanation. We normally begin with the supposition that a speaker speaks a certain language, and then infer facts about the nature of their language processing capacities. The Nyāya invite us to look at the matter the other way round: begin with the language processing mechanism, determine which word-object mappings it induces, and declare the totality of them to be the language actually understood by that hearer. The existence of the explanandum, a certain language processing faculty within a hearer, is a *given*, in just the same way as is the existence of their perceptual or inferential faculties. This way of proceeding has a good deal in common with what Chomsky (1995) calls the 'naturalistic approach' to language, an approach which studies the human language faculty as a natural object. Chomsky (1986, 1988, 1995) introduces a technical term 'I-language' for what I have been calling the hearer's idiolect, and distinguishes it from the linguists' 'grammar', which is a formal theory of an I-language:

> The I-language is what the grammar purports to describe: a system represented in the mind/brain, ultimately in physical mechanisms that are now largely unknown, and is in this sense internalised; a system that is intensional in that it may be regarded as a specific function considered in intension—that is, a specific characterisation of a function—which assigns a status to a vast range of physical events (1988: 513).

In a later paper, he emphasizes that 'this is a strictly internalist approach to language, analogous in this respect to studies of the visual system' (1995: 13).

The leading idea, then, is that each of us is endowed with a testimonial epistemic faculty, analogous to our perceptual faculty, which generates world-directed beliefs from perceived utterances. My testimonial faculty fixes, as it were, a mapping from utterances of a given language to belief contents. The 'meaning' of a statement for me is, by definition, the belief-content to which it is mapped by my testimonial faculty. If I am to be able to understand every statement I hear, the language processing mechanism which underpins this faculty must have a certain compositional structure, and that leads to an assignment of belief-content components to sub-sentential elements in the language.

The schema [I] is a causal or dispositional theory of meaning. As it stands, it is vulnerable to Kripke's arguments against dispositional theories (Kripke 1982; see also §2.2). Kripke raised two objections: the infinitary character of meaning, and the normativity of meaning. The totality of a person's dispositions are finite, for they are the dispositions of a finite creature existing for a finite time. Yet the meaning of a term has an infinitary character: it determines whether it is correct or incorrect to apply the term to an object for all past, present, and future, actual and non-actual objects. Indian philosophers had a good deal to say about the infinitary character of meaning, and we examined their discussion in §2.2.

Kripke's argument concerning normativity is this. Truths about meaning are normative truths: they concern how the term *ought* to be applied, not how it is or *will* be applied. Describing the hearer's dispositions, however, tells us only how the hearer will apply the term, and not how she ought to apply it. The issue of normativity is important, and the Nyāya philosophers of language have a good deal to say which is relevant to the problem. I will introduce a central aspect of the Nyāya theory, one which bears directly on the normativity question. This is the doctrine that public word-meaning is constituted by authoritative mandates. I will argue that although the doctrine cannot be defended in its original form, there is indeed a way to account for the normativity of meaning within an epistemological conception of language (§4.3).

Notice, finally, that the notion of word-meaning acquires significance, in the Nyāya theory, only within the context of a description of a language-user's ability to understand whole sentences. A sentence is the smallest linguistic unit capable of being true or false, the smallest unit from which information can be derived by exercising one's language-processing mechanisms. The language processing mechanism is, as we have seen, considered to be part of an epistemic faculty, testimony, and it is sentences, not words, which are capable of conveying knowledge. The fundamental feature of the language faculty consists in the correlations it sets up between whole sentences and the contents of beliefs. Dummett calls a theory of meaning 'atomistic' if it attempts to give an account of the meanings of words in isolation from their contribution to the meanings of sentences in which they occur; that is, of word-meaning as a primitive, building-block relation. He contrasts such theories with 'molecular' theories of meaning, which claim that an account of the meanings of words can be given only in terms of their contribution to the meanings of sentences of which they form part. Both of these are to be distinguished from 'holistic' theories, which claim that the meaning even of sentences can be given only in terms of an account of the entire language. Where does the Nyāya theory lie? Since, in the above explication, a word will only be correlated with an entity if that entity enters the content of every sentence containing the word, it seems that this theory is molecular rather than atomistic—the meaning of a word is explained in terms of its contribution to sentence meanings. The account lies between extreme atomism, exemplified in the Indian literature by the Bhāṭṭa school, and Bhartṛhari's semantic holism.[25] Words acquire meaning in virtue of making systematic contributions to the meanings of sentences in which they occur, rather than by having a causal link or primitive relation of some other kind with their referents.

The Nyāya are aware too that the behavioural evidence for a theory of meaning attaches to sentences, not to words. They sketch the following picture of language acquisition based on observing the speech-behaviour (*vyavahāra*) of members of the linguistic community. One person is observed to utter the sounds 'Bring a cow' and a second person is observed to going and fetching a cow. On a second occasion, a person utters the sound 'Bring a horse' and someone fetches a horse. On still another occasion, a person is observed to utter 'Tie up a cow', and a corresponding action is seen to ensue. Such evidence bears upon whole sentences, but now a process of positive and negative correlation (*anvaya-vyatireka*) leads the observer to infer the meanings of the sub-sentential components from the meanings of whole sentences.[26]

4.3 Public Meaning and the Role of Mandates

Suppose a population of speakers and hearers understands the same public language L. Each is capable, as a result of her language processing capacities, to move from an auditory perception of any uttered sentence σ of L to the tokening of a thought whose content at least partly concerns a thought-content *p*. Each, moreover, is able to do this in virtue of having internally represented a compositional I-language for L. Can we demand any more than this of someone who is a full participant of a public linguistic practice? In particular, can we demand that every participant ought to know the *same* I-language, that the public language imposes standards of correctness on the meanings of individual words? The Nyāya give an affirmative answer, and the basis for their reply is the claim that the public language is a body of authoritative mandates.[27] Gadādhara introduces the doctrine as a revision in the earlier definition of the meaning relation (1927: 5):

> A literal meaning-relation (*saṅketa*) is a mandate (*icchā*) [whose form is either] 'Let this word bring into thought this object' or 'From this word, this object should be brought into thought.'

The thesis is that there are mandates prescribing the way members of a public linguistic community ought to understand the sentences they hear. A mandate is allegedly an act of will (*icchā*), whose content is expressible as 'Let word *w* bring into thought object *x*', or else the corresponding passive version. This comprises a sentence '*w* brings into thought *x*', embedded in the imperative context 'It is mandated that ...'. The subject of the embedded sentence is the word *w*, while the predicate is expanded as 'being the cause of thoughts into whose content the entity *x* enters'. The structure of the mandate, therefore, is ⟨Let word *w* be the cause of [hearer's]-thoughts into whose content the entity *x* enters⟩.[28] The thoughts in question are the beliefs which constitute the hearer's understanding of an utterance by directly assenting to it.

Gadādhara is now able to define the notion of the meaning of a word in a public language. He says this (1927: 5–6):

> As far as the terms 'meaningful expression' (*vācaka*) and 'meaning-entity' (*vācya*) are concerned, the meaning of the verbal root [from which they derive, viz. √means] is [to be identified with a certain part of] the content of the mandate, namely, 'cause of a thought' (*bodhajanaka*). In [the sentence expressing] that [mandate], the agentive affix is attached to the word 'word', which is the agent *qua* substratum. Moreover, in such [locutions] as 'The word speaks about the object', 'the word "means" the object', the direct object affix is attached to the word 'object', and serves to indicate that the verbal root [viz. 'cause of a thought'], has as its [grammatical] direct object just that entity which [enters] the content of the [aforementioned] thought. [However], in such [locutions] as 'A cow is spoken of by the word ["cow"]', 'A cow is the "meaning" of the word ["cow"]', the relation between the meaning of the verbal root, which is located in the word, [and the object] is indirect. [Gadādhara shows how to construe such passive locutions.] When the mandate has the second form ['From this word ...'], the [above locutions] are to be construed the other way round. This is the established Nyāya view.

Later on, he summarises his view by saying that 'we use the term meaning (*śakti*) to denote just that relation which is the ground (*prayojaka*) for the understanding of sentences containing the word, as determined by a mandate'.[29] This statement insists that the notion of word-meaning is not merely derived from an explanation of a hearer's ability to understand utterances, but from public mandates governing the content of the beliefs which constitute that understanding. The meaning of an expression in the public language L of a population P is now as follows:

(S) A word *w* means an entity *x* in the public language L of a population P iff there is a mandate on P decreeing that *w* I-means *x* for every person in P.

Before evaluating the thesis, let us examine its origin. The Nyāya had a distinctive motivation for their doctrine that word-meanings derive from mandates. It was to defend an anti-essentialist thesis about meaning properties. At *Mīmāṃsā-sūtra* 1.1.5, Jaimini states that the meaning relation is 'uncreated' (*autpattika*). His commentator Śabara explains that this means 'not of human origin' (*apauruṣeya*). The Mīmāṃsā thesis is that bearing its referent is a non-conventional and sui generis property of a word. We might say that, for the Mīmāṃsā, all meaning is 'natural' meaning, using Grice's term 'natural meaning' to capture that sense in which, for example, black clouds 'mean' rain or red skies 'mean' fine weather (Grice 1989: 213). The doctrine was grounded in a special reverence for the Sanskrit language as the divine language of the Vedas, and a belief that Vedic meaning could not be a matter of human creation.[30]

The doctrine that all meaning is natural meaning is bound to sound strange to a modern audience. It is, after all, a platitude that words are arbitrary, in the sense that any noise is as good as any other in its capacity to act as a sign for an object. Putnam has labelled this platitude Trivial Semantic Conventionality: 'It is a triviality that we might have meant something other than we do by the noises we use. The noise "pot" could have meant what is in fact meant by the word "dog", and the word "dog" could have meant what is in fact meant by the word "fish"' (1975: 164). As a criticism of the Mīmāṃsā doctrine, this objection is hardly new. It was made first by the early Buddhists (cf. Jayatilleke, 1963: 314), who pointed out that the arbitrariness manifests itself in cases where the same word has different meanings in different languages. It was repeated by the earliest exponents of Nyāya under *Nyāya-sūtra* 2.1.56. Thus Vātsyāyana noted:

> Word-object relations are not natural but conventional, for words designate objects according to the desires of [name-introducers, such as] the seer (*ṛṣi*), the noble (*ārya*) and the foreigner (*mleccha*). If word-object relations were natural, words could not be used in accordance with their desires, any more than light has the capacity to reveal different colours to different groups of people.

Perhaps, however, there is a more interesting reading of the Mīmāṃsā doctrine. The idea might be that even if words qua noises could have had different meanings, the words as they in fact are, as part of an established language, cannot mean something else. Kaplan has recently drawn attention to this phenomenon: '[T]hough Alpha Centauri might have been named "Hesperus" ... it does not follow that our name "Hesperus" might have named Alpha Centauri' (1990: 118). In a similar vein Matilal remarks that 'the [Mīmāṃsā] has ... made one important point regarding the givenness of the language and the word-object connection. Within a linguistic community, the [word-object] connection cannot easily be tampered with' (1990: 30).[31] The Mīmāṃsaka might thus be understood as highlighting an important linguistic phenomenon, the fixedness of linguistic relations within a linguistic community, and as having proposed an explanation, that words are permanent, natural entities having their linguistic properties or powers intrinsically.

The Nyāya reject this theory in favour of a reductionist approach to meaning properties, and must therefore find an alternative explanation of the unrevisability-from-within of linguistic relations. Their claim is that the meaning relations are based on authoritative mandates. The mandates are authoritative in the sense that they are not revisable by individual members of the linguistic population. It is, by analogy, no longer open for chess players both to change the knight's move and still regard themselves as playing chess: the knight's move has been fixed by the game's inventor. A public language, for the Nyāya, consists in a set of objective, normative rules prescribing the way each word is to be understood.

Who produces these mandates, and on whose authority do they rest? In most cases, the mandates are said to have a divine origin and authority. The only exception is when a new word is introduced by explicit stipulation. Gadādhara (1927: 5–6) distinguishes the two categories—

> And here [there are two kinds of mandate]. A 'theoretical rule' (*paribhāṣā*) is a mandate which is explicit (*ādhunika*), and a designator [whose mandate is 'theoretical'] is [called] a 'theoretical term' (*pāribhāṣika*). For example, such words as '*nadī*' and '*vṛddhi*', which were introduced by an author [Pāṇini, as theoretical terms in his grammar]. The [other sort of] mandate (*śakti*) is a mandate which is of divine origin, and a designator [whose meaning rule is divine] is [called simply] a 'meaningful expression' (*vācaka*). For example, a word such as '(the) cow', which refers to [a thing] which is qualified by cowhood. The thing designated by that [word '(the) cow'], i.e. the cow etc., which is the referent [of the word], is [what we call] the *chief* meaning-relatum (*mukhyārtha*).

Gadādhara calls a newly introduced term a 'theoretical' term. Such terms are introduced by an explicit mandate or stipulation (see Chapter 8). The Nyāya in effect extend the same model to the whole language. When the originator of the mandate is unknown, the Nyāya expedient is to say that it is a 'divine desire' (*īśvarecchā*), where an appeal to divine origin serves to emphasize the fixedness of the rule.

The Nyāya theory of mandates is primarily directed towards two questions about the nature of language. The first is the reduction of meaning properties. Mandates are thoughts of a certain kind, namely the will or desire of the name-giver. Thus, the Nyāya hope is to reduce semantic properties to intentional ones. The second question is the normativity of meaning. Whatever account one gives of meaning properties, it must sustain a standard of correctness or incorrectness in the use of words. There must be some explanation of why it is correct for the hearer to understand a word as referring to some particular object and not another, even if they do not actually understand the word so. A Nyāya mandate appears to sustain a standard of correctness of just this sort. I will look at the issue of reductionism in the remainder of this section, and discuss the extent to which the Nyāya mandates can serve as norms of correctness in §5.3.

First, reduction. It will facilitate our discussion of this aspect of the Nyāya theory if we reformulate the theory in the idiom developed by David Lewis (1975) and Stephen Schiffer (1987). For Lewis and Schiffer, a language is a purely abstract object, a function from noises or written strings to propositions. There are infinitely many such abstract languages.[32] The question to be addressed now is: what makes one language rather than another the *actual* language of a given population of speakers and hearers? What property of speakers and hearers determines which language, which function from noises to propositions, is theirs? Lewis calls this property the 'actual language relation'. Setting the problem up this way suits the reductionist, and this includes the Nyāya, for we may insist that the relevant properties of speaker and hearers be non-linguistic ones; for example, their having certain conventions or interpretative practices.

We can now see the Nyāya as offering a distinctive account of the actual language relation. According to the Nyāya account, what makes a language actual for a given population is that there is a set of mandates on the language faculty of each member of the population. Let us reformulate (S) above as follows:

(Ś) A language L is actual in a population P iff for each word *w* in L, there is a mandate on P decreeing that *w* I-means *x*, where *x* is the meaning of *w* in L.

That is, if there is a body of mandates on P whose net effect is to decree that a certain language L is to be the I-language of every member of P, then L is the actual language of P.

The actual language L is here taken to be a particular recursive specification of a function from sentences to propositions, that is, what Lewis calls a 'grammar'. Lewis in fact considers what seems to be a proposal rather similar to the one we are attributing to the Nyāya:

> Why not say ... that a grammar Γ of L is used by P if and only if there prevails in P a convention to bestow upon each constituent in Γ the meaning that Γ assigns to it? (1983: 178-9).

Lewis's conception of a convention to 'bestowal upon each constituent in Γ the meaning that Γ assigns to it' is perhaps analogous to the idea of a mandate to understand each constituent in Γ as having the meaning it has in L. Lewis, however, rejects the idea (1983: 178-9):

> *Reply*: A convention, as I have defined it, is a regularity in action, or in action and belief. It is essential that a convention is a regularity such that conformity by others gives one a reason to conform; and such a reason must either be a practical reason for acting or an epistemic reason for believing. What other kind of reason is there? Yet there is no such thing as an action of bestowing a meaning (except for an irrelevant sort of action that is performed not by language-users but by creators of language). Neither does bestowal of meaning consist in forming some belief.

I believe that Lewis's argument here is mistaken. In particular, I think that there are indeed epistemic reasons to try to form one's testimonial beliefs in a way which conforms with that of the other members of the community. As this concerns the normativity of meaning, I will postpone discussion of the point. What about Lewis's comment that 'bestowing a meaning' can be neither an action nor the formation of a belief? Lewis is talking about the public meaning of a term, and it is of course true that no member of the linguistic population can bestow a public meaning to an already used term at will. That is what we earlier called the unrevisability-from-within of meaning. But let us apply his criticism rather to the I-meaning of each individual. In the terms of the Nyāya account, this would be equivalent to denying that hearers can be mandated to understand words in one way or another. There does seem to be a genuine difficulty here. If the mandate is to *regulate* the way hearers interpret the language, and not merely to specify how they *ought* to understand, then understanding a word a certain way rather than another must be an action hearers are able to perform. But it would be strange to describe the way the language faculty works as involving an act, for it does not come within our volitional control.

Nevertheless, there are at least two ways in which one can volitionally affect the deliverances of one's language faculty. First, one can revise one's understanding of a word in the light of evidence that others interpret the word differently. One might, for example, start to use a word having encountered it being used in specific context, and later learn that its scope of application is wider. Second, it is possible to act in ways whose intended consequence is a change in one's language faculty, even if one cannot directly will that the language faculty changes. This is how, generally, habits and dispositions are susceptible to intentional change.

The account of conventions as mandates of the name-giver is indeed plausible for terms which are introduced explicitly into an already existing linguistic practice. The language-user hears the mandate and uses the semantic information encoded in it in her understanding of any sentence containing the new term. She has, moreover, a good reason to obey the mandate, since she knows that by doing so she can align her interpretations with the rest of the linguistic community. Gilbert (1983) argues that we can account for authority within a conventionalist framework as a means of agreeing to a single solution to a co-ordination problem. Let us imagine that a number of people are in a room with two exits. A fire breaks out and everyone has to leave quickly. Suppose further that the only way for everyone to leave quickly without chaos is if they all agree to leave by the same exit. There are two solutions to this co-ordination problem: leave by one exit, or leave by the other. If someone gives an order to leave by one of the exits, it will be in everyone's interest to follow the command, as they will have a way of agreeing to a common solution to the co-ordination problem. Perhaps we can account for the authority of mandates along these lines. In agreeing to follow the mandate, the members the linguistic population can ensure that they hit on a common solution to the 'co-ordination in understanding' problem for that word.

This is a partial defence of the role of Nyāya mandates. However, in extending such an account to the entire language, the Nyāya seem to commit a quantifier-shift fallacy. For although it might be true, of any given term, that its use is prescribed by an authoritative mandate, it cannot be true that there are authoritative mandates for every term. The reason is that a mandate can only have a regulative function if it is learnable by the population, and the only way for such a mandate to be taught or learned is through language. Even if the divine will is revealed to the seers in intuition, *they* can only communicate it to the population at large in words.

Notes

[1] There are other ways of understanding the notion of a *pramāṇa.*

[2] See Schiffer (1987) for a development of the language-processing model of understanding.

[3] Just as a speaker performs one of a number of different type of act in producing an utterance, so too does hearer. The classification of 'hearer-acts', unlike that of speech-acts, has not been extensively studied. (An exception is Coady [1992: 46–7]; another, Coady notes, is Hobbes.) One main type involves recognition of the type of speech-act performed by the speaker (issuing in judgements of the form 'S asked whether *p*', etc.). If the Nyāya are right here, and I think they are, another main type of 'hearer-act' invloves direct assent to that which the speaker said. The Nyāya emphasize the hearer's perspective, and are consequently more sensitive to these distinctions than western philosophy of language, with its emphasis on the speaker, tends to be.

[4] One can hear the epistemic use of the verb 'to understand' in imperative constructions, such as 'Understand that I will not tolerate this behaviour', in corresponding passive constructions like 'It was understood that they could not leave', and in constructions like 'I understand from Jones that you have got the tickets'. The verb also has epistemic overtones when it takes a direct object, as in 'Jones understands the political situation'.

[5] It might be better, in this circumstance, to describe S as 'attesting' that *p.*

[6] See Grice's paper 'Meaning', in Grice (1989).

[7] The proposal has some resemblances to Sosa's idea that we distinguish between what he calls 'animal' knowledge and 'reflective' knowledge. Both sorts of knowledge are produced by truth-conducive belief-forming faculties ('intellectual virtues'), but in the second case, the knower has an 'epistemic perspective', which consists in meta-knowledge about the functioning of those faculties. See Sosa (1991, esp. p.240), and Chapter 2 below. Likewise, we might say that anyone capable of human communication must have a 'linguisic perspective', consisting in knowledge of a 'common sense' theory of language and the nature of communication. The capacity to play upon normal communicative practice, in lying or in fiction, depends on the existence of such reflective awareness.

[8] Coady (1992: 152–76); cf. Plantinga (1993: 80–1).

[9] For this criticism of the Nyāya account, see Mohanty (1992: 252–3).

[10] See A. Chakrabarti (1994: 121–2).

[11] A. Chakrabarti (1985: 314) suggests that the Nyāya explanation of fiction could proceed via their notion of 'quasi-understanding' (*āhārya-jñāna*). See also Ganeri (2001b: §6.4).

[12] Dummett later continues (1978: 132): 'The notion of informational content is plainly connected ... with that of what we recognise as justifying a statement, as establishing its truth: a statement with no informational content requires no

justification, and it is plausible to say that we grasp the information that is conveyed by a sentence just in case we know what is needed to establish it as true.' The argument depends on an internalistic conception of justification, according to which justification consists in having reasons or evidence for the truth of the statement. Only then does it follow that we have to understand a sentence in advance of knowing it to be true.

[13] For still another rendition, see McDowell (1980: 135).

[14] And there are no defeating conditions. Peacocke observes that S's knowing that *p* is not sufficient (1987: 149–50): 'Suppose Mary sometimes comes to believe that it is raining by looking, and sometimes by deduction from astrological principles. On occasions of the former sort, she knows it is raining; on occasions of the latter sort, she does not. But if on an occasion of the first sort, she tells her friend that it is raining, he does not come to know that it is raining.' The hearer's coming to know is defeated by the speaker's unreliability. Another sort of defeating condition involves the hearer falsely believing that the speaker is lying or unknowing.

[15] Thus, Audi (1998: 139) remarks: 'Testimonial knowledge seems ultimately to depend on knowledge grounded in one of the other sources .... To enable others to know something by attesting to it, I must know it myself; and my knowledge [or that of the attester from whom I acquired it, etc.] must ultimately depend at least in part on non-testimonially based knowledge'.

[16] They are even willing to countenance cases in which the hearer gains knowledge by testimony without there being any speaker! Examples include cases where the 'utterance' is generated artificially, for example my computer displaying the message 'the battery is low'. The occurrence of the message is highly correlated with the truth of the proposition that the battery is low, but the computer does not say and does not know this proposition. Gaṅgeśa makes the point with the example of a parrot's 'speech', although this is better seen as a matter of the parrot's relaying someone else's speech. Another sort of example considered by some Indian schools, but not the Nyāya, involves infinitely long testimonial chains and 'tradition' (*aitihya*).

[17] Evans (1982: 311) considers the idea: 'It is possible to use the [Testimony] principle the other way round, bringing our intuitions about knowledge to bear upon the explicitly semantical concepts—the concepts or reference, saying, and understanding .... [W]e might say that in order to say something, one must enable an audience to know what it is that one is saying (fn. Only so can we make it intelligible that by hearing and understanding one he might come to know *that it is so*). A speaker who is to say something must make it *manifest* which object it is that he intends to be speaking about—which object an audience must think of in understanding his remark.'

[18] This is the equation *śābdabodha* = *vākyārthajñāna*. See e.g. *Nyāyakośa* s.v. *śābdabodha*.

[19] The notion has clear connections with Chomsky's notion of an I-language, from which I derive the terminology. I discuss this below.

[20] *saṅketo lakṣaṇā cārthe pada-vṛttiḥ. vṛttyā pada-pratipādya evārtha ity abhidhīyate*; Gadādhara (1927: 1–4). Madhav Deshpande (1992: 2) renders the second sentence as: 'The term *artha* "meaning" stands for the object or content (*śābda-bodha-viṣaya*) of a verbal cognition (*śabda-jñāna*) on the basis of an awareness of the signification function pertaining to that word (*pada-niṣṭha-vṛtti-jñāna*)'. See also Gerschheimer (1996: 345).

[21] *Vivṛtti*, (1929: 1): *vṛttiḥ śābdabodhaupayikaḥ sambandhaḥ*. See also *Mañjūṣā*, (1927: 4): *śābdabodhānukūlārthopasthityanukūlaḥ padapadārthayoḥ sambandhaḥ vṛttiḥ* 'the relation between word and object is that relation which is conducive to such a presenation of objects as is conducive to testimonial knowledge'. The definition goes back to Gaṅgeśa. Nothing in this chapter depends on what we take the correlates of words to be. Likewise, nothing depends on what we take the contents of beliefs to be. In connection with this, I should stress that, in calling the content of a belief a 'proposition', I am merely employing a synonym. In asking what is the content of belief, one might equally and equivalently ask what is a proposition.

[22] *Ādarśa*, (1892: 2): *vṛtti-prayojya-pada-janya-pratīti-viṣayaḥ padārthaḥ, pratītiśca śābdabodhaḥ*. See also *Mañjūṣā*, (1927: 5).

[23] I shall follow the practice of using angle brackets to quote meaning-giving sentences.

[24] There has been considerable recent discussion about the nature of states of tacit knowledge, in particular concerning whether they are dispositional or genuinely intentional, and how such states draw upon the semantic information they encode (cf. Evans 1981, Wright 1986, Davies 1987). The Nyāya describe these states as states of *śakti-jñāna* ('cognition of a meaning relation'). They belong to a category of mental dispositional 'traces' (*saṃskāra*), and are grouped with the non-mental dispositional properties, elasticity and inertia. Such traces are the causal basis for occurrent mental events, especially rememberings. Clearly, as the dipositional bases of occurrent memories, they are thought of as states which store information.

[25] For these views, see Matilal (1990: 106–19). Quine was probably aware of Bhartṛhari's position: in *Word and Object* (1960: 9, n.2), he mentions an article by Brough on Indian theories of meaning (Brough 1953), in which Brough reports Bhartṛhari's holistic views. Quine, it might be noted, commented on a draft of Ingalls (1951), and exercised a considerable influence on the early work of Ingalls, Matilal, and Potter. Kahrs (2001) objects to my comparison of Bhartṛhari with Quine for reasons which are not entirely clear to me.

[26] See *Vivṛti*, (1929: 1), and also Cardona (1967) and Matilal (1990: 14).

[27] Here, the Nyāya depart company with Chomsky. Chomsky's explanation of I-language inter-subjectivity is that the compositional structure of the I-language is by and large innately fixed (e.g. 1995: 17). There is no trace of such an idea in the Nyāya.

[28] Gadādhara often uses the passive version of this analysis. Thus: *x* is in the content of such belief states as are caused by *w* (*ghaṭapadajanya-bodhaviṣayatā-niṣṭha-prakāratā-nirūpiteśvareccha-viśeṣyatā ghaṭaniṣṭhā*).

[29] *īśarecchāyās tatpadajanya-śābdabodha-viṣayatā-prayojakaḥ saṃbandha eva tatra tatpadaśaktir iti vyapadeśa-niyāmakaḥ* (1927: 44).

[30] See Lipner (1986, chapter 1).

[31] The claim that meanings 'cannot easily be tampered with' is, of course, rather weaker than the claim that they cannot change without the language itself changing. It is not clear to me which of these would better characterize the Mimāsaka position.

[32] I do not mean to attribute to the Nyāya any such conception of language, but simply to use it to make clear certain aspects of their doctrine.

5

Śabda-pramāṇa

Meaning and Knowing

5.1 Knowing: A Linguistic Analysis

Indian epistemology is a theory of the *pramāṇa*s: the faculties or capacities which lead to knowledge. Study of the sources of knowledge, as part of the Indian philosophers' general enterprise, stretches back even to the time of the later Upaniṣads and Buddhist Nikāya. Jayatilleke (1963: 64–5) reports that:

> [W]e find in the Maitrī Upaniṣad the use of the word *pramāṇa* (a valid means of knowledge) in a technical sense and a growing realisation that our claims to knowledge must be backed up by their being made on valid grounds. We talk about time but how do we know that such a thing called time exists. This Upaniṣad suggests that we measure or know time from observing the movements of the sun across the constellations. It is said: 'Because of its subtlety this (course of the sun) is the proof for only in this way is time proved (to exist)' (*saukṣmyatvād etat pramāṇam anenaiva pramīyate hi kālaḥ*, 6.14). This is followed by the significant statement that 'without a valid means of knowledge there is no apprehension of objects (lit. what is to be proved)' (*na vinā pramāṇena prameyasyopalabdhiḥ*, loc. cit.) .... There is also a reference to *pramāṇikāḥ* in the Aṅguttara Nikāya ...: 'In this matter the epistemologists [*pramāṇikāḥ*] argue thus: this person and the other have identically the same traits, why then is one of them (considered) inferior and the other superior' (A.V. 140).

Jayatilleke notes that at roughly the same time, the Greek Strabo referred to Indian philosophers as 'a class of Brahmins contentious and fond of argument called the *Pramnai*', the name '*Pramnai*' presumably derived from '*prāmāṇikāḥ*', the Sanskrit word for epistemologists.

For a systematic development of the notion of a *pramāṇa*, one may turn to the early Nyāya. The thesis they defend is that a *pramāṇa* is that through which things are 'established'.[1] What is it to 'establish' (*upa* + *labh*) something? The guiding analogy in the early Nyāya was between a *pramāṇa* as a means of establishing objects and a measuring instrument, such as a pair of scales, as a means of establishing weight.[2] The persuasiveness of this analogy is considerably strengthened in Sanskrit by the fact that the verbal root *mā-*, from which the term '*pramāṇa*' is derived, means 'to measure' as well as 'to know'. To establish an object, then, is akin to 'getting the measure' of it, in the sense of knowing it for what it is. The early Nyāya emphasize that we use a *pramāṇa* when we wish to resolve a doubt, which will usually have the form 'Is the object an *F* or is it a *G*?', where '*F*' and '*G*' are incompatible predicates. The doubt-free state (*nirṇaya*) at which we finally arrive must be the result of our 'measurement' of the disputed object by means of some *pramāṇa*. A means of knowledge is an instrument of measurement.

As well as the forms of knowledge attribution suitable for the ascription of knowledge of truths ('S knows *that* the sun is shining') and of objects ('S knows the Councillor'), English has a variety of 'know wh-' constructions: knowing which, knowing what, knowing whether, knowing who, and so on.[3] What is the proper form of knowledge attributions in Indian epistemology? We must note that their concern is with measurement and doubt resolution. Someone who resolves a doubt as to whether the object is *F* or *G*, thereby comes to *know whether* the object is *F* or *G*. I come to know whether my coffee is hot or cold by sipping it, whether it is time to leave by looking at my watch, and so on. So knowing *whether* is the proper form of knowledge here. The *pramāṇa* theory is indeed concerned with the knowledge of truths, however, for knowing whether the object is *F* or *G* consists in knowing *that* the object is *F* (or knowing *that* it is *G*).

Another influence on the *pramāṇa* epistemology was the need to find a reply to the Mādhyamika sceptic Nāgārjuna. Nāgārjuna asks the following question (1986: 115; translation by K. Bhattacharya):

> If such and such objects are established for you through the *pramāṇas*, tell me how those *pramāṇas* are established for you? If you think that such and such 'objects of true cognition' are established through the 'instruments of true cognition', just as the things to be measured (*meya*) are established through the measuring instruments, [we ask:] how are those 'instruments of true cognition', viz., perception, inference, comparison and verbal testimony, established? If [you say that] the *pramāṇas* are established without the help of *pramāṇas*, then [your] proposition that [all] objects are established through *pramāṇas* is

> abandoned. [But] if the *pramāṇa*s are established through other *pramāṇa*s, then there is an infinite series.

We cannot use something as an instrument for knowing unless we are sure that it is itself 'accredited', any more than we can use a ruler to measure lengths unless we are sure that it has been calibrated correctly. But in order to establish that the instrument is accredited, we must use still another instrument. How, asks Nāgārjuna, are we to avoid the regress that ensues? Nāgārjuna here gives an early statement of what Sosa calls the 'doxastic ascent' argument (cf. Sosa 1991: 181).[4]

Nyāya epistemologists break the regress by claiming that there are here two distinct attributions of knowledge: knowing p by means of π, and knowing that π is 'accredited' by means of π^*; and that the first does not entail the second (cf. Matilal 1986, esp. p. 63). Let us attend, then, to the logical form of such attributions of knowledge.

In §3.1, I described the Nyāya analysis of action sentences in terms of a thematic-role grammatical theory, the *kāraka* theory. The application of that analysis here depends on two assumptions that I shall not try to defend: that knowing is the tokening of a mental event, and that knowers are Agents of knowing-events.[5] Etymologically, a *pramāṇa* is the Instrument in connection with a knowing-event: a *pramā-karaṇa*. In this theory, (1) is initially paraphrased as (2):

(1) S knows that p by means of π.

(2) $\exists e$ [Agent (e, S) & Knowing$_T$ (e) & Patient (e, *that p*) & Instrument (e, π)]

The Patient of an event is the 'home' of the final effect (*phala*) instigated by the event. That is, Patient (e, N) $\leftrightarrow \exists f$ [home (f, N) & culminates (f, e)]. The final effect here is the tokening of an 'intransitive' knowing-event (*pramā*). The 'home' of a mental event is not its location but its content. So (2) is expanded as (3):

(3) $\exists e \exists f$ [Agent (e, S) & Knowing$_I$ (f) & Content (f, *that p*) & culminates (f, e) & Instrument (e, π)]

The Instrument of an event is an object whose 'functioning' (*vyāpāra*) constitutes the event. That is, Instrument (e, A) $\leftrightarrow$ functioning (e, A) & $\exists f$ [culminates (f, e)]. Inserting this analysis of an Instrument in (3) leads to (4):

(4) $\exists e \exists f$ [Agent (e, S) & Knowing$_I$ (f) & Content (f, *that p*) & culminates (f, e) & functioning (e, π)]

So 'S knows that *p* by means of π' is analysed as S is the Agent of a functioning of π which culminates in a knowing$_I$-that-*p* event. Recall that an event *B* is a 'functioning' or 'occupation' for event *C* just in case *B* and *C* occur, and *B* is a member of a causal chain from some prior event to *C*. The 'occupation' of an arrow is its flying through the air in order to hit a target. In coming to perceive that an object in one's field of vision is a book, one's perceptual system is 'occupied' in the production of that perceptual belief. Functionings are intermediary events in the causal chain which begins with the Agent's action and ends in the final effect, in this case a knowing$_I$-event.

The logical form of (1) is given by (4), but we do not yet have an *analysis* of knowledge attributions. The analysis will proceed via an explication of knowing$_I$ (*f*). Gaṅgeśa, the founder of Navya-Nyāya, stipulates that a knowing-that-*p* event is a true believing-that-p (that is, a believing-truly-that-*p*) event:[6]

(5) knowing$_I$ (f) iff true-believing$_I$ (*f*).

Gaṅgeśa, as Matilal (1986: 138) says, 'wants to restrict the primary (philosophical) use of "to know" (*pramā*) to designate simply any "truth-hitting" cognitive episode'. Substituting 'true-believing$_I$ (*f*)' for 'knowing$_I$ (*f*)' in (4):

(6) $\exists e \exists f$ [Agent (*e*, S) & true-believing$_I$ (*f*) & Content (*f*, *that p*) & culminates (*f*, *e*) & functioning (*e*, π)]

(6), however, is not by itself sufficient to give an analysis of (1), for we are not yet able to draw a distinction between knowledge and accidentally true belief, between warranted and unwarranted true belief.[7] We arrive at a sufficient condition when we place a further restriction on the Instrument in (4). Not every Instrument of true belief is an Instrument of knowledge. Indeed, whenever a true belief arises, there will be some functioning event which culminates in that true belief; the existence of an Instrument is entailed by *any* action statement which has the same logical form as (1). Consider, for example, (7):

(7) S believes that it will rain by consulting his tea-leaves.

The Instrument in (7) is the tea-leaves, the 'functioning' of which culminates in S's believing that it will rain. This follows from the logical form of (7). An Instrument of *knowing*, therefore, is not any Instrument in a statement like (6); the analysis of knowing$_I$ (*f*) necessitates a further condition on the functioning Instrument π.[8] Let us say that the functioning of the Instrument has to be a *well-functioning*, and look for a suitable explication of the notion of well-functioning. Our final formulation of the *pramāṇa* theory of knowledge is that S knows that *p* iff $\exists\pi$ [S knows that *p* by means of π, where:

(K) S knows that *p* by means of π iff $\exists e \exists f$ [Agent (e, S) & true-believing$_I$ (f) & Content (f, *that p*) & culminates (f, e) & well-functioning (e, π)]

What is for an Instrument to be well-functioning? The Instrument of knowing is described in Nyāya as being a 'fault-free' (*aduṣṭa*) and/or 'non-deviating' (*avyabhicāri*) cause of the final effect (cf. Matilal 1986: 135). The key to the Nyāya theory lies in the relation between these two notions. What we need is a distinction between the etiology of mere true belief, and the etiology of knowledge. The second sort of causal chain is what Sainsbury (1979: 38) calls an 'epistemic causal chain'. Let us consider an example he gives to illustrate the difference. The example concerns two scenarios, in both of which the following attribution is true:

(8) You truly believe that $2^8 = 256$ by means of your calculator.

In the first scenario, the calculator is working as it should. You press the buttons for $2^8 = ?$ (this is the 'functioning' of the calculator; *e*), the result '256' is displayed on the screen, and you come to believe, truly, that $2^8 = 256$ (this is the final effect; *f*). In the second scenario, you again press the buttons for $2^8 = ?$, the result '256' is again displayed on the screen, and you again come to believe, truly, that $2^8 = 256$. In this scenario, however, the calculator is malfunctioning: it displays '256' whatever buttons are pressed.

What is the difference between the two scenarios? Why do you know in the first case but not the second? Clearly, the answer lies in the properties of the calculator. In the first scenario, the calculator 'tracks' or 'follows' the truth; in the Nyāya terminology, it does not 'wander' or 'stray' from the truth. The calculator in the second scenario is malfunctioning or, as the Nyāya say, 'defective' (*duṣṭa*). It is important to notice here that the defect does not *consist in* its wandering from the truth. Rather, there is some defect *in virtue of which* the calculator fails to follow the truth.

The notion of 'wandering' (*vyabhicāra*) is, in fact, a technical one, defined as follows: a property H wanders from a second property S just in case H is located somewhere S is absent. Set-theoretically, $H \setminus S \neq \emptyset$.

In the present context, H is the property being-a-belief-produced-by–π, and S is the property being-true. So an Instrument follows (does not wander from) the true just in case the beliefs it produces when functioning are true. An Instrument of knowledge π therefore has the following property: *if e is a functioning of* π *, and e culminates in a belief f, then f is true provided there are no defects in the functioning of* π. In short, π is an Instrument whose normal function is to produce true beliefs: it produces true beliefs as long as there are no defects in its operation. This is the analysis of a means of knowing or *pramāṇa* in Nyāya. So, finally, an event *e* is a well-functioning of π iff *e* is a functioning of π and π is an Instrument whose normal (non-defective) function is to produce true beliefs. Being produced by such an Instrument is what distinguishes knowledge from merely true beliefs.

What is a defect (*doṣa*)? The standard definition of a defect as a special cause of false belief[9] can be only an extensionally true definition, for otherwise the mention of defects, in our analysis of an Instrument of knowing, would be redundant. In fact, there is, as Gaṅgeśa (Mohanty 1966: 128) stresses, no generic characterization of a defect. Gopinatha Bhattacharya (Annaṃbhaṭṭa 1983: 338) observes that, in the case of perceptual knowledge, the defects fall under three general headings: environmental, pathological, and 'psychical' or cognitive. Defects in the environment include haze, the object's being very distant, bad lighting; pathological defects are faults in the visual apparatus, such as myopia or jaundice; cognitive defects involve the mental state of the perceiver, such as being angry or inattentive. The notion of a defect, broadly construed, is that of a defeating condition. While all the environmental defects mentioned here are 'local' defects, in that they are possible faults in environment of operation of the Instrument on a particular occasion, I think we must also add to the list 'global' environmental defects, when the environment in its totality in some way defeats the operation of the Instrument. For example, a person trying to see things at the bottom of the ocean fails, not because of any local defect in the lighting, but because the human visual system is not suited for such environments.[10]

An Instrument of knowing functions to produce true beliefs in appropriate circumstances. The characterization of an appropriate circumstance is not purely negative (the absence of any defect): it is also described in a positive way, as an 'alethic virtue' (*guṇa*), a special cause of true belief. The Nyāya claim that, for each Instrument of knowing, there is just one alethic virtue, a particular factor whose presence is sufficient for the belief to be true in the absence of any defect. In the case of perception, it is the current existence of a sensory connection (*indriyārtha-sannikarṣa*) between the perceiver and the object perceived. (It may in fact be the case, as Stephen Phillips (2003) points out, that the term 'pramāṇa' has a normative use according to which it means 'well-functioning Instrument of knowing', so that in cases of misfire, the Instrument is not strictly described as '*pramāṇa*'. This terminological detail does not affect the substantive point here being made.)

I hope it is by now clear how the Nyāya epistemologist would reply to Nāgārjuna's sceptical regress. They would make the classic externalist move: a true belief is knowledge if it is produced by a well-functioning Instrument in the absence of defects; it is not a necessary condition for knowledge that the knower *knows* that it is so produced. The Instrument for one item of knowledge might become the Content of another. To continue the earlier analogy, a pair of scales is an Instrument for weighing a certain piece of gold, but becomes itself the thing measured when being tested or calibrated against a known weight. And although, when I see an object, my perceptual faculty is the Instrument, the same perceptual faculty becomes the *object* of measurement (*prameya*) when I am asked to read the optician's chart.

I conclude this section by considering three problem cases posed by another Indian sceptic, Śrīharṣa (see Matilal 1986: 136–7; 1991b). The first case is of a gambler who, when invited to say how many dice I have in my hand, correctly guesses 'five'. We may add that the gambler is sure of his abilities, and really believes that I have in my fist five dice. In the second case, I misperceive a dust cloud in the distance as a plume of smoke, and infer, correctly as it happens, that there is a fire at that place (see Ganeri, forthcoming, Chapter 5). The third case is of a person who correctly identifies an animal at a distance as a cow, having mistaken a piece of cloth around its neck as a dewlap. We can dismiss the first case easily, as the Instrument, guessing or guessing 'five', does not follow the truth. The similarity between the second and third cases and the examples introduced into the literature by Gettier (Gettier 1963) is striking. In both Śrīharṣa's cases, as in Gettier's, the person infers to a true belief from a false premise. The correct response of the Nyāya epistemologist, I suggest, should be to note that in each case there is a defect, indeed the same defect. The visual system, taken as a whole, has the capacity to discriminate objects of different sorts, but cannot discriminate types of object which are very similar in appearance, let alone from a distance. It is neither a defect of the environment that it contains objects similar in appearance (if it does), nor of the visual sense faculty that it cannot discriminate between them. But it is a cognitive defect on the part of the perceiver to assume that the object perceived is of one type rather than another. So there is a defect in the combined Instrument which, in these cases, leads to a true belief.[11]

If we are to situate the *pramāṇa* theory within contemporary discussions in epistemology, I believe that it has most affinity with the approach versions of which are developed by Alvin Plantinga (1993) and Ernest Sosa (1991). The leading idea in their work is that we are endowed with epistemic belief-producing faculties, and that it is the normal function of these virtues in the environments for which they are suited which confers epistemic warrant on the beliefs they produce. Plantinga employs the teleological notion of 'proper function': something is functioning properly if it is functioning in the way it was *designed* for, or, as Plantinga puts is, in accordance with its design plan. It is part of the design plan for the human circulatory system that the heart's purpose is to pump blood. An epistemic faculty is a cognitive process which has the production of true beliefs as its proper function (1993: 38). The notion of proper function is relative to an environment, for something which is designed to have a certain function in one environment need not have that function in another (a heart will not pump blood if it is in a jar; eyes designed to see on the surface of the earth will not perform that function at the bottom of the ocean). Even when situated in the environment for which it is designed, a thing's proper function can be overridden by defeating conditions (air in the blood stream; poor lighting for the eyes).

Plantinga's idea that the epistemic faculties are *designed* to produce true belief has no clear correlate in the Indian theory,[12] but neither is it essential to the approach. Sosa, more liberally, describes truth-conducive belief-forming faculties as 'intellectual virtues', where 'a subject's intellectual virtue V relative to an environment E may be defined as S's disposition to believe correctly propositions in a field [of propositions] F relative to which S stands in conditions C, in environments E' (1991: 140). He attaches importance to the thought that a virtue is a competence rather than an ability or a process; it is what makes true relevant counterfactuals, of the form 'if *p* were true, S would believe it' (1991: 274). Examples of epistemic faculties are vision, introspection, memory and deduction, and both Plantinga (1993:77–88) and Sosa (1991: 215–24) include testimony.

Any faculty-based approach to epistemic warrant must give due weight to the importance of the reflective nature of human knowledge. Epistemic warrant, it is alleged, supervenes on non-epistemic facts, facts about the cognizer's faculties and causal relations with their surroundings. Humans, however, are not merely information-processing machines. We are conscious of the origins and warrant of our beliefs, and hold ourselves responsible to ensuring them to be true. Sosa addresses the issue in his distinction between 'animal knowledge' and 'reflective knowledge' (1991: 240), between our 'animal endowments' and our reflective awareness of them, an 'awareness of one's persistent tendency to be right in field F when in circumstances C' (191: 282), and an ensuing inference to the best explanation of why this should be so. In the Nyāya theory, a perspective on one's own epistemic capacities is gained in the reflective justification of one's beliefs, based on an inference from their behavioural effects or an inference from the epistemic 'likeness' of one belief with another (cf. Matilal 1986: 153–67).[13] The point I wish to stress is that a faculty-based epistemology in no way has to represent the epistemological subject as a passive or unreflective register of information.

5.2 Towards a Theory of Testimony

The Nyāya theory of testimony is built upon two central doctrines. The first is that understanding an assertion normally consists in assenting directly (non-inferentially) to what is said. The second is that the beliefs we thereby form normally constitute knowledge. In Chapter 4, I formulated the account as follows:

H testimonially knows that *p* on hearing S's utterance σ iff

(i) H directly assents to σ, thereby believing that *p*,
(ii) *p* is true, and
(iii) there are no defeating conditions.

The Naiyāyikas themselves phrase the analysis in somewhat different technical vocabulary. They say[14] that:

H testimonially knows that *p* on hearing S's utterance σ iff

(i) H forms a language-based world-directed true belief (*śābdabodha*) that *p* on hearing σ,
(ii) σ satisfies four auxiliary conditions, namely:
 (1) *āsatti*: the sentence elements must be in physical and temporal proximity with one another.
 (2) *ākāṅkṣā*: the sentence must be syntactically well-formed.

(3) *tātparya*: the sentence must be unambiguous, or else disambiguated via consideration of the speaker's intended meaning.

(4) *yogyatā*: the sentence must be 'semantically fit'.

(iii) S is a 'credible witness' (*āpta*).

Of their four conditions mentioned in (ii), the first three are intuitive constraints on the type of utterance capable of being used to express a unique proposition. The first is self-explanatory: if the words in the utterance are uttered one at a time over a long period of time, or mixed in with the words of a distinct utterance, it will be impossible for the hearer to form a proper auditory perception of the utterance. Syntactic 'expectancy' is defined as the inability of one word to produce, without another word, an awareness of a connected sentence-meaning; an utterance which fails to possess such 'expectancy' is the sentence 'horse man elephant'. The idea is that the utterance must be grammatically correct. More than that, it is in virtue of the syntactical rules that the undesignated relations between the word-meanings are expressed. The third condition, 'speaker's intention', is appealed to when the sentence contains an ambiguous word—disambiguation proceeds via consideration of the speaker's intended meaning. The important theoretical concepts in the Nyāya account are those of 'semantic fitness' (*yogyatā*) and a 'credible witness' (*āpta*).

Let us begin by applying our analysis of knowledge attributions. Suppose a person hears an utterance and comes to believe truly the proposition it expresses. That belief is a case of knowledge if it is produced by the functioning of an Instrument of knowing. The functioning (*e*) here is the operation of the language faculty on the heard utterance, the processing of the utterance. The hearer draws on her knowledge of the meaning relation to assign, to each constituent of the utterance, a meaning-relatum, and on her knowledge of syntax to relate them in a single thought-content. Directly assenting to that thought-content, she thereby comes to believe the proposition expressed by the sentence. This belief is the final effect (*f*). The *pramāṇa* theory claims that the final belief is an item of knowledge just in case the Instrument—which we may take to be the entire process leading from an auditory perception of a spoken utterance, via the operation of the language faculty, to the tokening of a belief—is one whose non-defective functioning produces true beliefs. *Understanding* is an intellectual virtue.

A defect, I repeat, is not to be thought of merely as anything which prevents the Instrument from producing a true belief; rather, it is one of an antecedently specified set of environmental, pathological, or cognitive faults. An important 'local' environmental defect is if the speaker of that particular utterance is lying, or simply uninformed about the subject matter. Indeed, any salient deficiency on the part of the speaker will count here as an environmental defect. A possible 'global' environmental defect is that, within the linguistic population as a whole, lying is endemic; another is that false belief among speakers is endemic.[15] Pathological defects affect the functioning of the hearer's testimonial Instrument: mistaken knowledge of meaning, faults in the language processing faculty, poor hearing. The cognitive defects pertain to the hearer, and include: false beliefs about the speaker's truthfulness, mistrustfulness, false beliefs about the matter under discussion.

That we do indeed directly assent to what others say is what Reid calls the 'Principle of Credulity':

> The wise Author of nature hath planted in the human mind a propensity to rely upon human testimony before we can give a reason for doing so (Reid 1983: 281).

In agreeing that this is so, the Naiyāyikas are advocating an anti-reductionist account of testimony. The reductionist typically claims that the testimonial Instrument at least partly implicates a process of inference, by which we infer to the truth of the proposition expressed, perhaps on inductive grounds, such as that the speaker's utterances have been generally true in the past,[16] or perhaps as an inference to the best explanation of the speaker's speech-act. The Nyāya model of understanding and testimony avoids the tendency to 'ever-intellectualize' both, to see them as involving much more in the way of reason-giving and inferring than they in fact do. That tendency is found in both Gricean theories of understanding and Humean reductionist accounts of testimony. In the Nyāya model, direct assent is defeated only if the hearer knows of a defect in the process. We therefore take it that H directly assents to S's utterance σ just in case H non-inferentially believes that p on hearing σ in virtue of the functioning of her testimonial Instrument, and H does not know of any defect in that functioning.

The Nyāya theory of testimony consists in the following, normative, thesis: directly assenting to a true utterance in the absence of defects or defeating conditions is sufficient for knowledge. Another way to formulate the thesis is in terms of the Testimony Schema:

(T) if S tells H that p, and H understands S's utterance and thereby accepts it as true, then H comes to know that p.

In terms of this schema, the Nyāya thesis is: (there are no defects) $\rightarrow$ T.

Elizabeth Fricker (1994: 125) recommends that we formulate a claim of this sort in terms of what she calls a 'presumptive right':

> *PR thesis*: On any occasion of testimony, the hearer has the epistemic right to assume, without evidence, that the speaker is trustworthy, i.e. that what she says will be true, unless there are special circumstances which defeat this presumption.

She comments that

> the PR thesis is ... a normative epistemic principle, amounting to the thesis that a hearer has the epistemic right to believe what she believes an arbitrary speaker to assert, just on the ground that it has been asserted: she need not attempt any assessment of the likelihood that this speaker's assertions about their subject matter will be true .... [It] is an epistemic charter for the gullible (1994: 124–5).

Fricker's claim is that the absence of defeating conditions is not by itself sufficient for the transmission of knowledge. The hearer has an epistemic responsibility to be 'alert' to the presence of defeating conditions. This alertness is 'partly a matter of her being disposed to deploy background knowledge which is relevant, partly a matter of her monitoring the speaker for telltale signs revealing likely untrustworthiness' (1993: 150). It is quite clear that the hearer does have an obligation to hold himself open to the possibility that defeating conditions obtain. There are, however, two different ways to see the role of that obligation. One way is to demand that the hearer acquires, either in advance of or concurrently with her acquisition of a testimonial belief, information bearing upon the credibility of the speaker. The possession of such evidence, as a necessary condition for the transmission of knowledge from speaker to hearer, would place the hearer in a position to justify the beliefs she thereby acquires. Fricker (1994: 145) says, 'The thesis I advocate in opposition to a PR thesis, is that a hearer should always engage in some assessment of the speaker for trustworthiness'. That is, it is not sufficient for testimony that there are no defeating conditions; what is required in addition is that the hearer knows, or has a suitably well justified belief, that the current testimony is defect-free.[17]

There is, however, a different way for the hearer to discharge her obligation to be 'alert' to the possibility that defeating conditions obtain. The hearer might discharge the obligation in being *epistemically susceptible* to the existence of defeating conditions; notably by being such that the counterfactual 'if there were defeating conditions, she would come to know of them' is true. Imagine someone who has an internalized lie detector, a disposition to notice when speakers are lying, grounded perhaps in sensory cues of which she is barely or un- aware. It would be true of that person that if the speaker were lying she would notice it. She would, in a perfectly legitimate sense, be open to the possibility that the speaker is lying. However, in the normal case, when the speaker is not lying, she will not possess any information or beliefs about the speaker's credentials, nor should she need to in order to discharge her epistemic obligations.[18]

The hearer might, indeed, be able to exploit the fact that she is epistemically susceptible to the obtaining of defeating conditions in order to attain a reflective awareness that the speaker is trustworthy, for she might be in a position to perform the following inference *ad ignorantium* (comparable with the Indian *anupalabdhi-hetu*, 'reason based on non-observation'): if the speaker were lying, I would suspect she was, but I do not suspect she is; therefore, she is not lying. Performing that inference, however, is not a necessary part of what is required for the hearer to be alert to the presence of defeating conditions. Can we concede the possibility of quasi-perceptual capacities to detect a lie, but deny that there is nothing comparable in the case of a speaker who honestly expresses a false belief in a field about which she lacks competence? Something like this, though perhaps more extreme, was suggested by the Buddhist Kamalaśīla, who criticized the Nyāya account on the grounds that 'even if we agree that there are "credible persons" (*āptāḥ*), there is no accredited means by which to ascertain their good and bad qualities, since these [qualities] are imperceptible [dispositions], and [the same] bodily and verbal behaviour can be made on the basis of many different intentions' (*Pañjikā* under TS 1509 [1917: 537]).

There are ways of being epistemically susceptible to the *competence* of the speaker without having to have background knowledge of his curriculum vitae, an alertness perhaps to inconsistency in his testimony over time. I doubt that even this is necessary, however, at least in those situations in which the incompetence of the speaker is not, in Goldman's terminology, a relevant alternative. If our linguistic community were full of people who habitually made honest but false assertions about matters they had little competence in, then the possibility that the speaker is incompetent, on a particular occasion, would be a relevant one, and the hearer would be epistemically irresponsible not to consider it. The faculty of testimony is not designed to work in such an environment; reason must override it. *Our* linguistic community, however, is not like that. In our community, competence is the default position.

Similar remarks, I think, can be made about the other defeating conditions. So let us turn to consider some other problematic cases. The Nyāya account has no trouble with cases of 'mistaken liars' or 'deceived deceivers', people who believe something false but in lying end up saying something true. For although the hearer's belief is a true one, it is not warranted, since the speaker was not a credible testifier.[19] However, the notion of a mistaken liar can be used to construct a rather trickier, Gettier-style problem for the Nyāya account of testimony.[20] Suppose that S believes that *p*, is honest and sincere, and testifies to H that *p*. However, S learned that *p* from another person R, and R is a mistaken liar. R falsely believes that *not-p*, but lies that p. It would seem that the hearer H's belief counts as knowledge according to the Nyāya account, for it is true and produced by a credible speaker. We may suppose that H has no reason to disbelieve that *p*, and that *p* is a mundane unastonishing truth. Nevertheless, we should not want in fact to say that H has acquired knowledge, because of the element of chance in R's report. The only solution to this problem is, I think, to insist on some form of Transmission Principle for the acquisition of knowledge by testimony (cf. §4.1). That is, we must insist that the attestee H knows that *p* only if the testifier S knows that *p*. This would certainly rule out the present case; S here does not know, since her source was not a credible one.

Environmental defects in testimony are of two sorts: faults with the utterer, and faults with the utterance. The Nyāya say that the utterer must be a credible or authoritative witness, while the utterance must be 'semantically fit'. I have discussed the first sort in some detail, so let me now consider defects of the second sort. Here, too, the possibility of testimony (T) entails only that the defect does not occur, and not that it is known by the hearer not to occur.[21] In the last chapter, I considered a number of such defeating conditions, to do with the language shared by speaker and hearer. For many terms, the hearer must think of the referent under a conventionally determined mode if testimony is to be possible, and the speaker and hearer must know meaning theories with isomorphic derivational structures. Nothing in the arguments for these claims made it a necessary condition on the transmission of knowledge that the hearer have second-order knowledge about those properties of the language.

The Nyāya regard the 'semantic fitness' (*yogyatā*) of the utterance as another such condition. The notion of fitness has many epistemic and normative overtones. The traditional definition of fitness is as the absence of 'incompatibility' between the elements in the content of the putative final belief state.[22] A paradigmatic example of a statement which fails the fitness condition is the statement 'She sprinkles [the field] with fire' (*vahninā siñcati*). This is contrasted with the sentence 'She sprinkles [the field] with water' (*jalena siñcati*), which passes the test. This definition of fitness has been the source of considerable controversy, both among the Naiyāyikas and their latter-day interpreters. Its primary significance is within a framework of ontological categories. It is claimed that the sentence 'She sprinkles with fire' is unfit because, though grammatically proper, it violates a principle of ontology: sprinkling is an activity capable of being performed only with water and other fluids, not with fire. The idea, then, is that there is an ontological framework, for example the Vaiśeṣika system of categories, which determines some notion of physical possibility, and a putative statement is fit iff the state-of-affairs it describes is physically possible.

Clearly the notion of what is physically possible is relative to a physical theory. So, generalizing, we may take fitness to refer to the coherence of the new statement with the background theoretical, or deeply-entrenched, beliefs of the hearer. It may mean something like 'likelihood of the utterance to be true in the lights of the hearer', or 'coherence with the hearer's general beliefs'. Utterances are fit if they 'make sense'. Knowledge of what is ontologically possible will, no doubt, inform this conception. Once again, the fitness constraint is regarded as a defeasibility condition: it is not that a testimonial belief is warranted only if the hearer ascertains that it fits with her other beliefs, but rather that the belief's warrant is overridden if and when she discovers that it does not. The condition appears designed to rule out so-called 'astonishing reports', assertions which strike the hearer as extremely implausible or contrary to her accepted schema. John Abercrombie, in his discussion of testimony, gives a nice example (1830: 77): 'When the king of Siam was told by a Dutch traveller that in Holland at certain seasons of the year water becomes so solid that an elephant might walk over it, he replied, "I have believed many extraordinary things which you have told me, because I took you for a man of truth and veracity, but now I am convinced that you lie".' It may also be recalled that Hume, one of the first to discuss testimony in the West, did so in the course of a discussion of reports of miracles. The Nyāya quite sensibly restrict the domain of testimony to natural extensions of our already existing beliefs. They are interested in the role of testimony in every-day life, and not in the special epistemological problems posed by religious witnesses.

Some authors have found the problem of understanding *false* sentences to pose particular problems for the Nyāya account.[23] For if understanding a sentence is a matter of acquiring knowledge of the proposition it expresses, then how can we understand false sentences?

Matilal alludes to the problem, and suggests that the fitness constraint supplies an answer:

> The fitness condition is broadly defined to take care of at least two major cases of 'misfires' in testimony: (a) when the objects referred to by the elements do not fit, an impossible combination—e.g. 'a barren woman's child', and (b) when the objects may fit in a possible world, but not in actuality, as somebody saying 'there is a snake in the next room' when I know that there is none. The second case takes care of the cases of the so-called meaningful but false utterances (1990: 66).

I do not think that there is in fact a genuine problem here, given a sufficiently careful description of the Nyāya theory of understanding. There are two scenarios to consider. First, the scenario where the sentence is false and the hearer knows or at least believes that it is false, the second case referred to by Matilal. As I have reconstructed the Nyāya model, this will be a situation where the hearer's direct assent to the statement is defeated: we do not assent to things we firmly believe to be false. That would indeed fall within the remit of the fitness constraint. The 'understanding' the hearer achieves of the sentence in such a case is not belief in what it expresses, but rather belief that the speaker believes or said it.[24] The other scenario to consider is one in which the sentence is false, but the hearer does not believe it to be false and has no reason to suppose that it is false. In this situation, the hearer will directly assent to the statement. If the speaker is lying, the belief so formed will not be warranted; but if he is sincere but himself deceived, it will be a warranted, though false, belief. In neither case will it constitute knowledge, any more than a non-veridical perception does. Nevertheless, the speaker will have understood the sentence, in directly assenting to what it expresses.

I conclude that the Nyāya theory of testimony fits well into the epistemological perspective which sees knowledge acquisition in terms of an individual's possession of truth-following cognitive capacities non-defectively functioning in the absence of defeating conditions. Whether or not that perspective can find adequate answers to well-known problems, such as deciding the correct level at which to specify the capacities, is a matter for further investigation.

5.3 Testimony and Semantic Structure

The rules of language are normative in the sense that they determine conditions of correct use. By 'use' I mean both speakers' use of words in referring to objects, and hearers' 'use' of words in interpreting utterances as being about objects. A speaker uses the word 'pot' correctly to refer to a pot; incorrectly to refer to a cup. A hearer uses the word 'pot' correctly if she forms a belief about a pot; incorrectly if she forms a belief about a cup. The difficulty in accounting for the normativity of meaning has been brought into sharp focus with Kripke's (1982) discussion of rule-following and meaning scepticism. Boghossian (1989: 513) summarizes the problem: 'Any proposed candidate for the property in virtue of which an expression has meaning, must be such as to ground the "normativity" of meaning—it ought to be possible to read off from any alleged meaning constituting property of a word, what is the correct use of that word'.

The Nyāya claim that a word's meaning something consists in its having been introduced by a divine mandate of the form ⟨let this word be construed as this object⟩. Clearly, mandates of this form impose conditions for correct usage; the account of meaning in terms of mandates is indeed addressed directly at the normativity problem. I see, however, two main problems with this account. The account asserts that a word is correctly interpreted as concerning a particular object because it is God's will that this be so. The normativity of meaning is derived from imperative mental acts: divine acts of will. The claim is, of course, analogous to the claim that moral norms have a theistic basis. The first problem is that divine acts of will, even if they exist, would give the rules of language the wrong sort of normativity. Divine mandates are categorical imperatives: ⟨Understand by this word this object!⟩. The norms of meaning, however, are hypothetical. They are of the form ⟨if you wish to speak or understand Sanskrit, understand by this word this object⟩. The second problem is that divine mandates could not be regulative, for the reason considered above—the mandates will not be learnable. They give no account of what is involved in following a rule as opposed to simply acting in accordance with it. There is, in fact, considerable debate about whether the rules of language are regulative or only descriptive. My point here is just that the Nyāya must regard them as regulative, since knowledge of the mandates is constitutively involved in the hearer's language faculty.

Mohanty too criticizes the 'divine decree' doctrine as an explanation of the existence of linguistic norms. He says (1992: 91 -2):

> [O]n the Nyāya view ... the connection between a word and its meaning is conventional, and 'convention' is explicated by 'the desire "let this word mean such and such thing"'. To say that the desire which

> assigns meanings to words in a language is but God's—as the Naiyāyikas often said—is to escape from subjective relativism, but at what cost? There is not only the problem whether one act of desire on God's part can objectify all things by assigning names to them, there is also the problem about languages in the plural: which vocabulary did God sanction, which names did he choose? No, appealing to God's desire won't do, but at the same time we may admit that there must have been some original 'baptism' (to borrow Kripke's term) or some *Urstiftung* (in Husserl's sense). However, once such a baptism has been performed, the *Urstiftung* established, the connection becomes objective .... We assume, unless otherwise indicated, that the speaker intends to use the words he utters in the sense in which the community uses them.

I agree with Mohanty's criticism of Nyāya mandates, but not with his attempt to reinterpret them as baptismal reference-fixing acts. Reading the decrees as baptismal acts is, of course, a way to make word-meaning a more robust notion in the Nyāya theory, but what makes reference a robust notion in Kripke's account is that there is a causal relation between the word and its reference, and such a claim is largely absent in Nyāya writings. The Nyāya are explicit that it is the hearer's knowledge of the decree governing the term which guides her understanding; yet, on the causal theory, her use of the term is guided by something quite different, an intention to co-refer with the other members of the population. Neither does the idea that hearers are able to discriminate the referent have anything like the prominent role it does for the Nyāya in the causal theory.

Matilal has another solution to the normativity problem. He suggests (1985: 407–8, 418; 1990: 54–5) that the interpretations of an 'ideal hearer' are the benchmark against which to measure actual language use: 'We can conceive of an "ideal" hearer ... who reacts rationally and mechanically ... This rational and mechanical reaction, according to the Indian theorists, is produced by the utterance generating a particular direct cognition in the hearer, very much as blowing a horn produces a particular vibration in the air' (pp. 407–8). 'In this way, it is claimed that an attempted account or analysis of the knowledge of such an ideal hearer would be an account of the *meaning* of the sentence' (p. 418).

Matilal's claim is that the meaning of an expression in the public language just is the meaning it has in the I-language of an ideal hearer.[25] An actual hearer understands the expression correctly just in case, or to the extent that her understanding coincides with that of the ideal hearer. Matilal makes no reference here to the doctrine of authoritative mandates, and I take it that his proposal is intended as a revision of the Nyāya account, in which the talk of mandates is replaced by talk about an ideal hearer. What then makes a hearer 'ideal'? We should not say that an ideal hearer is one whose interpretations accord with the mandates, for that would render the mention of an ideal hearer superfluous—the mandates would still be appealed to as the source of normativity. An Euthyphro-style problem threatens: is a hearer ideal because he conforms with the mandates, or are the mandates those rules which describe the ideal hearer? Matilal must have some other account of an ideal hearer in mind, and his suggestion is that she is a hearer whose language processing mechanism is working 'rationally' or 'mechanically'. The implication here is that an ideal hearer's language faculty is free from error, that it is functioning perfectly. However, this still does not help much, since we are now in need of an explanation of what constitutes erroneous and non-erroneous functioning. The problem of normativity returns.

I think that we can do better if we look, not for a hearer whose language faculty is functioning *perfectly*, but for one whose language faculty is functioning *properly*. As I have argued, the concept of a 'knowledge-yielding Instrument' (*pramāṇa*) is that of a faculty whose function is the production of true beliefs. Non-defective function, unlike perfect function, does not preclude the possibility of error. Perhaps then we can give an alternative account of the normativity of meaning within the conception of language as a means of knowing. We might try, in particular, to derive linguistic norms from the epistemic norms involved in understanding. A possibility along these lines is hinted at by Gadādhara's nineteenth-century commentator Sudarśanācārya (1892: 2):

> The meaning of a word is an object of a presentation (*pratīti*) caused by the word as governed by the meaning relation. A 'presentation' here is an item of testimonial knowledge (*śābdabodha*). Here, if the phrase 'by the meaning relation' were not uttered, but it were simply said that 'the meaning of a word is an object of an item of testimonial knowledge caused by the word', then [consider] the sentence 'the pot is blue'. [From this sentence], an item of testimonial knowledge can arise whose qualificandhood is delimited by being a pot, whose qualifierhood is delimited by being a blue thing, and whose relation is identity. Just as the pot is an object of this item of testimonial knowledge, so too is the blue thing. So the blue thing too could be the meaning of the word 'pot'. It is in order to exclude this that the phrase 'by the meaning relation' is uttered. Thus, even if the blue thing is an object of an item of testimonial knowledge caused by the word 'pot', there is no meaning relation between the word 'pot' and the blue thing. So the blue thing is not the object of an item of testimonial

> knowledge caused by the word 'pot' as governed by a meaning relation between the word 'pot' and the blue thing. So the blue thing is not the meaning of the word 'pot'.

Sudarśanācārya imagines the possibility that two hearers could have different internalized grammars but attach the same meaning to every whole sentence. One construes the term 'blue' as standing for a blue thing, and the term 'pot' as standing for a pot. The other takes the term 'blue' as standing for a pot, and 'pot' as standing for a blue thing. If we assume with the Nyāya that the sentence 'the pot is a blue thing' is an identity statement, both hearers apparently could acquire the same belief, that the pot is blue, on hearing this sentence.

Sudarśanācārya in effect observes that facts about sentence–proposition correlations are consistent with attributions of tacit knowledge of different semantic theories. Of course, his point is made for the meaning of a single word, but the argument can easily be generalized. Indeed, the generalization is a version of Quine's criticism of the very notion of internalized grammar: how could there be empirical evidence justifying the attribution of tacit knowledge of one semantic theory rather than another, extensionally equivalent, theory? (Quine 1970)

If I am right, Sudarśanācārya's reply is that a speaker and hearer who agree on truth-conditions for every sentence in the language while assigning different meanings to the words will not be able to communicate knowledge. The idea rests on the following Testimony Principle:

T → S and H tacitly know derivationally equivalent semantic theories.

Before trying to defend this principle, let us consider how, if at all, it might lead to an answer to the normativity problem. The idea is that we can appeal to the epistemic norms under which methods for belief-formation fall. Goldman (1986) usefully distinguishes between a system of rules of justification ('J-rules'), and the criteria that make a system of J-rules 'right'. Examples of J-rules are: 'a cognizer is permitted to believe anything he is told on a Tuesday', and 'a cognizer is permitted to believe that things are as his senses represent them as being'. Now beliefs formed in accordance with the first rule will not be justified, while those formed in accordance with the second will be: the first is a wrong J-rule and the second a right one. Goldman therefore formulates the principle that:

> S's believing *p* at *t* is justified iff S's believing *p* at *t* is permitted by a right system of J-rules and this permission is not undermined by S's cognitive state at *t* (p. 63).

What makes a system of J-rules right or wrong? Popular answers in the past have been: a system of J-rules is right iff the rules are derivable from logic; if they are accepted by the members of one's linguistic community; if they guarantee a coherent set of beliefs. Goldman himself is a process-reliabilist, and therefore proposes that:

> A J-rule system R is right iff R permits certain (basic) psychological processes, and the instantiation of these processes would result in a truth ratio of beliefs that meets some specified high threshold (greater than 0.50) (p. 106).

A *pramāṇa* epistemology agrees with the form of this proposal, but replaces the second clause 'and the instantiation of these processes would result in a truth ratio of beliefs that meets some specified high threshold (greater than 0.50)' with its favoured description of what makes a process a *pramāṇa*, an 'accredited' belief-forming process. This is that the non-defective function of the process, in appropriate conditions, is truth-following.

Consider now the unrestricted testimony J-rule: 'A hearer is permitted to believe that *p* when the speaker tells him that *p*, and he understands the speaker's utterance and thereby accepts it as true'. No account of the rightness of J-rules ought to permit this rule in an unrestricted form. Indeed, each testimony principle (other than the facticity of testimony, which reflects the truth-clause and not the justification clause) states a restriction on the rule. Suppose that a testimony principle asserts that testimony occurs only if the speaker is trustworthy. The testimony J-rule ought then to take a restricted form 'A hearer is permitted to believe that *p* when the speaker tells him that *p*, and he understands the speaker's utterance and thereby accepts it as true, and the speaker is trustworthy'. Testimony principles, therefore, are consequences of rightness criteria for J-rule systems. A process-reliabilist would derive the testimony principle just mentioned by considering the reliability of utterances of an untrustworthy person.

Testimony principles are thus normative truths, truths which are consequences of rightness criteria for J-rule systems. Suppose that it is indeed a testimony principle that speaker and hearer tacitly know structurally equivalent semantic theories. The testimony J-rule the hearer follows will be right only if his internalized grammar is derivationally equivalent with that of the speaker. Conformance with the epistemic norm demands conformity in derivational structure. The speakers of the language now face a co-ordination problem: they must achieve conformity in the derivational structure of their internalized grammars if their testimony-based beliefs are to be justified. Lewis says that it is 'essential that a convention is a regularity such that conformity by others gives one a reason to conform'. If the members of the population were to achieve a conformity in the semantic theory they each tacitly know, then each would have a clear 'reason' to conform: conformity is what gives them access to the community of knowledge by testimony. More precisely, the 'reason' they have to conform is this: conformity is what makes beliefs formed from testimony permitted by a right J-rule, and so what makes testimony a way of acquiring justified beliefs. Once the co-ordination problem has been solved, and a conventional tacitly known semantic theory fixed upon, we can take the conventional semantic theory to be the standard of correctness against which to compare any individual's tacitly known semantic theory. It will serve in the same capacity as the I-language of Matilal's ideal hearer.

Let us now see if we can make plausible the testimony principle upon which this argument rests. To clarify the proposal, consider a slightly different example (the example is taken from Evans 1985: 327). Consider a language with just one hundred sentences. Each sentence is composed of one of ten names along with one of ten predicates; that is, each is of the form '$F_i a_j$'; $1 \geq i, j \leq 10$. Suppose further that most of the linguistic community understands this language by tacitly knowing meaning axioms for each of the ten names, each of the ten predicates, and a rule of composition. They have an articulated, structured understanding of the language. In virtue of their tacit knowledge of the meaning axioms, they are able to associate each of the one hundred possible sentences with one of the one hundred propositions $p_1, \ldots, p_{100}$. Let us take a typical member of this community, and call him Saṃvyūha (from the Sanskrit for 'structure').

Now suppose that one of the members of the community, call him Avyūha ('structureless'), understands the language simply by tacitly knowing a hundred distinct axioms, each of the form ⟨'*Fa*' means *p*⟩. This person has an unarticulated, list-like understanding of the language. The tacit knowledge of this semantic theory consists in having a set of causally operative states, one for each of the axioms in the theory. A hearer tacitly knows a particular semantic theory just in case the structure of the causal explanation of his understanding a sentence 'mirrors' the derivational structure of the semantic theory. The explanation of Saṃvyūha's coming to understand an utterance of the sentence '*Fa*' will implicate operative states containing the information that '*a*' refers to *a*, and that '*F*' is true of *F*s. The explanation of Avyūha's coming to understand an utterance of the sentence '*Fa*' will implicate the single operative state containing the information that '*Fa*' is true iff *Fa*.

Evans (1985: 331–3) points out that empirical evidence for possession of one or the other competence can be found in two areas: patterns of acquisition and patterns of loss.[26] The first concerns the effect of coming to understand new sentences. Suppose that a hearer, having never previously encountered any sentence containing the name '*f*', hears the sentence '*Ff*' in a context in which they are able to learn its meaning. If the hearer is now able to understand any sentence containing the name '*f*', we would have strong evidence that the hearer has a structured understanding of the language. Likewise, if a hearer who loses the ability to understand a sentence, '*Fa*' say, also loses his ability to understand any sentence containing the name '*a*', we would again have strong evidence that his understanding was structured. The loss would be explained by the decay of the state containing the information that '*a*' refers to *a*. We would expect to see neither pattern of acquisition nor loss of competence if the hearer's understanding were unstructured (these points are clearly related to the arguments considered in §2.2).

Martin Davies (1987) suggests an important further sort of evidence: patterns of revision. A hearer who on revising his belief about the meaning of one sentence, for example '*Fa*', also revises his beliefs about the meaning of every sentence containing the name '*a*' is likely to have a structured understanding of the language. Davies (1987: 457) indeed regards facts about revision as not merely evidential but also constitutive in attributions of tacit knowledge:

> Tacit knowledge of an articulated semantic theory requires a match between the derivational structure of the theory—constituted by facts about canonical derivations of meaning specifications—and the causal explanatory structure of speakers—... constituted by facts of the following form: the operative states implicated in the explanations of the speaker's beliefs about $s_1, s_2, ..., s_n$ are jointly sufficient for a causal explanation of the speaker's belief about *s*; *and* those first states together with the revision of the speaker's belief about *s* provide an explanation of the speaker's corresponding revisions in his beliefs about $s_1, s_2, ..., s_n$.

Facts about revision will be especially important to my argument.

We have seen already that knowledge cannot rest on chance. Knowledge is not produced by lucky guesswork, or gazing into crystal balls, even if the belief so produced happens to be true. One way to satisfy the 'no-accident' requirement is to demand that the belief-forming methods and processes are sensitive to the difference between circumstances in which the belief is true and relevant alternative or non-actual circumstances in which it is false. Goldman's celebrated 'barn' example illustrates this point (Goldman 1976). Imagine a person driving through countryside in which there are located both real barns and look-alike fake ones. Her perceptual faculties cannot discriminate between the two types, but glancing out of the window she sees a real barn and forms the belief that it is a barn. Though true, this belief does not constitute knowledge. The reason is that she might just as easily have glanced out a moment later and seen a fake barn, thereby forming a false belief. Her belief-forming process in fact produces a true belief, but in relevant alternative circumstances (looking at a fake barn rather than a real one) it would have produced a false one.

Avyūha has a testimony-based belief-forming method based on direct assent to the utterance of other speakers. Does this method reliably follow the truth? I prescind here from any questions about the general reliability of such a method, being concerned only with what follows from the fact that Avyūha has an unstructured understanding of the language. The question is whether Avyūha's belief-forming method is sensitive to relevant alternatives in scenarios involving patterns of acquisition, loss and revision. Let us fix our attention on a language having these four sentences among others: 'Pablo is bald', 'Pablo is happy', 'Jacob is bald', and 'Jacob is happy'. Saṃvyūha and Avyūha tacitly know the semantic theories T_1 and T_2 respectively:

T_1: (i) 'Pablo' refers to Pablo,
(ii) 'Jacob' refers to Jacob,
(iii) 'ξ is bald' is true iff the referent of 'ξ' is bald,
(iv) 'ξ is happy' is true iff the referent of 'ξ' is happy,
etc.

T_2: (i) 'Pablo is bald' is true iff Pablo is bald,
(ii) 'Jacob is bald' is true iff Jacob is bald,
(iii) 'Pablo is happy' is true iff Pablo is happy,
(iv) 'Jacob is happy' is true iff Jacob is happy,
etc.

Let us first imagine a linguistic community where the introduction of new elements into the language is a common occurrence. How reliable is Avyūha's belief-forming method, 'believe that *p*, if a speaker asserts sentence *s* and *s* is true iff *p*' relative to that of Saṃvyūha's structured method? It is clear, first of all, that this method is not going to lead to false belief. Suppose that a new sentence 'Lucy is happy' is uttered in a context in which its meaning is plain. Avyūha acquires the ability to understand this sentence, without, unlike Saṃvyūha, acquiring the ability to understand an utterance of, for example, 'Lucy is bald'. Hearing an utterance of this latter sentence will not lead Avyūha to form a false belief, but to form no belief at all. So Avyūha's method would be a reliable if deficient method of acquiring beliefs. The more new terms were introduced, the more deficient it would become, and Avyūha may soon find himself unable to understand, let alone gain knowledge from, much of what is said. But although his testimonial belief-forming method would become increasingly limited in scope, it would remain reliable.

Imagine next a community where speakers are congenitally liable to the decay of states of tacit knowledge. The unstructured understander Avyūha is here in a better position than before, and better indeed than the structured understanders in the community. They are liable to lose their grasp on whole classes of sentences simultaneously; by losing, for example, the state that contains the information that 'Pablo' refers to Pablo. Avyūha's belief-forming method will again be reliable, although now an increasing greater proportion of Avyūha's tacit knowledge will become redundant. Here too, there is no reason to think that lacking a structured understanding is an epistemic deficiency.

The crucial case is the third. We are now to imagine a community in which revision in belief about meaning is rife. Let us suppose that the members of the community revise their belief about the meaning of 'Pablo is bald', taking it now to be true iff some other person, Anton, is bald. The structured understanders will revise their beliefs about the meanings of all other sentences containing the word 'Pablo'; as Davies puts it, 'We shall expect the speaker to keep his meaning assignments in step with each other—to preserve systematicity under revision' (1987: 455). They do this by revising the content of the state which contains information about the meaning of the word 'Pablo': its content will now be that 'Pablo' refers to Anton. The unstructured understander, Avyūha, is insensitive to the preservation of systematicity. He will revise his belief about the meaning of the sentence 'Pablo is bald' without revising his belief about the meaning of any other sentence containing the name 'Pablo'. So, if after the revision Saṃvyūha were to utter 'Pablo is happy', Avyūha's testimonial belief-forming method would lead Avyūha to come to believe that Pablo is happy. This might be true, but if it is true, it would only be by accident; for the belief that Savyūha expressed in uttering the sentence is that Anton is happy. In short, in a community in which revision is widespread, the unstructured understander's method of accepting what he hears as true leads often, and increasingly often, to false belief.

Given that Avyūha cannot tell whether an utterance to which he is about to assent is subject to revision or not, his testimonial beliefs even in the cases where he believes truly do not constitute knowledge. His justification is undermined by the possibility that the speakers' belief about their meaning might have changed without his knowing. Like Goldman's fake barns, sentences containing words about whose meanings the structured understanders have revised their beliefs will be ever-present pitfalls for Avyūha's belief-forming method. Thus, the beliefs formed by an unstructured understander on assenting to the utterances of a structured understander are not warranted, even when the sentences concerned are not in fact subject to revision.

There can thus be no state operative in the causal explanation of the speaker's competence which is not operative in the causal explanation of the hearer's competence, if the hearer is to be in a position to acquire knowledge from the speaker's utterance. So the semantic theory tacitly known by the speaker must be a sub-theory of that tacitly known by the hearer. Speakers, however, are also hearers—every member of the community is both source and recipient of testimonial knowledge. From this symmetry, it follows finally that speaker and hearer must tacitly know the same semantic theory.

This then is the argument for the testimony principle to which Sudarśanācārya appealed. The argument, however, is not quite complete. It depends on the assumption that revision is a relevant alternative; that revision is a common, widespread feature of linguistic practice, or at least sufficiently widespread to be relevant. That might be questioned. Consider again Goldman's 'barn' example: the moral of this example is not that we do not have perceptual knowledge because we might have been in an environment surrounded by fake objects perceptually indistinguishable from genuine ones. The moral is rather that if we were in such an environment, we would not have perceptual knowledge. More generally, we do not expect our epistemic capacities to function well in all circumstances no matter how bizarre, but only that they function well in the circumstances for which they are suited. The unstructured understander's method of believing others' utterances works well in linguistic communities where revisions in beliefs about meaning are not widespread, and if that is true of actual linguistic communities, it constitutes an adequate method of forming beliefs. My reply to this is that for a community in which most speakers have a structured understanding, the very fact that their understanding is structured makes the possibility of revision a relevant one. It is particularly relevant if, as Davies claims, the notion of systematic revision has a constitutive role in an account of tacit knowledge. Furthermore, while the extent to which such revision does occur is, of course, an empirical matter, I would conjecture that the sorts of revisions in belief about meaning being considered here occur rather frequently and over relatively short periods of time. An unstructured understander would, even in actual linguistic communities, be at a serious epistemic disadvantage.

Notes

[1] See the comments by Vātsyāyana and Uddyotakara above *Nyāya-sūtra* 1.1.1.

[2] See *Nyāya-sūtra* 2.1.16.

[3] For an analysis of 'knowing who' locutions, see Boer and Lycan (1986).

[4] Sosa: 'It is sometimes held, for example, that perceptual or observational beliefs are often justified through their origin in the exercise of one or more of our five senses in standard conditions of peception. The advocate of doxastic ascent would raise a vigorous protest, however, for in his view the mere fact of such sensory prompting is impotent to justify the belief prompted. Such prompting must be coupled with the further belief that one's senses work well in the circumstances, or the like. For we are dealing here with *knowledge*, which requires not blind faith but *reasoned* trust. But now surely the further belief about the reliability of one's senses cannot rest on blind faith but requires its own backing of reasons, and we are off on the regress'. The force of the argument, Sosa notes, derives from its denial that epistemic justification can supervene on non-epistemic facts.

[5] For an extended defence of these claims, see Matilal (1986), especially chapter 4.

[6] *tadvati tatprakārakatva pramātvam.* See Mohanty (1966: 9-41, 100-101); Matilal (1986: 138-40; 1990: 70-2).

[7] Matilal argues that the thesis that knowledge is merely true belief is defensible, if a suitable distinction is drawn between knowing and knowing that one knows. Someone who by chance comes to believe truly that *p*, and so 'know' that *p* will not be in a position to know that he knows that *p*, i.e. truly believe that he truly believes that *p*. He attributes the view to Gaṅgeśa (see the references in the previous footnote). The thesis that knowledge is merely true belief has also been defended recently by Crispin Sartwell (Sartwell 1991, 1992). He argues, in rather the same spirit as Matilal, that we should think of 'knowledge' as the goal or purpose of our epistemic inquiries, and what we aim for is true

belief. Justification is to be thought of as an instrumental notion, as something which we seek, not for itself, but because it helps us in the project of acquiring true beliefs. See also Williams (1978, chapter1).

[8] The additional condition is apparent in the paraphrases of the *pramāṇa* analysis offered by both Matilal (1986: 135) and Mohanty (1992: 230). Mohanty says: 'S knows that *p* if S has a cognitive state having the form *p*, this cognitive state is true, and it is brought about *in the right sort of way*' (my italics).

[9] *apramāsādhāraṇa-kāraṇaṃ doṣaḥ*, Annaṃbhaṭṭa (1983: XXXVIII); *Nyāya-kośa* s.v. *doṣa*.

[10] That is, we need something like Sosa's distinction between 'conditions' and 'environments' (Sosa 1991: 139).

[11] For another response to the Gettier cases from within a similar approach, see Plantinga (1993: 31–7).

[12] I am unaware of any explicit discussion of teleological processes in Nyāya. One must be cautious in regarding the notion of 'functioning' (*vyāpāra*) as teleological, since a functioning event is defined just as a causal intermediary. The theory of defects (*doṣa*), however, brings with it the idea of a *dysfunctional* process, and hence of a process functioning 'normally' (i.e. without any defect).

[13] Matilal's repeated emphasis of the importance in Nyāya of knowing that we know derives, I believe, from his recognition of the need to give an account of reflective justification within a faculty-based epistemology.

[14] The main source is Gaṅgeśa (1901), but the position is reported in many of the books and manuals written by later Naiyāyikas, such as Annaṃbhaṭṭa (1983) and Viśvanātha (1988).

[15] So the absence of what Lewis (1975) calls a *convention of truthfulness* is a global environmental defect.

[16] Hume is a classic reductionist. Thus:

> There is no species of reasoning more common, more useful, and even necessary to human life, than that which is derived from the testimony of men and the reports of eye-witnesses and spectators .... Our assurance in [it] is derived from no other principle than our observation of the veracity of human testimony, and the usual conformity of facts to the reports of witnesses. It being a general maxim that ... all the inferences which we can draw from one [object] to another are founded merely on our experience of their constant and regular conjunction; it is evident that we ought not make an exception to this maxim in favour of human testimony (Hume 1975: 111).

Coady (1992) gives a series of highly persuasive arguments against the reductionism of Hume and others, in particular noting that the phrase '*our* experience' already imports a prior appeal to testimony. For the Nyāya arguments against reductionism, see the articles by Chakrabarti and Matilal in Matilal and Chakrabarti (1994).

[17] This way of formulating the point presumes that defeating conditions do not take the form: the hearer does not have a suitably justified belief that the

speaker is trustworthy (and so on). Defeating conditions have the form illustrated by my examples.

[18] Compare Audi (1998: 132): 'There is another account that can explain the psychological role of background beliefs. On this account, beliefs about the credibility of the attester and beliefs pertinent to the attested proposition play a mainly filtering role: they prevent our believing testimony that does not "pass", for instance because it seems insincere; but if no difficulty strikes us, we "just believe" (non-inferentially) what is attested. These filtering beliefs are like a trapdoor that shuts only if triggered; its normal position is open .... The open position is a kind of trust. The absence or laxity of filtering beliefs yields credulity; excessively rigorous ones yield skepticism'.

[19] The example of a mistaken liar (*bhrānta-pratāraka*) is mentioned by Gaṅgeśa (cf. Mukhopadhyay 1992: 284 - 5). Gaṅgeśa himself regards the hearer's belief as knowledge, because of his technical use of the term *pramā*. Gaṅgeśa's view is not, however, definitive of the whole Indian epistemological tradition (contra Phillips 2003).

[20] Some other interesting Gettier cases involving testimony are discussed by Plantinga (1993: 82–8).

[21] Cf. Matilal (1985: 405, fn. 3); Bilimoria (1988: 207–8).

[22] E.g. Annaṃbhaṭṭa (1983: § 67): *arthābādhao yogyatā.*

[23] A. Chakrabarti (1986), and Mohanty's Foreword to Bilimoria (1988).

[24] Compare Gadamer (1975: 262): 'Just as the recipient of a letter understands the news that it contains and first sees things with the eyes of the person who wrote the letter, i.e. considers what he writes as true, ... so we understand texts that have been handed down to us on the basis of expectations of meaning which are drawn from our own anterior relation to the subject. And just as we believe the news reported by a correspondent because he was present or is better informed, we are fundamentally open to the possibility that the writer of a transmitted text is better informed than we are .... It is only when the attempt to accept what he has said as true fails that we try to "understand" the text, psychologically or historically, as another's meaning'.

[25] For example, Matilal (1990: 55): 'The ideal hearer is like a computing machine, where the input would be the utterance and the output would be a corresponding uniquely structured knowledge-episode'.

[26] Evans mentions a third sort of evidence, which I will ignore here: evidence from experiments on the perceptual processing of sentences. The structured understander *perceives* the sentence '*Fa*' as containing the name '*a*' and the predicate '*F*'.

Part III

The Cognitive Basis of Meaning

6

Pravṛtti-nimitta
The Basis of Linguistic Practice

6.1 The Basis of Meaning

The authors of Navya-Nyāya identify a central problem for the realist theory of meaning. According to that theory, the linguistic meaning of a descriptive noun 'A' is given by the clause ⟨objects which are A are meant by 'A'⟩. The property **A**, to which earlier grammarians and Naiyāyikas had given the name 'basis for usage' (*pravṛtti-nimitta*), functions as a restrictor on the scope of the term 'A', restricting it to the class of As. Quantified sentences of this form are reparsed in the regimented technical language (§2.3). The paraphrase leads the later philosophers to redefine the notion of a basis for the use of word as the property *delimiting* the meaning relation (*śakyatāvacchedaka*).[1] The meaning-giving clause for 'A' now reads:

(1) $\mathcal{M}$|'A' $\subseteq$ A.

(i.e. only As are meant by 'A'.) We have seen in Chapter 4 how clauses of this form are constructed both for simple terms and for complex terms compounded in any of the ways distinguished by the Sanskrit grammarians. Further consideration of such compounds, however, reveals a difficulty implicit in the account. Take 'A' to be the descriptive noun 'the* pot'. If **P** is the property being-a-pot, then the meaning clause for this term is:

(2) $\mathcal{M}$|'pot' $\subseteq$ P.

(i.e. only pots are meant by 'pot'.) The class of pots, however, can be picked out in a number of different ways: there are many descriptions which have as their extension this same class. For example, the class of pots is also the class of objects with a certain mereological structure (*ākṛti*), expressed perhaps by the description 'utensil with a handle and a conch-shaped neck'.[2] Now, if giving the meaning of a descriptive noun is simply a matter of fixing the domain of objects to which it can refer, it would seem to follow that the meaning clause for 'pot' could be equally well stated by

(3) $\mathcal{M}$ |'pot' $\subseteq B \cap C \cap D$,

where B is the class of utensils, and C is the class of things having handles, and D is the class of things having a conch-shaped neck. That is to say, utterances of the word 'the* pot' refer only to members of the class of utensils with handles and conch-shaped necks. This, however, is just the clause the realist theory would like to give for the complex description 'utensil-with-handle-and-conch-shaped-neck'. The realist theory therefore entails that all co-extensive descriptions are synonymous.

Vardhamāna (*c.* AD 1440), the son of Gaṅgeśa, offers a solution. His influential claim is that the property which delimits the extension of the term is itself a meaning-relatum (*vācya*) of that term. This thesis is stated in his celebrated analysis of a term's 'basis-for-use':

> A basis-for-use is [a property] which (i) is a meaning-relatum, (ii) occurs in each meaning-relatum [other than itself], and (iii) regulates the presentation of the meaning-relata.[3]

So, in the meaning-clause for 'A', the property A occurs, not merely as delimiting the scope of the term, but as itself a relatum of the meaning relation (I discuss the third clause in this definition in §8.3). Vardhamāna's claim concerns the proper form of meaning clauses. The idea is that a description is associated by linguistic convention with a property, and, since properties are intensionally individuated, two co-extensive terms can be associated with distinct but co-extensional properties. As a consequence, they have different meanings. I will call the thesis that an intensionally individuated property has to occur as a relatum of the meaning relation of a description 'Vardhamāna's Thesis'.

Gadādhara, in his discussion of Vardhamāna's definition of a 'basis for usage', links the thesis with the older Nyāya doctrine that meanings are structured complexes, propertied particulars. In §1.4, we traced this idea right back to the *Nyāya-sūtra*, where at *NS* 2.2.66, it is asserted that 'the meaning of a word is a universal-*cum*-form-*cum*-individual'. Later Naiyāyikas took this to signify that its meaning is a 'determinative complex' (*viśiṣṭa*) of the three.[4] As Gadādhara puts it (1927: 40):

> The meaning relation obtains between a word like 'pot' and [a particular] as determined (*viśiṣṭa*) by a property like pothood, which

> is the delimitor of word-meaning. It does not [obtain between the word and a particular] merely as 'indicated' (*upalakṣita*) by pothood. If pothood were a mere indicator of the [pot], then, since properties like being-a-thing-with-a-conch-shaped-neck or being-a-substance would do equally well, the regularity between the word 'pot' and [hearers'] thoughts of a thing as being-a-pot, not as being-a-thing-with-a-conch-shaped-neck or as being-a-substance, could not arise.

This view is traditionally known as the theory that the meaning of a term is a property-determined particular (*jāti-viśiṣṭa-vyakti-śaktivāda*). I will return below to the distinction between 'determiners' and 'indicators', and to the regularity Gadādhara mentions. Gadādhara now (1927: 40–1) says:

> But surely, since a particular pot is both a pot and a substance [or a thing with a conch-shaped neck], the meaning of the word 'pot' is a thing determined by being-a-substance [or being-a-thing-with-a-conch-shaped-neck] just as it is a thing determined by being-a-pot. So what is the import of the claim that the meaning relation holds [between the word 'pot'] and [a particular] as determined by pothood, but not [a particular] as determined by substancehood?
>
> This is what they [scilicet Vardhamāna] say. The meaning of [my above assertion that] the meaning relation holds [between a word like 'pot'] and [a particular] as determined (*viśiṣṭa*) by a property like pothood is that it holds between [the word] and each of three things: the property, the substratum of that [property, i.e. the pot individual], and the qualifier-qualificand relation [between the two]. So, even though the relata of the meaning relation for the word 'pot' are [by virtue of being pots] qualified by substancehood, since substancehood is not an [explicit] meaning relatum, it is [said to be merely] an indicator (*upalakṣaṇa*) [of the pot]. [On the other hand,] since pothood is an [explicit] meaning relatum, it is a determiner (*viśeṣaṇa*). Thus, in [Vardhamāna's] definition of a basis-for-use, as 'that which is (i) [itself] a meaning-relatum, (ii) located in the meaning-relata, and (iii) the way which the meaning-relata are presented', the clause 'in itself a meaning-relatum' is given so that the basis-for-use too is a meaning-relatum. The *Nyāya-sūtra* [2.2.66] 'The meaning of a word is a universal-*cum*-form-*cum*-individual' also makes a universal such as cowhood a meaning (*padārtha*) of the word 'cow'.

The significance of Vardhamāna's Thesis lies in its recognition that meanings are intensional. I do not mean by this a recognition of such specific phenomena as, for instance, the substitution-failure of co-referring expressions in opaque contexts, but simply a denial that the relata of the meaning relation can be purely extensional entities.

Vardhamāna's Thesis asserts that this affects the form of meaning specifications. In order to specify the meaning of a description, uttered on a particular occasion, we must state both the referent of the description on that occasion and the intensional property with which it is associated. Vardhamāna's Thesis entails that a meaning theory can no longer be constructed as a theory of reference alone, containing clauses of the form ⟨'Hesperus' refers to Hesperus⟩ or ⟨'The* pot' refers only to pots⟩. A meaning-theory should include an *explicit* statement of the intensional element.

Gadādhara, in the above passage, says that the thesis entails a change in the meaning relation itself. The meaning relation must relate an utterance with both an object, the referent, and a property. That is, the relata of the meaning relation are now ordered pairs, ⟨*x*, *y*⟩, where '*x*' ranges over particulars and '*y*' over properties. I will call this the 'two-component' theory of the meaning relation. In the next section, I will consider the relationship between this two-component theory and Fregean and neo-Fregean accounts of meaning.[5]

6.2 The Adverbial Modification of Thought

Let us return to Gadādhara's observation cited above:

> If pothood were a mere indicator of the [pot], then, since properties like being-a-thing-with-a-conch-shaped-neck or being-a-substance would do equally well, the regularity between the word 'pot' and knowledge of a thing as being-a-pot, not as being-a-thing-with-a-conch-shaped-neck or as being-a-substance, could not arise.

The regularity here is a claim about what is involved in correctly understanding an utterance of the word 'pot'. When we spell out what it is to understand the term, it is not sufficient to state *which* object is to be thought about: we must also specify *how* that object is to be thought of. Someone who hears the sentence 'The pot is blue', but thinks of the referent of 'the pot' merely as being a substance, or even as being a thing with a conch-shaped neck, has not understood the sentence correctly. Gadādhara repeats the idea later in his discussion (1927: 59):

> In the mandate [for the word 'substance'], having the form ⟨Let there be a thought of a substance from the word 'substance'⟩, the content of the thought is specified as being [of a substance] as being-a-substance, and not as being-a-pot. So [pseudo-]knowledge of the meaning of 'substance', in which the semantic relation is in the form of a mandate which prescribes that thoughts produced by the word 'substance' are of objects as being-a-pot, is erroneous.

So the mandates which govern how words are correctly to be understood prescribe that someone who understands an utterance of the word 'substance' thinks of its reference as being-a-substance, or, as I will say, under the 'mode' being-a-substance. The idea of a mode under which an object is thought about is a technical one in the Nyāya theory of content; the mode is the 'delimitor of the property of being the object of thought' (*viṣayatāvacchedaka, dharmitāvacchedaka*). Let me try to explicate this notion.

Thought contents are analysed in Nyāya as having a relational structure. Every thought has three elements: a subject or 'qualificand' (*viśeṣya*), a 'qualifier' (*viśeṣaṇa*), and a relation (*saṃsarga*), which connects the qualificand and qualifier. Thus, the content of the thought expressed by 'The pot is on the ground' is a relational triple comprising a pot, the ground, and a relation of location. Thoughts stand in a content-relation $\mathscr{V}$ (*viṣayatā*, 'contentness') with each member of the triadic complex. We may represent the situation (cf. Bhattacharyya 1990: 162; 1996: 39) in Figure 6.1.

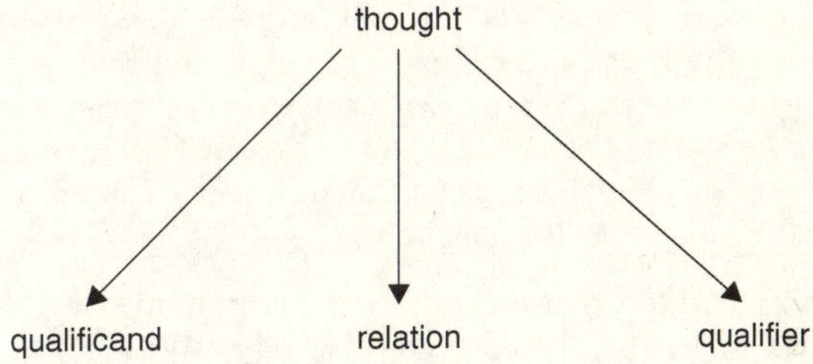

FIGURE 6.1

So Harry's belief that the Eiffel Tower is in Paris, for example, would be described by saying that he has a belief whose qualificand is the Eiffel Tower, whose qualifier is Paris, and whose connecting relation is location. This mode of content ascription is called the ascription of a 'conditional content' (*nirṃūpya-nirṃūpaka-bhāvāpanna-viṣayatā*), a content independent of the truth-value of the belief (cf. Matilal, 1968: 28-9).[6] When the belief is true, there exists, in addition to the ⟨qualificand, relation, qualifier⟩ triple, a 'determinative complex' (*viśiṣṭa*) of the three, and the thinker stands in a distinct contentness relation to this complex, over and above her relation to each member of the triple. Harry's belief would now be described as a belief concerning the presence of the Eiffel Tower in Paris, where the mention of the presence of the Eiffel Tower in Paris is something to which the ascriber can appeal only because the belief is true. Such ascriptions are called the ascription of a 'determinative content' (*viśiṣṭa-viṣayatā*) (cf. Matilal, 1968: 28-9; Mohanty, 1966: 34, n.69; 1992: 148).

The Nyāya theory of error is a 'mislocation' theory (*anyathākhyāti-vāda*; cf. Matilal 1986: 201–20; 1994). A belief is false if it has as its content a triple ⟨*a*, R, *b*⟩, and ~ *a*R*b*. The qualifier, *b*, is mistakenly located in or ascribed to the qualificand, *a*, in the content of the belief. All falsehood is explained on the model of 'mistaken identity' illusions: my mistaken belief that the object in front of me is a snake, when in fact it is a piece of rope, mislocates the qualifier being-a-snake in the qualificand of my belief, the object in front of me.

There is a rather striking similarity between the early Nyāya theory and a view once held by Russell (1912: 72–5):

> The relation of judging or believing must, if falsehood is to be duly allowed for, be taken to be a relation between several terms, not between two .... that is to say, Desdemona and loving and Cassio must all be the terms in the relation which subsists when Othello believes that Desdemona loves Cassio. .... [I]f Othello believes *truly* that Desdemona loves Cassio, then there is a complex unity, 'Desdemona's loving Cassio', which is composed exclusively of the *objects* of the belief, in the same order as they had in the belief, with the relation which was one of the objects occurring now as the cement that binds together the other objects of the belief.

Later authors introduce an important new element into the Nyāya theory of content. The new idea follows from the recognition that we do not in general simply think about objects as such, but only insofar as the objects are presented to us in certain 'ways', 'modes', or 'guises'. I might think of an object as a pot, but also of the same object merely as a substance, and so on. This was tantamount to a critique of the myth of the 'given', to which the earlier Naiyāyikas had fallen prey, that there is such a thing as the bare presentation of objects to the mind.[7]

The modes are conceived of as adverbially modifying the contentness relation: a mode is a delimitor of the property of being the object of a thought (*viṣayatāvaccedaka*). The modes, therefore, are not predicative—the truth or falsity of my thought depends on what I think about the pot, not how I think about it. The Nyāya name the modes by using an intensional abstraction device: if I think of some object as a pot, the Nyāya say that I think of it by way of the mode *pot-hood.* This use of the abstraction device carries no implication that the modes are reified into physical kinds or universals.

We must be careful to note an ambiguity in the Nyāya use of the term 'delimitor' *avacchedaka*. Its use here, as describing the mode element in belief content, is quite distinct from its use above (§2.3), as giving, in effect, the bound on the range of a quantifier. Suppose I am thinking of a certain object, a pot say. Let us distinguish now two quite different senses that can be given to the claim that pothood is a delimitor of $\mathscr{V}$(*ghaṭatvāvacchinna-viṣayatā*):[8]

(L1) Only a pot is the object of the thought *t*.

(L2) The thought *t* is about the object under the mode P.

The first of these says that the thought is about an object which is in fact a pot. The second says that the thought is about an object by way of the mode being-a-pot.

That the two notions are distinct is clear from the fact that (L1) does not entail (L2): one can think of an object which is in fact a pot, without thinking of it as a pot. However, it is a principle of great importance to the Nyāya concept of a mode that (L2) does entail (L1): one cannot think of an object by way of a mode being-an-F unless that object is F. A Nyāya mode of thought is a property of the object thought about. I will call this the 'Fundamental Principle' of Nyāya modes:

(Fundamental Principle) Thinking of an object *a* by way of its being-F $\rightarrow$ F*a*.

It is a consequence of the Nyāya theory of error that every belief is of an object, its qualificand, even if the attributes it represents the object as having are not indeed properties of that object. All falsehood is the result of misapplication of qualifiers to a given qualificand. The Nyāya authors therefore say that there can be no error as far as the qualificand of the thought is concerned: all error is traceable to the misascription of qualifiers.[9] To put this another way: if it is true that a thought *t* has a triple $\langle a, R, b\rangle$ of thought-contents, then even if $\langle a, b\rangle \in$ R, it will still be the case that $\langle t, a\rangle \in \mathscr{V}$. For what makes it true that the thought *t* has a triple $\langle a, R, b\rangle$ of thought-contents is that the determinative complex of *a*, *t* and $\mathscr{V}$ exists. Again, Russell (1912: 74) expresses a very similar[10] idea:

> Among the objects, as we saw in considering 'Othello believes that Desdemona loves Cassio', one must be a relation—in this instance, the relation 'loving'. But this relation, as it occurs in the act of believing, is not the relation which creates the unity of the complex whole consisting of the subject and the objects. The relation 'loving', as it

> occurs in the act of believing, is one of the objects—it is a brick in the structure, not the cement. The cement is the relation 'believing'.

There is, then, a sharp distinction between the roles of the two relations, $\mathscr{V}$ and R, in a singular thought about an object *a*, to the effect that it is R to *b*. For the same reason, there is a sharp distinction between a mode and a qualifier: a mode is an adverbial modifier of $\mathscr{V}$, while a qualifier is a thought constituent like *b*, which the thought locates or mislocates in *a* by the relation R. In his *Viṣayatāvāda*, Gadādhara is explicit about this (1990: 140–1; see also Guha 1968: 203–4):

> The property being-the-qualificand [V] is sometimes delimited and sometimes not. In the case of a thought which does not have a mode (*nirdharmitāvacchedake*), such as [the one-word sentence] 'Pot!', the qualificand-hood, which is restricted by a qualifier-hood [resident in] pothood, is not delimited [by any mode]. In a determinate thought which has a mode, such as 'This is a pot', the qualificand-hood, which is restricted by a qualifier-hood [resident in] pothood, is delimited by thisness. Thus, thisness is called a mode (*dharmitāvacchedaka*), since a mode is the same thing as a delimitor of qualificand-hood. To be a delimitor of qualificand-hood is not to be a qualifier of the qualificand. For, if it were, then in both the thought 'Pot!' and the thought 'This is a pot', pothood would be the mode, and there would be no determinate thoughts without a mode.

A mode is not a property which is ascribed or misascribed to the object of a singular thought. Rather, its role is to do with the relation between the object and the thought. It seems clear that its significance is in 'securing' an object for the thought. The problem is to understand the nature of this role.

We see now how the Fundamental Principle comes in. Suppose I look at a bowl, and mistakenly judge 'this is pot'. One might naturally describe the case as one in which the object is mistakenly identified as a pot, and locate the error in the way the object is identified. This might therefore look like a counter-example to the Fundamental Principle. Gadādhara, however, describes the case rather differently. It is described as one in which an object which is already identified is mistakenly ascribed the qualifier being-a-pot. The mode under which the object is thought about is not being-a-pot but simply *being-this*. Error is thereby always located in the predication, and never in the mode under which the subject is brought into the thought. The Fundamental Principle imposes strict requirements on what can be a mode.

Let us see what recent interpreters have said about the nature of the Nyāya modes. Sibajiban Bhattacharyya says (1996: 97) that 'When one cognizes a jar under the mode of jar-ness, jar-ness becomes the limitor of the qualificand-ness resident in the jar. This simply means that the thing jar has become the qualificand of the cognition only in so far as it possesses jar-ness, that is, in so far as it is an instance of the universal jar-ness.' Mohanty (1992: 65–6) also regards the Fundamental Principle as constitutive of the notion of a mode, and argues that the Nyāya delimiting mode therefore cannot be anything like a Fregean 'mode of presentation': 'Every cognition not only has its object, but cognizes its object in a certain manner, qua such and such, or again, in Nyāya vocabulary, as limited by some property or other .... The problem we are encountering is the problem of identifying the sense as the mode of presentation with a property of the referent, for one must have to keep the possibility open that a thing *x* is presented as *y*, even if the property of being *y* does not belong to *x*.' It is not clear to me that Mohanty's conclusion follows, at least for those Fregean senses which are 'routes to the reference', and in particular for Fregean senses which are definite descriptions; for then the reference just is whatever the sense leads to. I will return to this in the next section.

Matilal (1985a) argues that a mode is an item of identifying information possessed by the thinker. He formulates two principles about the nature of awareness in Nyāya; the first (P1), that 'whenever an object *x* figures (or floats, or swims = *avagāhate*) in my awareness, it figures there as something, that is, under some guise or mode, distinguished in some way or other' (p.373), the second (P2), that 'to generate an awareness in which the object *x* is presented as qualified by *f*, a prior awareness of *f* is needed' (p. 377). He claims that P1 'actually leads to a theory of identification of objects through descriptions or information about them. I cannot identify an object unless I already possess some information about it.' In his (1985a) paper, he goes on to say that 'We identify (pick out, single out) an object *x* in various ways, and a particular way (a particular mode of singling out) in a given context would be called the *dharmitāvacchedaka*, the delimiting character of the qualifiable object. These ways or modes are usually governed by bits and pieces of information the person has gathered about the object.' However, the article as reproduced in his (1986: 342–54), omits this passage and three paragraphs in which the informational aspect of the notion is developed. What replaces it is a stress on the idea that there need be no prior awareness of the *qualificand* in a thought (1986: 351):

> Nyāya emphasizes that we construct here with characteristics or qualifiers as the building-blocks, but we construct, to continue the metaphor, upon the subject of characterization as representing the

> building site. We need therefore a prior grasping of the qualifiers or characteristics, but we need not have a prior acquaintance with the subject or *dharmin*. For we can become acquainted with it at the same time we 'construct' the judgement. For example, we may have to obtain the prefabricated materials as building-blocks beforehand, but the building-site is required only at the time of construction. In other words, Nyāya says that a prior awareness of the qualifiers is all that is logically needed to formulate a 'qualificative' judgement. We may know the subject or the substratum or the qualificand only as qualified by the said characteristics or qualifiers as we identify such a subject.

Matilal's 'building-site' metaphor is suggestive, and reminiscent of the passage from Russell cited above. Matilal has in mind, I think, a restriction on a version of the principle of acquaintance which states that we must be acquainted with each of the objects in a thought content triplet in advance of 'knitting them together' (Russell 1912: 73) in a judgement. The restriction is that we might be acquainted with the *qualificand* only at the time of the judgement, and in virtue of our prior acquaintance with the *mode* by way of which the qualificand appears. Matilal is explicit that this does not mean that the thinker's knowledge of the qualificand has to be by description (1986: 352):

> Sighting an object from a distance in dim light we may speculate in various ways whether it is *F*, *G* or *H*, where we are already acquainted with the 'meanings' of *F*, *G* and *H*. The object sighted enters our speculation only as an 'it'. It is something 'we know not what', but we attempt to characterize it with one or other known characteristics .... The situation envisaged here by Nyāya seems to have a parallel in the 'name-predicable' analysis of the atomic sentence, where the name is believed to be a logically proper name or a rigid designator (that is, it must be non-connotative), but the predicables must have a meaning.

This is a 'maypole' theory of judgement. It takes seriously the Nyāya theory of error, according to which all error is due to the misapplication of a qualifier to some given qualificand. Matilal's oblique reference to the Lockean idea that we have knowledge only of an object's qualities is, I think, unfortunate, since in the Nyāya conception, the object is itself a constituent in the content of a judgement. The idea is rather that an object does *not* become the qualificand in virtue of the thinker having a uniquely identifying conception of the object (if we take it that 'having a prior awareness' is best explicated in terms of possessing a concept, so that having a prior awareness of the qualifier cowhood = possessing the concept *cow*). Rather, the thought-qualificand relation in these cases is a real relation between two objects, possibly grounded in a physical connection or causal link between the object and the thought.

What, then, is the role of the mode in 'securing' that relation? I will take my cue from an alleged feature of perceptual experience. Matilal (1986: 203–4; see also 1995) claims that it is a feature of the Nyāya account of our perception of objects that one can see an object without seeing its parts or properties, even though one sees it because of its parts or properties. Thus, when someone sees an object as a piece of silver 'the Nyāya position is that we see the opaque physical object, the piece of silver for example, because of the presence of these properties, but not necessarily because we see these properties, features, parts, etc. as a preliminary'; and again, 'I see [the car] because it has a colour, but not necessarily because I see that colour'. Matilal draws attention to an important distinction, between seeing an object *because* it is *F*, and seeing *that* it is *F*. The application of the idea to the perception of wholes enables the Nyāya to maintain that we see wholes without seeing their parts, and thereby to block a sort of mereological slide in the content of perceptual experience.

Let us try to account for the role of adverbial modifiers of the thought-object relation as follows. We will draw a distinction between a person thinking of an object *because* it is *F*, and a person thinking of an object *that* it is *F*. A mode is a property of the first sort, a property of the object in virtue of which that object is the relatum of the thought-object relation. A qualifier is a property of the second sort, a property which enters the content triple as a purported relatum of the relation R.

We therefore have the following schema:

(M) S thinks of *a* under mode **F** iff S thinks of *a because a* is *F*.

The difficulty is to make sense of the 'because of' here. It points to a relation of *sensitivity* between a thought's being of *a* particular object, a say, rather than any other, and the fact that *a* is *F*. There are three ways to explicate the concept of sensitivity: as a counterfactual notion, as an explanatory notion, or as an epistemic notion. The counterfactual construal is that a person S's thinking of *a* is sensitive to *a*'s being *F* just in case if *a* were not *F*, S would not be thinking of *a* (but of some other object, or no object at all). The explanatory construal appeals to the idea that *a*'s being *F* is implicated in the explanation of S's thought being about *a*, rather than some other thing. Finally, the epistemic construal appeals to a notion of warrant, which distinguishes knowledge from accidentally true beliefs. As we saw in Chapter 5, one does not have knowledge unless one's epistemic methods discriminate between true propositions and relevant alternative false ones. One might then say that S thinks of *a* because it is *F* to be understood as saying that *a*'s being *F* is implicated in S's beliefs about *a* being warranted.

We need not, however, think of these three ways of explicating the notion as competing with one another. For, first, counterfactuals of the relevant sort are likely to be grounded in the causal laws or correlations which sustain the explanatory model. Second, as I will argue, the sort of explanation that is relevant here will also sustain epistemic relations. So I will assume that the way to understand (M) is as saying that *a*'s being *F* *explains*, in some suitable sense, S's thinking of *a*. We have seen two main cases where the Naiyāyikas talk about modes: perceptual judgements about objects in one's visual field, and understanding sentences containing descripive nouns. Let us reconsider these cases in the light of (M).

Consider again Gadādhara's example of the perceptual judgement 'this is a pot', in which the thinker perceives say, an object *ã* in front of her and identifies it as a pot. Gadādhara's claim is that the mode here is the property thisness (*idaṃtva*), and not pothood. What might he mean? The relevant question, if what we have said is correct, is: why does the thinker's perceptual judgement concern the particular object *a* and not some other? It is clear first of all that, if some other object, *b*, had been in the place where the perceiver was looking, then her perceptual thought would have been about *b* rather than *a*. The Nyāya regard all perceptual judgements as resting on a physical connection between the perceiver's sense-faculty and the object of the perception (*indriyārtha-sannikarṣa*; cf. Potter 1977: 161–2; Matilal 1986: 207). So the reason that *a* is the object of the thought and not *b* is that *a* is *this* particular object, the demonstrative identifying that object to which the perceiver's gaze is related, in virtue of its being located in the place to which the gaze is directed. *This* object is the object which is the adjunct of *this* sensory relation, the object of *this* gaze. Thus, the fact that *a* is *this object* enters the causal explanation of S's perceiving it.

It is idiomatic in English to describe such a perceptual identification as a case of seeing-as: seeing the object as a pot. I repeat, however, that one must not be led by this into thinking that the Nyāya mode here is pothood. For that would be inconsistent with the Fundamental Principle, since in this sense one can see an object as *F* even if it is not *F*. So the mode has to be thisness, and being-a-pot has to be a predicative qualifier. Notice too that the perceiver's thought about *a* is counterfactually sensitive to *a*'s being this object: if *a* had not been *this object* (the object at the end of this gaze), *it* would not have been the object perceived by

S. Some other object, or no object at all, would have been. The truth of the counterfactual is grounded in a causal law of the form 'whatever is at the end of the perceiver's gaze causes a perception of it'.

The example shows that the type of explanation needed in (M) is a 'contrastive' explanation (cf. Lewis 1986; Lipton 1990). Contrastive explanations are answers to 'Why *P* rather than *Q*?' questions, and not to 'Why *P*?' *simpliciter*. Typically, a contrastive explanation 'addresses the question of how one selects, out of the total causal history leading up to the event to be explained, that part of the history which is of explanatory interest' (Ruben 1993: 9). Lewis's analysis of explanatory contrast is by appeal to a counterfactual difference: an event explains why *P* rather than *Q* if it is a cause of *P* that would not have been a cause of *Q*. Lipton argues that explanatory contrasts select causes by means of what he calls the 'difference condition': 'To explain why *P* rather than *Q*, we must cite a causal difference between *P* and not-*Q*, consisting of a cause of *P* and the absence of a corresponding event in the history of not-*Q*', where 'a corresponding event is something that would bear the same relation to *Q* as the cause of *P* bears to *P*'. Thus, my ordering coffee rather than juice is explained by my needing a dose of caffeine. The explaining event 'needing caffeine' is indeed a cause of my ordering coffee. Moreover, my needing caffeine cannot be cited as a cause of my ordering juice, had I done so. So it is a source of explanatory contrast between the 'fact' *P*, and the 'foil' *Q*.

In (M), what we are trying to explain is not why S is thinking about *x simpliciter*, but rather why S is thinking about *x* rather than another object *y*. S thinks about *x* rather than *y* because *x*, and not *y*, is *F*. While the event '*x*'s being *F*' is in the causal history of S's thinking about *x*, it cannot be cited as a cause of S's thinking about *y*, had she done so. This answers a possible objection to the sufficiency of (M). For one might argue that many of the object's properties are implicated in the explanation of S's thinking about it; in the perceptual case, for example, the object's being opaque. Yet we do not want to say that S thinks of the object as opaque. The reply is that the object's being opaque is not implicated in the explanation of why S thinks about one object rather than another: it is not a source of explanatory contrast.

Let us consider another example. In his discussion of Russell's principle of acquaintance, Sainsbury (1979: 38) considers explicating the notion of acquaintance between a thought and an object in terms of what he calls an 'epistemic contact' or 'epistemic causal chain', a causal relation capable of grounding an epistemic relationship with the object.

Imagine two scenarios, in both which you truly believe that $2^8 = 256$, as a result of tapping out the sum $2^8 = ?$ on your calculator. In the first scenario, the calculator is working as it should. You press the buttons for $2^8 = ?$, the result '256' is displayed on the screen, and you come to believe truly that $2^8 = 256$. In the second scenario, you again press the buttons for, the result '256' is again displayed on the screen, and you again come to believe truly, that $2^8 = 256$. In this scenario, however, the calculator is malfunctioning: it displays '256' whatever buttons are pressed.

This example is interesting for several reasons. It seems right to say that, in the first case, you think of 256, rather than some other number, *because* it is 2^8. So the fact that $256 = 2^8$ enters into the contrastive explanation of your thinking of 256. In the second case, on the other hand, the fact that $256 = 2^8$ does not explain why you think of 256 rather than some other number: whatever buttons you press, you still think of the number 256. So, if (M) is correct, you think of 256 under the mode being-2^8 in the first case, but not the second.[11]

Second, as Sainsbury emphasizes, the contrast between the two cases is epistemic: in the first case, you have knowledge, but in the second case not. The knowledge in question is that $256 = 2^8$, in which the mode has become a qualifier. A general conjecture about the epistemology of modes, then, is that *someone who thinks of an object* a *under a mode F is thereby in a position to know that* a *is* F. The thought of the object does not itself constitute such knowledge, for one has to formulate a thought in which the mode has become a qualifier (as we have seen, modes are not predicates). Sainsbury's example suggests that the reason one has knowledge in the first case but not the second is linked to the existence, in the first case, of a contrastive explanation. In general, a knowledge-forming process or method is one which is sensitive to the truth or falsity of the proposition known. Believing the deliverances of the malfunctioning calculator is not a method which is *sensitive* to the truth or falsity of the proposition that $256 = 2^8$. The notion of an explanatory contrast can be used to explicate the notion of sensitivity appealed to here. In saying that a belief-forming method is insensitive to the truth-value of a proposition P, we mean that P is not a source of explanatory contrast between forming the belief that P rather than *not-P*.

Let us now turn to the second type of mode considered by the Nyāya, the modes involved in understanding. Consider the case of someone who hears and understands the sentence 'The* *F* is *G*'. Gadādhara asserts the mode in the hearer's language-based thought (*śābdabodha*) is the property being-an-*F*. Assume that the speaker is referring to an object in the speaker's and hearer's shared conversational environment, an environment which contains a number of objects of various sorts. We might imagine, for example, that the speaker is talking about her collection of ceramic artefacts, and says, 'The *pot* is Ming'. What we want is an explanation of the fact that a hearer who understands this utterance comes thereby to think of a particular object, the pot, and not any other artefact in the conversational context.

If it is to accord with the Fundamental Principle, the explanation must be such that one can correctly understand an utterance of the term 'the* pot' only by thinking of a pot. That is indeed just what the mandate governing correct understanding of the term prescribes. To see how the explanation might go, we must appeal to the idea that the hearer has antecedent knowledge about the objects in the conversational environment. The idea is that the hearer is only in a position to understand an utterance of the term if she already knows of some object in the surroundings, that it is a pot. Then the explanation of S's thinking of the pot rather than any other object runs as follows. First, S knows, concerning the various objects which are salient in the conversational context, which one is a pot. One main way to come to know this is to perceive the objects, and form perceptual judgements of the form 'this is a pot', and so on. There are, however, other ways for S to have singular thoughts about a range of objects in the conversational context. Second, on hearing the speaker's utterance 'The* pot is Ming', S comes to believe, of the object which she knows to be a pot, that it is Ming. The fact that a certain object is a pot is implicated here in the explanation of the hearer's believing of it, rather than something else, that it is Ming. So we have the first part of a contrastive explanation of why the hearer thinks of the pot rather than another object.

Suppose, instead, that the hearer had come to think of another object, say a bowl. The causal explanation of this occurrence will be in terms of a false belief; either the false belief that the bowl is a pot, or a false belief that 'pot' means bowls. In the first case, the hearer misidentifies the objects around her, and thereby misunderstands the utterance. In the second case, the misunderstanding has a more serious origin, in a lack of semantic competence. Either way, it is clear that the fact that our object is a pot does not enter the explanation of her thought about the bowl, that it is Ming. So the object's being a pot is the source of the explanatory contrast which explains why the hearer's final thought is of that object rather than some other object. Given (M), Gadādhara is right to say that, in the thought formed by the hearer who understands an utterance of the sentence 'The* *F* is *G*', the mode under which the hearer thinks of an object is being-*F*.[12]

It is interesting to compare this explanation of understanding with the one given by Evans (1982: 311–12):

> A speaker who is to say something by uttering a sentence containing a referring expression must make it *manifest* which object it is that he intends to be speaking about—which object an audience must think of in understanding his remark .... A very important factor [in making his intention manifest] is the choice of referring expression. The conventions governing referring expressions are such that, as uttered in a context of utterance, they are associated with a property which an object must satisfy if it is to be the referent of the fully conventional use of that expression in that context; I call such a property '*the referential feature* which the expression conventionally has in that context'... 'this ϕ' and 'that ϕ' are clearly associated with the referential feature *being* ϕ. When an expression in a context of utterance has the property of being ϕ as its referential feature, it will generally be at least partly in virtue of the audience's *knowing*, of an object, that it is ϕ that the audience will be able to know, of that object, that it is the object to which the speaker intends to refer.

A difference between the two accounts is in what constitutes correct understanding. For Evans, the *right* interpretation is the interpretation intended by the speaker (pp. 310, 332). So the hearer can only understand the speaker's utterance if she knows which object the speaker intends to refer to. The speaker manifests her intention to refer to the pot in her choice of expression 'the* pot', and the hearer, in virtue of knowing of a certain object that it is a pot, comes to know that that object is the speaker's intended reference, and hence the object about which to judge that it is Ming. The Nyāya do not take this detour via speaker's intentions. The right interpretation, they claim, is the interpretation mandated by the conventions. The hearer can only understand the speaker's utterance if she knows which object is the referent of the term. She comes to know that a certain object is the referent of an utterance of 'the* pot' in virtue of her 'antecedent' knowledge of that object that it is a pot, together with her 'semantic' knowledge that only a pot is the referent of an utterance of 'the* pot'. In fact, this difference is rather less important than it seems, because of Evans' claim that being the intended referent is a necessary (but not a sufficient) condition for being the referent (p. 318).

I am arguing that someone who, on hearing an utterance of 'The* *F* is *G*', judges of a certain object rather than some other, that it is *G*, does so because she *knows* of that object that it is *F*. In order to *know* of an object that it is *F*, the object must be *F*; and so the explanation implicates the fact that the object is *F*. One might wonder at this point whether merely *believing*, of the object, *a* say, that it is *F* would be enough. We would, it seems, still have an explanatory contrast, for if the hearer were to judge of some other object, *b*, that it was *G*, it would be on account of her belief that that object were *F*. So the belief that *a* is *F* has a role in the explanation of the hearer's judging that *a* is *G*, but no analogous role in the explanation of her judging that *b* is *G*, were she to do so. Yet, if merely believing of *a* that it is *F* is sufficient, then it would not follow that *a*'s actually being *F* is implicated in the explanation, and we could not claim that *F* is a mode in the hearer's judgement, in accordance with (M).

The reply to this is that judging that *a* is *G*, on hearing 'The *F** is *G*', puts the hearer in a position to know that *a* is *G* only if she knows, of *a*, that it is *F*. We appeal again to the constraints imposed by the possibility of testimony on understanding. Let us return to our example involving a collection of ceramics, and imagine now that the audience comprises two people. Both hear the utterance 'The* pot is Ming'. One is an expert in pottery, and can discriminate between pots and all other ceramic artefacts. She knows of one object, that it is a pot, and judges of the pot that it is Ming. The other has only the haziest idea about the difference between pots and other ceramic objects, but whimsically believing of the same object that it is a pot, likewise judges that it is Ming. Let us suppose further that the speaker, who is a world authority on Ming dynasty pottery, speaks truly and sincerely, and that all the other defeasible conditions necessary for testimony are met. The first hearer, by way of hearing and understanding the speaker's assertion, comes to know that the object is Ming, while the second hearer does not. The second hearer is not in a position to gain knowledge from the speaker's utterance, for it is purely accidental that her belief concerns the object to which the speaker referred.[13] The situation is analogous to Sainsbury's example of the calculator, and we might well say that the first speaker is in 'epistemic contact' with the pot (or its being Ming), while the second speaker is not. This case again supports our general conjecture about the epistemology of modes, that someone who thinks of an object *a* under a mode *F* is thereby in a position to know that *a* is *F*.[14]

To conclude our discussion, let us suppose now that the speaker is using the noun in a purely descriptive way, to refer to whoever or whatever has a certain property. She may say, for example, 'The largest pot in the world is Ming', without any acquaintance or other knowledge of the object which is in fact the largest pot in the world. It is in only a very loose sense that it is correct to describe the speaker or hearer as thinking of an object; rather, their thought has a quantified content. Such thoughts, and quantified thoughts generally, do not stand in the contentness relation to particular objects, and so do not have modes as we have understood them here. The Naiyāyikas do, however, say that a property is the delimitor of qualificand-hood (*viṣeśyatāvacchedaka*) in quantified thoughts as much as in singular thoughts. While the terminology is unfortunate, there should be no confusion as long as we keep in mind the ambiguity of the term 'limitor' mentioned above. A delimitor of qualificand-hood in an existential or general thought is the property which restricts the scope of the quantifier. For example, when the noun in the sentence 'A pot is a nice present' is used indefinitely, the property pothood restricts the scope of the existential quantifier and is in that sense alone a delimitor of qualificand-hood.[15]

6.3 Nyaya Modes, Fregean Senses, and Discriminatory Capacities

The introduction of cognitive modes into the Nyāya theory has been thought to resemble Frege's introduction of a distinction between the 'sense' (*Sinn*) of an expression and its 'meaning' (*Bedeutung*) or reference into his theory of meaning.[16] In this section, I will examine the question afresh. Fregean semantics asserts that there is a single entity which is at once (i) the meaning of a sentence, (ii) the bearer of truth-value, (iii) the object or content of thought, and (iv) that by which thoughts having different cognitive significance are individuated. Frege called such an entity a Thought or the sense of a sentence. It was the last of the above properties which, in the first instance, motivated the introduction of the notion of sense. Frege observed that it is possible for someone to believe different things about the same object, at the same time, if presented with the object in different ways. As Stephen Schiffer (1978: 180) points out, we can take this idea of a 'mode of presentation' or 'way of thinking' about an object to be defined by the following condition, which he calls Frege's Constraint:[17]

> Necessarily, if m is a mode of presentation under which a minimally rational person x believes a thing y to be F, then it is not the case that x also believes y not to be F under m. In other words, if x believes y to be F and also believes y not to be F, then there are distinct modes of presentation m and m' such that x believes y to be F under m and disbelieves y to be F under m'.

Do the Nyāya modes meet Frege's Constraint? Let us consider again our two cases, the case of perceptual modes and the case of modes implicated in understanding descriptive nouns. Imagine first a scenario in which someone is perceptually presented with a single object in two different ways. Let us suppose that the person, looking at a particular object on the table, judges 'this$_1$ is a pot'. Suppose further that she also sees the same object horribly distorted in a mirror, and, not realizing that it is the same object as the one on the table, judges 'this$_2$ is not a pot'. If the Nyāya modes meet Frege's Constraint, then the mode in the first judgement, thisness$_1$, must be distinct from the mode in the second judgement, thisness$_2$. I think, indeed, that they are. Recall that 'thisness' is unpacked as 'being the object at the end of this gaze'. So the claim that thisness$_1$ $\neq$ thisness$_2$ is the claim that being the object at the end of this$_1$ gaze is not the same property as being the object at the end of this$_2$ gaze, where 'this$_1$ gaze' refers to the perceiver's direct sensory contact with the pot on the table, and 'this$_2$ gaze' refers to their indirect sensory contact with the pot via the mirror. These are clearly two distinct relational properties, which happen to have the same relata in the present example. The properties are implicated in two different explanations of the perceiver's coming to see the object, directly and through a mirror.

Our main interest is in the modes implicated in understanding. It is not enough merely to claim that these modes are distinct on the basis of some metaphysics of properties (for example, Udayana's account above). We must show how they are implicated in two distinct explanations of the hearer's coming to think of a certain object. The explanans in (M) is intensional: it is the object's *being-F*, and not merely the fact that the object is *F*. But how can an intensional difference between the properties enter the explanations? The answer must lie in what it is for the hearer to know which object is *F*. So let us examine the account of such knowledge in Nyāya.

The ability to know which object is *F*, is a *discriminatory* capacity, an ability to discriminate the object as belonging to a given type or sort. The notion of discrimination (*vyāvṛtti*) in Nyāya is prominent, first, in their theory of perception, and second in their account of language acquisition. At *Nyāya-sūtra* 1.1.4, Gautama defines a perception as that which is (i) produced from 'contact' between sense-faculty and object (*indriyārtha-sannikarṣa*), (ii) 'non-verbal' (*avyapadeśya*), (iii) non-wandering (*avyabhicāra*), and (iv) 'definite in nature' (*vyavasāyātmaka*). The final clause was addressed to cases in which one sees an object but only indistinctly, without being able to tell what it is or classify it.

Vātsyāyana's example is of seeing a haze in the distance, unable to tell if it is a cloud of smoke or a dust-ball; another is of being unable to tell whether a shape seen at dusk is a person or the stump of a tree. In neither case does the perceiver know what the object is. Later Naiyāyikas therefore set down, as a condition for knowing what a perceptually presented object is, that the perceiver be able to ascribe a qualifier (*prakāra*) to it, a qualifier being defined as a 'discriminator' (*vyāvartaka*; Gaṅgeśa 1897: 824) of the thing qualified.[18]

In a typical case, then, discriminating knowledge of an object takes the form of a judgement 'this is a pot', in which the discriminator is the qualifier in the content of the judgement. The nature of such discriminatory capacities is clarified in the Nyāya discussion of the acquisition of terms like 'pot' and 'cow'. The Nyāya theory depends on the notion of 'analogical identification' (*upamāna*),[19] and is specifically of the acquisition of natural kinds terms.[20] A person who does not know the meaning of the natural kind term '*gavaya*' is told that a *gavaya* is an animal like a cow (*gosādṛṣya*). Later, coming across an object which fits this description, she judges 'This is what "*gavaya*" refers to' (*ayaṃ gavayapadavācyaḥ*). Knowledge of the likeness does not itself constitute an understanding of the term '*gavaya*'. That comes about only when the person, having used the description to identify at least one of its instances, acquires the capacity to judge of new instances 'this is a *gavaya*'. Gaṅgeśa asserts emphatically that the *meaning* of '*gavaya*' is being a member of the natural kind *gavaya*-hood. So mastery of the term consists, not in the knowledge of analogical or other properties of the kind, but in the acquisition of a capacity to discriminate members of the kind, having acquainted oneself with some of its members. The role of the comparative description 'an animal like a cow' is one of enabling the person to identify for the first time an object belonging to the right kind.

There is a resemblance here with Leibniz's notion of clear but indistinct or confused knowledge. He says (1902: 41): 'When I am able to recognize a thing among others, without being able to say in what its difference or characteristics consist, the knowledge is confused .... Such knowledge is not yet distinct. It is when I am able to explain the peculiarities which a thing has, that the knowledge is called distinct. Such is the knowledge of an assayer who discerns the true gold from the false by means of certain proofs or marks which make up the definition of gold'. Wiggins (1993: 207) paraphrases: 'In Leibniz's account of ordinary human knowledge, a clear idea of horse is ... that by the possession of which I recognize a horse when I see one. A clear idea of a horse is confused (or non-distinct) if, even though I can recognize a horse when I encounter one, I cannot enumerate one by the marks which are sufficient to distinguish that kind of thing from another kind of thing. My understanding is simply practical and deictic. What I possess here I possess simply by having been "brought into the presence of the thing"'.

Understanding a natural kind term, for the Nyāya, is a matter of possessing a discriminatory capacity grounded, not in knowledge of the defining properties of the kind, but in direct acquaintance with some of its instances.[21] Definitions do, nevertheless, have an important function. We must keep in mind that the Nyāya definition of a definition is extensional: a definition of a thing is any property which excludes the thing defined from other things.[22] The following are both definitions of a cow: a hoofed animal with a dewlap; a perissodactyl quadruped belonging to the genus *Bos*. Definitions of the first sort are 'syndromic', while those of the second type are by 'own-nature':

> Definition is of two sorts, definition by own-nature (*svarūpa-lakṣaṇa*) and definition by syndrome (*taṭastha-lakṣaṇa*). Here, as to the first case, it is said that the definition by own-nature of Brahman is given by 'Brahman is reality, knowledge, infinite'. As to the second case, it is thought that the definition of Brahman is as the cause of the world (*Nyāyakośa* 1928: 307).

I will return to the role of syndromes a little later. What I want to attend to here is the idea of a definition by own-nature.[23] What is the relation between a definition of this sort and the following *homophonic* definition of a cow: a cow is a thing which instantiates cowhood. This definition seems to be tautologous, but is not. For 'cowhood' is a name for whatever is the natural kind to which cows belong (in fact, the biological genus *Bos*). Someone who understands the term 'cow' has the capacity to discriminate the members of this genus, even if, as is likely to be the case, they know nothing about their biological or genetic structure. So the sort of discriminating knowledge of a natural kind which based on acquaintance with instances of the kind can be *redescribed* as knowledge of a homophonic definition, where the redescription does not entail that the person has any explicit knowledge of a definition of the kind.

So let us distinguish between two roles for definitions. One is to specify a piece of information the explicit knowledge of which grounds a capacity to discriminate the thing defined. Such definitions are necessarily non-homophonic, and are illustrated by the definitions of Brahman mentioned above. The other role for a definition is to describe what someone who has an acquaintance-based capacity to discriminate the thing defined implicitly knows. The distinction is due to Udayana (1971: 29-30; see also Tachikawa 1981: 113–14.):

> What then is this thing called definition?
>
> A definition is a sign based on a 'negative pervasion' (*kevala-vyatireki*). The Teacher [Uddyotakara] said that the function of definition is to exclude the thing defined from similar and dissimilar things.
>
> A definition is also used in the proper application of words (*vyavahāra-siddhi*). Thus [we can infer as follows]:
>
> The thing under discussion is called 'earth' by people, due to the mark earth-hood.
>
> Whatever is not called 'earth' is not earth, for example water.
>
> [But] it is not the case that this [thing under discussion] is not earth.
>
> Therefore, it is called 'earth'.
>
> The logical fault of 'not establishing the subject term' (*āśrayāsiddhi*) does not occur [in this inference] because the object to which the word is used to refer is established by its own-nature (*svarūpataḥ*). Nor does the fault of 'having an unfamiliar predicate term' (*aprasiddhaviśeṣaṇa*) occur, because [even] uninformed people [are able to] use the term 'earth'. [Moreover,] the inference is not useless, since it demonstrates that the subject term [that is, this thing] is pervaded by a particular occurrence of the predicate term [that is, the word 'earth'].

Notice Udayana's assertion that even 'uninformed' people are able to use the term 'earth'. These people are neither scientists, who can describe the physical and chemical structure of earth, nor are they 'assayers' who have reliable diagnostic information about the kind. Nevertheless, they can apply the term successfully; they have what Leibniz called a clear but indistinct conception of the kind. Their ability to use the term correctly is a product of their practical ability to discriminate instances of the kind earth-hood, together with their knowledge that things of that kind are called 'earth'. The homophonic definition of earth, that earth is what possesses earth-hood, is a way of describing that ability.[24]

Udayana tries to make sense of the idea that we can describe the discriminating knowledge of such people as the knowledge that earth is earth. He suggests that we can hear that ascription as non-vacuous if we formulate it negatively, as the knowledge that earth is distinct from non-earth, for it is clear then that we are ascribing a discriminatory capacity.[25] I too think that there is a way of hearing 'S knows that earth is earth' as ascribing discriminating knowledge, if we hear it as entailing that S knows what earth is. This reading has to be distinguished from the reading under which it means that same as 'S knows that the sentence "earth is earth" is true', which does not entail that S knows what earth is. One can know, for example, that the sentence 'a *gavaya* is a *gavaya*' is true without having any idea of what a *gavaya* is, or any acquaintance with *gavaya*s.

Let us now consider the function of a 'syndrome' (*taṭastha*). In a syndromic definition, the thing is defined by means of a co-extensive property; for example, earth is defined as a thing having an odour. The role of such 'definitions' is diagnostic: the information they encode is the sort of information one can appeal to, to detect the presence of the kind. There is a corresponding type of discriminatory capacity. Consider someone who has the capacity, when presented with a range of ceramic artefacts, to identify one of those objects is a Ming. This capacity is grounded in knowledge of the characteristic traits of Ming dynasty pottery, such as its having a particular sort of blue glaze, and so on. It is a diagnostic capacity, a capacity based on knowledge of traits and tell-tale signs.[26]

When someone's discriminatory capacity is based on knowledge of a syndrome, the discriminating knowledge they have is said by the Nyāya to have as its qualifier an 'indicator' (*upalakṣaṇa*). This idea goes back at least to the grammarian Bhartṛhari, who illustrated his point with an example. Suppose that I see a number of houses, but do not know which house belongs to Devadatta. I am informed, or otherwise come to know, that it is the house with the crow sitting on its roof (perhaps Devadatta is well-known for feeding the birds). Then the property of having a crow on its roof serves to distinguish the house in question from all other nearby or salient houses. That is what makes it an 'indicator' of the house. Another standard example is the knowledge that, among a group of assembled people, the ascetic is the one with matted hair. Having matted hair does not make one an ascetic, but it is an indicator, a symptom of being one (cf. Gaṅgeśa 1897: 824–38; Saha 1991: 216–68).

Although formulated as a distinction between two kinds of qualifier (*prakāra*), the distinction between determiner (*viśeṣaṇa*) and an indicator (*upalakṣaṇa*) is not an ontological one. It has little to do with either Aristotle's distinction between essential and accidental properties, or the distinction between sortal and non-sortal properties. It is a distinction in the content of two sorts of discriminating knowledge. Let us try to find a formulation of the distinction. A person S who has discriminating knowledge can distinguish, among a collection of objects, which one has a certain property. Attributions of discriminating knowledge thus have the form 'S knows which of the *F* is *N*'. I will call the extension of '*F*' the *field* of the attribution; among the possible substituents for 'the *F*' are: 'the objects in my perceptual field', 'the houses here', 'the people in this assembly', 'the artefacts on this table'. 'The *F*' is a plural description, and, as with many descriptions, the scope will be determined in part by salience considerations. '*N*' denotes what I will call the *target* of the discriminating knowledge. Among the possible substituents for '*N*' are: 'a pot', 'a cow', 'belongs to Devadatta', 'the ascetic', 'is Ming'.

Someone whose discriminating knowledge is diagnostic knows which of the *F* is *N* by knowing, for some *M*, that *N* is *M*. I know which of the houses belongs to Devadatta by knowing that the house belonging to Devadatta is the one with a crow on the roof. I know which of the assembled people is the ascetic by knowing that the ascetic is the one with matted hair. So, if S is a person who knows which of the *F* is *N*, then (1) is true:

(1) $(\exists M)$ (S knows that *N* is *M*).

The statement '*N* is *M*' is a definition of *N*, an extensional equivalence between *N*s and *M*s. So what (1) states is that S knows a definition for *N*. We have distinguished three types of definition: syndromic, own-nature or essential, and homophonic. There are likewise three types of discriminatory knowledge.

In discriminating knowledge of the first sort, S knows which of the *F* is *N* by knowing a syndromic definition (*taṭastha-lakṣaṇa*) '*N* is *M*'. For example, S might know which of the objects in the field is a cow by knowing that cows have dewlap (and seeing a dewlap). When a person has discriminating knowledge of this sort, the qualifier *M* is said to be an indicator (*upalakṣaṇa*).

In discriminating knowledge of the second sort, S knows which of the *F* is *N* by knowing by knowing a definition by own-nature (*svarūpa-lakṣaṇa*) '*N* is *M*'. In one sort of example, S knows which of the objects in the field is a cow by knowing that cows are members of the species *Bos* (and running a DNA test). S here knows the essential definition of the kind. In another sort of example, the definition constitutes an analysis of *N*. For example, S might know which of the objects in the field is a beast by knowing that beasts are hairy animals with long tails (and seeing an object with those features). This is Udayana's distinction between a 'natural kind' (*jāti*) and a 'synthetic property' (*upādhi*). A definition by own-nature of the former is a theoretical identity statement, a statement like 'water is H_2O' or 'gold is the element with atomic number 79'. A definition by own-nature of the latter is an analytical truth, a statement like 'a bachelor is an unmarried man' or 'a weed is an uncultivated garden plant'.

The third sort of discriminating knowledge is purely practical. S knows which of the objects in the field is *N* but does not have any propositional knowledge of a non-homophonic definition for *N*. We have seen, however, that Udayana thinks we can describe such a person as knowing that an *N* is an *N*, or rather, knowing that an *N* is not non-*N*. The statement 'an *N* is an *N*' is a homophonic definition, and the value of '*M*' for which (1) is true is *N* itself.

In non-diagnostic discriminating knowledge (of either sort),[27] the qualifier is said to be a determiner (*viśeṣaṇa*). Why is the division drawn this way? It is because the ability to understand a descriptive noun '*N*' is held to consist in having a non-diagnostic discriminating knowledge of *N*s, together with the knowledge that *N*s are called '*N*'. Udayana, as we have seen, distinguishes two primary types of descriptive noun: natural kind terms and synthetic kind terms. The natural kind terms are nouns in order to understand which it is sufficient to have a practical capacity to discriminate objects of a certain kind, a capacity based on acquaintance with some of the kind's members. One need have no propositional knowledge about the members of the kind, although it is likely that one will come to know a gradually improving set of diagnostic properties of the kind, and perhaps eventually even the own-nature of the kind. That, however, is not a necessary condition on understanding. It is sufficient that someone who understands an utterance of the natural kind term 'cow' is able to think of its referent because they have a practical discriminatory capacity to identify members of the kind cowhood. Wiggins (1993: 204), I think, has in mind a similar account of natural kind terms, when he says:

> When we fix the sense of an expression with a predicative role by giving its reference and give its reference by demonstrating or alluding to exemplars, what we need to impart to one who would learn the sense is both factual information and a practical capacity to recognize things of a certain kind, the information sustaining and regulating the recognition, and the recognition making possible the correction and amplification of the very information that first sustained the recognition. What we need to impart, we might say, is an identificatory or recognitional conception. It is this that corresponds to the sense of a natural kind term.

Synthetic kind terms are nouns in order to understand which one has to know an essential or an analytic definition. For example, in order to understand the noun 'weed', one has to know that a weed is an uncultivated garden plant. This group includes nouns which are what Putnam calls 'one-criterion' words, words like 'bachelor', 'vixen', or 'hunter', which either 'admit of an explicit definition straight off ... [or] are derived by transformations from verbal forms' (1975: 139). Someone who understands one of these terms knows a set of necessary and sufficient conditions for something to be a member of its extension. Here too, they may come to know diagnostic properties, indirect methods of establishing whether some object falls into the relevant sort. Again, however, the ability to understand this sort of term is in the first instance a *non-heuristic* discriminatory capacity.[28]

Discriminatory capacities are indexed by the properties whose instances they discriminate. When someone who understands a term thinks of its referent by exercising a discriminatory capacity of one of these properties, that property, qua index of the capacity, is the adverbial modifier of the thought-object relation. It is clear that someone might have two quite different ways of discriminating a certain class of objects, and so might think of an object, discriminated in one way, that it is G, and think of the same object, discriminated in a different way, that it is not G. So, the property, qua mode, meets Frege's Constraint.

What we take as constituents in propositional content will be represented by ordered pairs $\langle x, F \rangle$, comprising the object thought about and the property which indexes the way it is discriminated. Such ordered pairs of objects and properties, trivially 'determine' referents, as Frege required: the referent is the first member of the ordered pair. I conclude that a Nyāya mode, or rather an ordered pair of an object and a mode, fulfils the criterion for being the sense of a term, at least for anyone who regards the notion of sense as a theoretical one not tied to specifically *Fregean* doctrines about it.[29]

Notes

[1] See Raghunātha (1932: 47); Gerchheimer (1996: 79).

[2] See Vardhamāma (1911: 334), and Mathuranātha's comments.

[3] *pravṛtti-nimittaṃ ca vācyaṃ sad-vācya-vṛttitve sati vācyopasthāpakaṃ gotvādi*, (1933: 34). Elsewhere, he tries a variant of this definition: *pravṛtti-nimittatvaṃ śakyatve śakya-vṛttitve ca svabhinnaśakyānadhikaraṇatvam* (1911: 333). See Gerschheimer (1996: 77–8).

[4] The 'form' (*ākṛti*) of the early Nyāya is, for exegetical purposes, identified by later Naiyāyikas with the relation, inherence, between the individual and the property.

[5] Gadādhara states that the relation between the two is a further component, and so strictly one would need an ordered triple as the relatum of the meaning relation. However, as I have specified that the first component is an object and the second a property, the relation between the two is implied. I will therefore ignore the third component.

Let $\mathcal{M}_2$ denote the new meaning relation, and let U be the class of objects, V be the class of properties, and W be the class of word tokens. Then $\mathcal{M}_2 \subseteq (\mathrm{U} \times \mathrm{V}) \times \mathrm{W}$ is such that for each nominal type 'A':

(4) $\mathcal{M}_2 |\text{'A'} \subseteq \{\langle \mathrm{A}_i, \mathbf{A} \rangle : \mathrm{A}_i \in \mathrm{A}\}$.

Here $\{\langle \mathrm{A}_i, \mathbf{A} \rangle : \mathrm{A}_i \in \mathrm{A}\}$ is the set of ordered pairs having some A as first member and the property **A** as second. In standard set-theory, it is the Cartesian product A × {**A**}. The proper form of a meaning clause, according to the new theory, is thus that:

(5) $\mathcal{M}_2 |\text{'A'} \subseteq \mathrm{A} \times \{\mathbf{A}\}$.

Suppose now that 'B' is a term co-extensive with 'A', that is, such that A = B. The new meaning clause for 'B' would be:

(6) $\mathcal{M}_2 |\text{'B'} \subseteq \mathrm{B} \times \{\mathbf{B}\}$.

Now, the fact that A = B does not entail that **A** = **B**, and so does not entail that A × {**A**} = B × {**B**}, for the second member of each ordered pair will be different. The new meaning clause no longer turns co-extensives into synonyms.

[6] A note on Nyāya terminology. Let us suppose that ⟨*a*, *R*, *b*⟩ is a qualificand-relation-qualifier triple. The Nyāya say that the *qualificand-hood* resident in *a* is *conditioned by* (*nirūpita*) the *qualifier-hood* resident in *b*. I translate this use of nirūpita as 'conditioned by', to distinguish it from the quantificational 'restricted by' noted in §2.3.

[7] For a detailed analysis of the Nyāya critique of the myth of the 'given', see Matilal (1986: 342–54) and (1991a).

[8] The use of the same term 'delimitor' to denote both the extensional notion and the intensional one is the source of considerable confusion, and it took a philosopher of the stature of Gadādhara clearly to separate the two. The distinction is noted by S. Bhattacharyya, (1987: 240; 1996: 97). See also Guha (1968: 23–55) and Matilal (1968: 74; 1986, §12.5).

[9] Udayana (1967: 81): *sarvasya jñānasya dharmiṇy avisaṃvādād.* Mathuranātha (Gaṅgeśa 1897: 374): *dharmiṇi sarvam abhrāntam iti nyāyena.* See also Mohanty (1966: 57) and Matilal (1986: 208).

[10] See, however, Bhattacharyya (1987: 229–30), for reservations about the comparison.

[11] That shows that the notion of thinking of an object under a mode is an externalist notion, depending not on what is 'in the head' of the thinker, but on facts about the causal explanation of the content of her thoughts.

[12] What is the mode in a case of misunderstanding? When the misunderstanding results from a misidentification, the mode has to be being-believed-to-be-a-pot, for it is the (false) belief that the object is a pot which explains why S thinks of it. When the misunderstanding results from semantic incompetence, the mode has to be being-believed-to-be-the-meaning-of-'pot', for it is the (false) belief that the object is a meaning of the term 'pot' which explains why S thinks of it. Notice that both modes satisfy the Fundamental Principle.

[13] A similar argument is given by Heck (1995: 94–5) for understanding proper names: '[P]reservation of reference alone is not sufficient for transmission of knowledge. Suppose that Tony does not know that George Orwell is Eric Blair and that Alex asserts, in Tony's presence, "Eric Blair is Eric Blair". Suppose further that, in reaction to Alex's assertion, Tony forms the belief she would express as "George Orwell is Eric Blair". This belief does concern the correct objects. Reference is preserved. Truth is preserved. Has Tony then come to know that George Orwell is Eric Blair? Obviously not'.

[14] It reveals too a sense in which the statement 'The* *F* is *G*' *presupposes* but does not *state* that the object is *F*. See also Evans (1982: 312, fn. 10) and Davies (1982).

[15] Bhattacharyya (1996: 100) says that the 'sense of "limitor" as the mode which an object is cognized so that it can be related to another object does not give us any indication of the quantity of the cognition. Thus to say "cognized under the mode of fire-ness", that is, "limited by fire-ness" (*vahnitvāvacchinna*), does not give us any indication whether the object cognized is just one particular fire or all fires. Here an adjective of quantity like "all" has to be added.' If by this he means that saying that fireness is the mode does not yet tell us whether the thought is singular or quantified, on account of the ambiguity of the term 'mode' or 'delimitor of qualificand-hood' (*viṣayatāvacchedaka*), then I can agree. I would not agree, however, if the implication is that quantified thoughts are themselves of objects; for even if we can make sense of saying that the universally quantified thought 'all pots are blue' is of all pots, we would be quite unable to distinguish between the singular thought 'that pot is blue' and the existentially quantified thought 'a pot is blue'. See also Matilal (1968: 78).

[16] I believe that the resemblance was first pointed out by Matilal (1968: 26–7); it has since been the subject of some controversy. To some degree, the controversy rested on the espousal of too narrow a conception of Fregean sense. This notion permits of elaboration in various directions, as the considerable work in the neo-Fregean tradition bears witness.

[17] The Constraint has been formulated by many authors. See, for example, Peacocke (1986: 5).

[18] This cuts short a very long story! For details, see Potter (1977: 160–8).

[19] One of the four Instruments of knowing (*pramāṇas*) in the Nyāya system. See Potter (1977: 174–6) and Potter and Bhattacharyya (1993: 238–9).

[20] Given the frequency with which pots and cows are discussed, it is rather surprising but no sharp distinction appears to have been drawn between natural kinds and artifact kinds. But cf. Putnam (1975: 244) for a suggestion that the distinction is not a sharp one.

[21] I believe that we have here the beginnings of an explanation of the Nyāya claim that if the qualifier in the content of a thought is a simple universal (*jāti*), then it can appear unqualified by any further qualifiers. This exception to Matilal's principle P1 blocks a threatened regress of qualifiers. See Matilal (1986: 344).

[22] Uddyotakara (Gautama 1967: 183–4): *lakṣaṇasyaitaretara-vyavaccheda-hetutvāt.* See also Tachikawa (1981: 27–31), Staal (1988: 88–92), and Matilal (1985b: 176–202).

[23] Lipner (1986, esp. pp. 29–33) has an interesting discussion of the 'definition by own-nature' of Brahman, based on Rāmānuja. Rāmānuja claims that the definition states that Brahman is *nothing but* what is determined by those determiners (*tattadviśeṣaṇaviśiṣṭam eva brahma*), adding that 'by such texts as "Whence these beings are born..." [*Taittirīya Upaniṣad* III.1.1] Brahman is described through secondary characteristics (*upalakṣaṇa*), as the cause of the world and so on; but by "Brahman is reality, knowledge and infinite" [*Taittirīya Upaniṣad* II.1.1] and "Brahman is bliss" [*Taittirīya Upaniṣad* III.6.1] etc., Brahman is described essentially (*svarūpato*)'. Lipner comments that for Rāmānuja (unlike Śaṅkara), the verse provides a definition 'not only by excluding the *definiendum* from all else but also by describing it through its essential properties' (p. 33).

[24] Knowledge that earth is what possesses earth-hood is therefore to be distinguished from genuinely trivial knowledge, that the sentence 'earth is what possesses earth-hood' is true. This can be known by someone who has no ability to discriminate the instances of the kind earth-hood.

[25] See also Matilal (1990: 165; 1985b: 190).

[26] How do the Nyāya 'syndromes' compare with Putnam's 'stereotypes' (Putnam 1975: 148, 204–6, 249–52)? There are two important dissimilarities. First, Putnam does not regard having a discriminatory capacity as necessary for understanding a natural kind term (p. 205). Second, Putnam says that knowing the stereotype is *obligatory* for understanding a natural kind term (p. 251). For these reasons, no simple comparison between the two notions is possible.

[27] The distinction between the two sort is this. When the discriminating knowledge is based on knowledge of an essential or analytic definition, the object discriminated is qualified by a property which is itself further qualified. For example, the weed is qualified by being-a-plant, and that qualifier is further qualified by being-uncultivated. However, when the discriminating knowledge is purely practical, the qualifier is not itself further qualified. If someone who

has a purely practical ability to discriminate cows, judges of some perceptually presented object 'this is a cow', the qualifier cowhood is not itself further qualified.

[28] It follows that if someone understands an utterance of 'the* *F*', thereby thinking of an object under a mode F, and then goes on to judge that the object is *F*, the qualifier in the judgement has to be a determiner (*viśeṣaṇa*), and not an indicator (*upalakṣaṇa*). Perhaps, however, there are also terms to understand which a diagnostic discriminatory capacity is both necessary and sufficient. We will see in Chapter 6 that some Naiyāyikas, Udayana included, thought that there are terms of this sort. Udayana's position, indeed, is that there are three types of term: *naimittikī*, *aupādhikī*, and *pāribhāṣikī*, the latter requiring the understander to have only a diagnostic discriminatory capacity. It does not follow, however, that a mode can ever be derived from an indicator; rather, in the case of such terms, Udayana claims that the understander thinks of the referent in a pure, non-qualificative way.

[29] I agree with Mohanty, who says that the Nyāya modes sustain a notion of *quasi-Sinn* (1992: 67, 83, 88), in at least being modes of presentation. I think it is only a terminological matter as to whether we reserve the term 'Sinn' for entities in Frege's original theory, or take it as a term concerning entities about which there can be many theories, of which Frege's was one. I hope that it is clear that the Nyāya would not share Frege's theory of communication, which requires that the speaker and hearer entertain the *same* thought. In Nyāya, the thought tokened by a hearer is determined by epistemological and conventional contraints on understanding; any coincidence with what thought the speaker thinks has to follow from those constraints. See also the discussion of the Transmission.

7

Śakyatāvacchedaka

Delimiting the Reach of Reference

7.1 On the Form of a Meaning Theory

Having introduced the idea of a mode into the theory of meaning, the question which has to be addressed is how that introduction affects the specific form of a meaning theory. It is Gadādhara's position that we need to give meaning clauses which correlate words with object-property pairs, along the lines recommended by Vardhamāna. Let us see how he proceeds (1927: 44–5):

> Now [a worry is that] the divine mandate +Let a pot be known from the word 'pot', is the content of a particular belief [that of the divine will] and the qualificand [of that belief], whose qualifier is being-in-the-content-of-[a hearer's]-thought, is a pot alone, and not pothood; [this is so] even if every object is an object of [divine] cognition. So how can it be said that the meaning of the word 'pot' is in three things, pothood [a pot, and the relation]?
>
> We use the term 'meaning' (*śakti*) to designate just that relation which is the regulator (*prayojaka*) of the content of [hearers'] thoughts produced by the word, as determined by a mandate. In the divine mandate ⟨Let a pot be known from the word 'pot'⟩, [the qualifier] being-in-the-content-of-[a hearer's]-thought appears by way of being delimited by pothood, [and further] the mode in [the hearer's] thought appears as pothood, with the delimiting relation inherence. Or [to put it another way], being-in-the-content-of-[the hearer's]-thought appears as modified by pothood via inherence.
>
> And so three things come to be recognised as pertaining the content of [hearer's] thoughts produced by the word—
>
> (1) a pot, as the locus of the qualificand-hood [of the divine mandate] whose qualifier-hood is in the property being-in-the-content-of-[a hearer's]-thought.

> (2) pothood, either (i) as the qualificand of a delimitation relation whose qualifier is that property being-in-the-content-of-[a hearer's]-thought which [by (1)] is a qualifier of the pot, or [conversely] (ii) as the qualifier of a being-delimited relation [whose qualificand] is that property being-in-the-content-of-[a hearer's]-thought which [by (1)] is a qualifier of the pot.
>
> (3) inherence, as that which appears as the delimiting relation when pothood appears in a delimitation relation with the property being-in-the-content-of-[a hearer's]-thought.
>
> Thus, the three things become meaning relata.
>
> In spite of the different ways in which the pot, pothood and the relation enter into the content of the mandate, we say that the meaning [of the word 'pot'] is univocal, because there is a single content relation between the mandate and the property of being-in-the-content-of-[a hearer's]-thought. [We do not say that the meaning is univocal] because there is a single mandate, for then a word would not be ambiguous even if it has different delimitors of scope (*śakyatāvacchedaka* = modes), since the divine mandate would be the same.
>
> Knowing [the meaning of the word, in the form of knowing that the pot is] the qualificand of a mandate whose qualifier is being-in-the-content-of-a-[hearer's]-thought and whose relation is the substratumhood relation, is what governs [a hearer's] understanding [of a sentence] in which one word-meaning is connected with another. So, unless a semantic error occurs, one word-meaning cannot get connected with the delimitor of another word-meaning.

Gadādhara is trying to reconcile three theses. The first thesis is that the meaning of a word-token is whatever the mandates on correct understanding prescribe as entering the content of an understander's thought. As we saw in Chapter 4, this thesis is at the heart of the Nyāya approach to meaning. The second thesis is that in order correctly to understand a token of the word 'pot', the understander must think of a pot under the mode being-a-pot. This is what we have established in the previous chapter. The third thesis is that the mandate for the word 'pot' only states that a pot is to enter the content of an understander's thought. The form of the mandate is ⟨Let a pot be known from the word 'pot'⟩, and not ⟨Let a pot be known *under the mode pothood* from the word 'pot'⟩. Yet if the mandate does not state that the understander thinks of the referent in a particular way, how can we reconcile the first two theses?

In the next section, I will consider two Nyāya authors whose response to the quandary was to deny that the mandate needs to *state* the mode under which an understander has to think of the referent; to use Wittgenstein's metaphor, it can prescribe by showing, not stating.

Gadādhara's response is different. He argues that the mandate does indeed state which mode the understander must employ. The issue concerns the logical form of the mandate (1):

(1) Let hearers form beliefs about pots when they hear the word 'pot'.

Now (1) suffers from a distinctive sort of ambiguity. To see it, let us take a simpler example with an analogous logical form:[1]

(2) Hindus believe that God is like a spider.

On one reading, (2) is wholly specific about the content of the attributed belief: it states not just that Hindus have a belief, concerning God, to the effect that He is like a spider, but that they think of God in a certain specific way, the way the ascriber thinks of God when she uses the name 'God'. On another reading, the ascriber states only that there is some way or other of thinking about God, under which Hindus think that He is like a spider.[2] Letting 'Pxy' mean 'x is a mode of y', corner quotes indicate names of senses, and '^' the concatenation of senses, the two readings are (3a) and (3b) respectively:

(3a) B (Hindus, ⌜God is like a spider⌝)

(3b) $(\exists\alpha)$ (P(α, God) & (Hindus, α ^ ⌜is like a spider⌝)).

If we denote the mode of presentation the ascriber attaches to the word 'God' in (3a) by 'γ', then we can write (3a) as:

(3c) B (Hindus, γ ^ ⌜is like a spider⌝)).

In the standard terminology for the ambiguity in (3), the occurrence of the term 'God' is said to be opaque in (3a) and transparent in (3b). Since these terms have been used in a variety of ways, McGinn suggests that it would be better to call the first reading 'internal' and the second 'external'.

Gadādhara wants to recover the 'opaque' reading of (1). On this reading, the content of the mandate is that anyone who hears an utterance containing the word 'pot' must form a belief which has pothood as its mode. Gadādhara's point, I think, is that it will then follow from the Fundamental Principle that the belief is about a pot. For belief is only about an object under a mode F if the object is F.

One might be forgiven, at this point, for suspecting that Gadādhara relies on an equivocation between the two notions of a delimitor. The qualifier in (1) is the property being-in-the-content-of-hearers-thoughts (*bodhaviṣayatva*), and since (1) is a quantified sentence, we can say that its extension is delimited by another property, in this case pothood. So pothood is the delimitor of the property being-in-the-content-of-hearers-thoughts (*bodhaviṣayatāvacchedaka*). That very same phrase, when the term 'delimitor' is construed intensionally, is how the mode in the hearer's thought is described. Has Gadādhara simply traded on the ambiguity of the phrase in asserting that pothood is the mode in the hearer's thought? In fact, I think not. It is rather that, when (1) is disambiguated, there is a 'delimitation' relation between the way the ascriber picks out the object of the belief (viz. as pots), and the mode in the belief so ascribed.[3] Indeed, that is the characteristic of the opaque reading (cf. 3c).

What bearing does this have on the form of a meaning theory? If the mode under which an understander must think of the reference is indeed stated by the divine mandate, then, Gadādhara, concludes, it will be itself a meaning relatum. So the meaning relation is a relation between tokens of the word 'pot' and ordered pairs $\langle x, X \rangle$.[4]

Gadādhara has arrived at a 'two-component' theory of meaning, with modes of thought taking the place of intensionally individuated properties. He summarizes his theory in the following passage (1927: 58):

> A hearer's thought [of an object *y*] whose qualifying [mode] is **Y** by the relation *r* is produced by their having knowledge of a meaning relation, the qualificand [in the knowledge of the meaning relation being] *y* and the relation being one of being-in-the-content of a particular sort; it is a knowledge in which the qualifier is a word, and in which the mode of qualificand-hood (*dharmitāvacchedaka*) is the property **Y**, related [to *y*] by the relation *r*. The relation [in the knowledge of the meaning relation] is: being the qualificand of a divine mandate whose qualifier is being-in-the-content-of-thought-produced-by-its-[word], where there is a delimitation relation resident in the property **Y**, and [further] delimited by the relation *r*.

This recapitulates what we have said. Gadādhara, it seems, has few qualms about the 'paradox of analysis', that the analysans of a concept can employ concepts not possessed by someone who possesses the analysandum concept; Gadādhara is happy to regard someone who knows a meaning theory for his language as knowing a very complex analysis of the meaning relation, one which employs highly technical concepts from Navya-Nyāya logical theory. The paradox of analysis, however, is a problem for anyone engaged in conceptual analysis. More interesting is Gadādhara's demonstration of the way to construct a 'two-component' meaning theory, along the lines first suggested by Vardhamāna. We will see in subsequent chapters how that theory is applied.

7.2 Raghunātha's Austere Theory of Meaning

Gadādhara, we have seen, claims that a meaning theory must include both a statement of the referent of each referring expression and a statement of the mode under which the referent is to be identified. The second of these is what we might call, following Frege, the theory of sense. But could we not argue instead that, although we must specify the mode-element in meaning, given the constraints on understanding, we can do this via a theory of reference? This line of thought has become fairly standard in recent Fregean literature:

> Although a theory of meaning for a language must give the senses of expressions, we are not to think of the theory of sense as a separate tier, additional to and independent of the theory of reference .... Rather than look for a theory quite independent of the theory of reference, we must take one formulation of the theory of reference—the formulation of the theory which identifies the references of expressions in the way in which one must identify them in order to understand the language—and make it serve as a theory of sense (Evans, 1985: 294-5).

And again,

> [A] limited recognition of sense comes in with our claim that understanding the remarks we are concerned with requires not just that the hearer thinks of the referent, but that he thinks of it in the right way. But we recognize the primacy of the referent by recognizing that the hearer always confronts just one question, 'Which object does the speaker mean?'—not two questions, 'Which object does the speaker mean?' and 'How am I intended to think of it?' The second question is answered in passing; for if he understands the remark, he will know which object is meant; and in the normal course of events, he will know which object is meant only if he thinks of it in the particular way intended by the speaker (Evans, 1982: 315–16).

A theory of meaning, these theorists argue, should not be thought of as having two independent components, one specifying the reference of each expression, and the other specifying its sense. For, precisely because the sense of an expression is a mode of presentation of its referent, we cannot specify the sense except by stating the referent. How then do we 'specify' the sense of an expression in stating its reference? Dummett describes the idea that 'in saying what the referent is, we have to choose a particular way of saying this ... [to] stipulate the sense of the expression, we shall choose that means of stating what the reference is which displays the sense' (1981: 227). The idea, to use a familiar example, is that although the clauses

(1) 'Hesperus' refers to Hesperus, and

(2) 'Hesperus' refers to Phosphorus,

are extensionally equivalent reference specifications, only the former can be part of a theory of reference which is to 'serve as' a theory of sense, for only it identifies the reference in the way one who understands the name must identify it.

Theories of this kind are known as 'austere' theories of meaning. The radical Naiyāyika Raghunātha Śiromaṇi (fl. AD 1510), whose brilliant and revolutionary ideas led to the formation of a new faction within the Navya-Nyāya community,[6] suggested a view of just this sort. Raghunātha categorically rejects Vardhamāna's thesis, that the basis-for-use or delimitor of the scope is a relatum of the meaning-relation; or, as we are now saying, that meaning specifications have two components, one of reference, the other of discriminatory mode. In his *Pratyakṣa-maṇi-dīdhiti*, he says (1951: 135–6):

> Between the meaning relation (*śakti*) and the delimitor of its scope (*śakyatāvacchedaka*) there is a relation of regulation (*prayojakatva*), that is, of causing to be grasped an object in cognition.
>
> Since even something which is not [itself] a meaning-relatum (*śakya*) can be in the content of [the hearer's] thought (*śābdabodha*), the over-extension [of the meaning relation] to the delimitor of the scope of the reference [of the term, *śakyatāvacchedaka*] can be removed. [So] even if the meaning relation were in the delimitor of its scope, the knowledge that it is there is useless.

In his commentary on this passage, Gadādhara explains that what Raghunātha means is that a property, pothood for instance, regulates the mode under which the hearer thinks of the pot when he understands a sentence, by being the mode under which the hearer thinks of the referent in his knowledge of the meaning relation. Someone whose knowledge of the meaning of the term 'pot' consists in the knowledge that pots alone are the meanings of the word 'pot' thinks of the subjunct of the meaning relation under the mode pothood, and that explains his thinking of the meaning under the same mode in the judgements he makes on hearing sentences containing the word uttered.

Raghunātha describes his position again in the *Kiraṇāvalī-prakāśa-dīdhiti* (1932: 49):

> This is the fact of the matter. When someone knows of a relation between two objects, each object grasped under a mode, cognizing one of those objects under its mode makes them aware of the other object under the other mode. This is like the elephant and the elephant-driver. This too is the way a word and its meaning are related. When the meaning of a word is presented in a certain way, then it is presented that way in the [hearer's utterance-derived] thought as well. There is no such thing as non-qualificative memory, and neither do non-qualificative states enter with words. For if they did, the words could not be syntactically connected. In the hearer's knowledge of the meaning relation, and the ensuing presentation of the word meaning, the qualifier is not itself a meaning relatum. So cowhood is the same. For, even though it is not a meaning relatum, it can still be the constant element (*anugama*) [running through] the meanings. So even if the knowledge of the meaning is of a determinative complex (*viśiṣṭa*), that does not have to be a meaning-relatum, because its presentation is regulated.

The idea is that there is a way for our knowledge of the meaning relation to regulate the contents of our understanding without every element in that content explicitly being a meaning relatum. Raghunātha observes that our language-processing capacity has a certain causal structure. Knowledge of the meaning relation is dispositional, memory-like knowledge. If one tacitly or habitually knows that two items are related (*aRb*), being made to think about one relatum *a* triggers a thought about the other *b*, provided that the way one is made to think about *a* is the same as the way it was originally presented and is now presented in the memory-trace. Then one thinks of the other relatum *b* in the way it too was originally presented. Raghunātha cites as an example someone who knows that elephants are ridden by elephant-drivers. Seeing an elephant puts such a person in mind of a driver, but only if the elephant is recognised as such. If the person saw an elephant but did not identify it as one, they would not be put in mind of the presence of an elephant-driver. The point then is that knowledge of the meaning rule can regulate the way we understand a term, and particularly the mode under which we identify its reference, without explicitly stating what that mode is.[7]

The two meaning clauses (1) and (2) are extensionally equivalent, and yet 'Hesperus' and 'Phosphorus' are not synonyms. That led Vardhamāna to introduce two-component meaning clauses, like (3) and (4):

(3) 'Hesperus' means ⟨Hesperus, Hesperus-hood⟩

(4) 'Phosphorus' means ⟨Phosphorus, Phosphorus-hood⟩

Even though Hesperus = Phosphorus, the meanings of 'Hesperus' and 'Phosphorus' are distinct, because the associated properties are intensionally individuated. Raghunātha, however, points out that the *hearer's knowledge* of (1) and (2) differs in content:

(5) S knows that 'Hesperus' refers to Hesperus.

(6) S knows that 'Hesperus' refers to Phosphorus.

(5) and (6) are not extensionally equivalent, since knowledge ascriptions generate opaque contexts. This intensional difference is expressed in the Nyāya technical language by citing the mode (limitor of qualificandhood, *viśeṣyatāvacchedaka*) under which the object appears in the hearer's thought. The suggestion is that it is this difference which provides grounds for distinguishing the first of the two meaning clauses, and consequently that there is no reason to modify the referential meaning relation. In our notation, (7) and (8) can have distinct truth-values, even if A = B:

(7) S knows that ($A \supseteq \mathcal{M} \mid$ 'A').

(8) S knows that ($B \supseteq \mathcal{M} \mid$ 'B').

The Nyāya modes are, as we have seen, merely indexes for discriminatory capacities, and the difference between (7) and (8) is a difference in the sorts of discriminatory ability demanded of someone who understands the term. The ability to discriminate pots on the basis of acquaintance with a few specimens is quite distinct from the ability to discriminate utensils with a conch-shaped neck, on the basis of their defining properties. So, given clauses like (7) and (8), understanding the term 'pot' does not entail a capacity to understand the term 'utensil-with-a-conch-shaped-neck', and vice versa. Only one of the two clauses will be implicated into the causal explanation of a hearer's ability to understand the term.[8]

In reporting Raghunātha's view, Jagadīśa (1934: 119–20) gives it a twist:

> Since the [hearer's] knowledge of a meaning relation in which the qualificand is *indicated* (*upalakṣite*) by clothhood is the cause of a [hearer's] thought about a cloth under such a mode, [even though] we let it be that the meaning of the word 'cloth' is in what is delimited by clothhood, others [say] that it is in an object *indicated* by clothhood. This is what [Raghunātha] Śiromaṇi said.

Jagadīśa's commentator Kṛṣṇakānta says that the meaning is *indicated* 'because, in Raghunātha's view, the mode of the qualificand in the [hearer's] knowledge of the meaning relation regulates what is the qualifier in the understanding [of a sentence utterance]'.[9]

We need to look again at the way a mode property **A** is implicated in the causal explanation of S's ability to understand utterances of 'A'. In the explanatory models of both Raghunātha and Gadādhara, the referent's being A enters the explanation of the hearer's knowing which object is the referent of a given utterance of 'A'. This is an item of discriminatory knowledge, one whose field is the class of salient objects in the context of the utterance of the term, and whose target is the referent of the utterance of 'A'. Raghunātha claims that the hearer knows which object is the referent of the utterance of 'A' because she knows (i) that the referent of the utterance 'A' is an A, and (ii) that a certain object in the context is A. So she takes 'A' as applying to that object because it is A. Now **A** is indeed an indicator in this theory, in accordance with the definition of an indicator given in §6.2. The hearer knows which of the salient object is the referent of 'A' by knowing that the referent of an utterance of 'A' is an A. Her ability to discriminate the referent is a diagnostic discriminatory capacity, grounded in her knowledge of the meaning of 'A', that utterances of 'A' mean As.

This theory treats the meaning clause, that As are meant by 'A', as a *diagnostic* definition, a merely extensional equivalence. It 'regulates' the mode under which the hearer thinks of A, when she understands an utterance of 'A', only because it is the content of an item of propositional knowledge possessed by the hearer, the knowledge *that* 'A' means As. An important feature of Raghunātha's theory follows from this: its ability to fix the mode associated with a word *only idiolectically*. There is nothing in the account which requires different hearers to identify the referent of a term in the same way as each other. All it does is to solve the synonymy problem for an individual's idiolectical meanings. For what Raghunātha's theory entails is that, for each person S, there is a mode α such that S interprets the term correctly iff S identifies its referent under α. The role of the property is purely within the causal explanation of a given hearer's capacity to understand the term.[10]

With this in mind, recall Gadādhara's remark, while explaining Vardhamāna, that if the property were a mere indicator of the referent, then it would not be part of the hearer's understanding of uttered sentences at all. I repeat the passage (1927: 40):

> The meaning relation obtains between a word like 'pot' and [a particular] as determined (*viśiṣṭa*) by a property like pothood, which is the delimitor of word-meaning (*padārthatāvacchedaka*). It does not [obtain between the word and a particular] merely as 'indicated' (*upalakṣita*) by pothood. If pothood were a mere indicator of the [pot], then, since properties like being-a-thing-with-a-conch-shaped-neck or being-a-substance would do equally well, the regularity between the word 'pot' and thoughts of a thing as being-a-pot, not as being-a-thing-with-a-conch-shaped-neck or as being-a-substance, could not arise.

The linguistic conventions for a nominal like 'the* pot' associate the term with just one way of identifying the reference for the entire community: there is a mode α such that, for each person S, S interprets the term correctly iff S identifies its referent under α. That certainly seems to be the content of the divine mandate as has been discussed. If Raghunātha were correct, this regularity would be inexplicable; indicator properties are implicated only in the intra-personal explanation of understanding.

Gadādhara uses this fact to redefine the term 'indicator' in his theory of meaning. He defines an 'indicator' as a property which might figure in the hearer's knowledge of the meaning relation, but does not figure in specification of the content of the thoughts which constitute their understanding of particular utterances.[11] We will see subsequently how Gadādhara puts this notion to very good effect, arguing, for example, that the property 'being the speaker' enters the hearer's knowledge of the meaning of the indexical 'I', but not the content of thoughts produced by particular utterances of it. How might we incorporate this distinction between indicating and descriptive features into the semantic theory we have been developing? Notice that indicators always seem to be dependent clauses in a compound description: 'the house *with a crow on the roof*', 'the ascetic *with matted hair*'.

As we will see in the next chapter, there is a view about proper names which claims that there are no conventional restrictions on how hearers think about the referent of the name, as long as whatever mode they use uniquely picks out the right object. That view is properly described in terms of the notion of an indicator: any property used to state the meaning of the term is only an indicator of the referent.

Contrast this notion of an 'indicator' with Donnellan's (1966) notion of a referentially used description. Consider his example: standing beside me at a party, you say 'The man *in the corner drinking a martini* is a philosopher'. In fact, I know that the individual in the corner is drinking water from a martini glass. Nevertheless, in spite of the error in your description, you are able to communicate to me the fact that that individual is a philosopher. Communication has occurred without me identifying the reference in the way your utterance instructed me to. Donnellan takes the example to show that descriptions have a 'referential' as well as an 'attributive' use, and that they can be used to refer even to objects which do not possess the property associated with the description.

The existence of a non-semantic role for the matrix of a description has been remarked on by a number of authors. Kaplan expresses the idea well (1989: 584): '[T]he idea of finding a role for non-semantic, communication facilitators, and accounting for referential uses of definite descriptions in this way is appealing. The theory of direct reference, with its prepropositional semantics, seems especially open to such off-the-record elements in language'. Note that it is not essential to this account that the description is erroneous—cases involving error simply dramatize the point being made.

The role of indicators, and their associated diagnostic definitions, shows a way in which descriptive information about the referent can enter systematically into in the explanation of a hearer's knowing which object is the referent of a term, without it following that the term is used attributively.

We have seen that Raghunātha's theory is unable in its current form to account for terms whose correct understanding requires any hearer to think of the referent under the same mode. This might explain a remarkable fact about Gadādhara's description of Raghunātha's account in the *Śaktivāda* (1927: 61–2). For there he ascribes to Raghunātha a view quite different to the one we have so far been considering:

> Now [an objection to my position might go as follows]. The delimitor of the scope of a term (*śakyatāvacchedaka*) is [by definition] whatever is the regulator (*prayojaka*) determining which property of the referents is the mode (*prakāra*) in the hearer's thought. So the delimitor of the scope is the mode of qualificandhood conditioned by a qualifierhood

> in the property being-in-the-content-of-[a hearer's]-thought; it is not a meaning relatum qua determiner (*viśeṣaṇa*), a content of the mandate by way of being the delimitor of the property being-in-the-content-of-[a hearer's]-thought (*bodhaviṣayatāvacchedaka*).[12] Moreover, let it be that the cause of a hearer's thought, in which the mode is the property Y, is the hearer's knowledge of the meaning relation for the word, where the relation is being-in-the-content qualified in this way by being delimited by the property Y. That is, in the divine mandate for the word 'substance', the qualificand is under the mode substancehood, the qualifier being the property being-in-the-content-of-[a-hearer's]-thought-produced-by-the-word-'substance'. Even though the qualificanda are [in fact] pots, pothood is not the mode of qualificandhood conditioned by such a qualifierhood. This is acceptable, and there is no [risk of the] above-mentioned over-extension [of a term to what it does not apply to]. So [making] the delimitor of the scope a meaning relatum must be a mistake. This is the view of [Raghunātha], the author of the *Dīdhitis*, as displayed in the *Pratyakṣamaṇidīdhiti*.

He also explains Raghunātha's view in the *Gādādharī* (1970: 60):

> According to the author of the *Dīdhiti*, the cause of a [hearer's] thought having a property **Y** as the mode, is in all cases their knowledge of **Y** as being a delimitor, the delimitor of the scope [of the term], namely its being a delimitor in the mandate by being the delimitor of such a qualificandhood as is conditioned by a qualifierhood resident in [the qualifier] being-in-the-content-of-[a-hearer's]-thought. This is so of pothood and tailhood, in the case of the words 'pot' and 'beast'. And in the case of the word '*gagana*' [= '*ākāsa*', a theoretical name for the postulated substratum of sounds], since the property being-the-substratum-of-sounds is a delimitor of scope in the sense specified, a hearer can think [of *ākāśa*] under the mode being-the-substratum-of-sounds without there being any semantic deviance. So there is no difference between the words 'pot' and '*gagana*'.

The position described here is clearly different from the one we have been examining; to distinguish them, I shall call this the theory of Raghunātha*. Raghunātha* agrees with Gadādhara that the way *any* hearer must think of the referent is prescribed by the mandate governing the term. The disagreement is in the nature of that prescription. While Gadādhara argued that the mandate literally states which mode hearers must employ if they are to be credited with understanding, Raghunātha* claims that the mode is prescribed by the mandate in virtue of being the mode under which the *mandator* thinks of the reference (mandates, recall, are 'desires' or 'acts of will' on the part of the mandator, who is usually but not necessarily divine).

We took Gadādhara to be giving the mandate an internal or opaque reading. So we should take Raghunātha* as construing it as having an external or transparent reading. Consider again the mandate, and take the underlined term '*pots*' as having external occurrence:

(9) Let *pots* be what hearers must form beliefs about when they hear 'pot'.

The intensional difference Raghunātha* wishes to exploit derives from the fact that the word 'let' here is itself an intensional operator, meaning 'it is mandated that'. So (12) expands as:

(10) It is mandated that *pots* be what hearers must form beliefs about when they hear 'pot'.

In (10), the term 'pots' has an external occurrence with respect to the embedded propositional attitude verb, but an internal occurrence with respect to the mandate. So (13) and (14) differ, even if the underlined terms are co-extensive:

(11) It is mandated that *utensils-with-conch-shaped-necks* be what hearers must form beliefs about when they hear 'pot'.

Someone whose knowledge of the meaning of the term consists in knowledge of (10) knows something different from someone whose knowledge consists in (11). So the new theory explains just as well as the earlier one how hearers' knowledge regulates the modes in understanding. The important difference between the accounts of Raghunātha and Raghunātha*, however, lies in the fact that, since knowledge of (10), but not knowledge of (11), is sufficient (together with knowledge of a general sort) for understanding the term 'pot', *anyone* who understands the term must think of the referent under the same mode.

Gadādhara, Raghunātha, and Raghunātha* each gives a different reading to the following knowledge-of-meaning ascription:

(12) S knows that G mandates that hearers believe that As are denoted by 'A'.

The term 'A' can occur within all the intensional contexts, within the first two or within the first alone. So we have:

(Raghunātha) S knows that As are mandated by G to be believed by hearers to be denoted by 'A'.

(Raghunātha*) S knows that G mandates that As be believed by hearers to be denoted by 'A'.

(Gadādhara) S knows that G mandates that hearers believe that As are denoted by 'A'.[14]

Gadādhara stresses that we have to attend to the specific semantic properties of different kinds of referring expression. He argues that the sort of knowledge implicated in the causal explanation of a person's competence depends on the type of term. It is possible that there are terms for which the requisite item of knowledge must have the form of (Raghunātha), other terms for which it has the form of (Raghunātha*), and still other terms for which it has the form of (Gadādhara). Gadādhara (1927: 73) calls terms the understanding of which has to be explained on the model of (Gadādhara) designators-of-the-determined (*viśiṣṭa-vācaka*), and includes in that category the descriptive nouns, like 'pot' and 'cow'. Terms for which the correct explanatory model is (Raghunātha) are called non-designators-of-the-determined (*viśiṣṭāvācaka*). Ordinary proper names presumably belong here, for it can hardly be right to say that everyone who understands a proper name has to discriminate its reference in the same way. As for terms for which (Raghunātha*) supplies the correct model, the most likely candidates are theoretical terms, terms introduced by stipulation but not, perhaps, synonymous with the description in that stipulation. The term '*ākāśa*' (= '*gagana*') was introduced into the language of Vaiśeṣika proto-physics via the stipulation: ⟨Let '*ākāśa*' denote whatever it is that is the substratum of sounds⟩. The Naiyāyikas point out that we do not want to say that '*ākāśa*' is synonymous with 'the substratum of sounds', as then the sentence '*ākāśa* is the substratum of sounds' would be trivial in ways it does not seem to be. Neither would we want to say that its semantics are those of an ordinary proper name, semantically associated with *no* description at all. Perhaps then, the explanatory model based on (Raghunātha*) is right for such terms. Indeed, it is in the context of a discussion of these terms that the proposal arose. The account would claim that someone who understands the term has a diagnostic discriminatory capacity. A hearer knows which object is the referent of the term '*ākāśa*' by knowing that the referent of '*ākāśa*' is the substratum of sounds. Notice how the fact that *ākāśa* is the substratum of sounds enters the explanation here. It does not enter the contrastive explanation of why the hearer thinks about *ākāśa* rather than some other object, and so is not a mode in the hearer's understanding. It enters the explanation as an item of background, collateral information, on which the hearer draws when deciding which, of a number of antecedently presented objects, is the referent of '*ākāśa*'. Anyone who correctly understands the term must know this same item of background knowledge (that is what distinguishes Raghunātha* from Raghunātha). But it is not implicated in the explanation of the hearer's ability to think of the object *ākāśa* (that is what would distinguish Raghunātha* from Gadādhara).[15]

Where Raghunātha* goes astray, according to Gadādhara, is in his claim that the same explanatory model is true for the understanding of *all* referring expressions. Gadādhara's criticism is that we cannot give a univocal explanation of what is involved in understanding. He argues, in particular, that Raghunātha*'s theory will not do for certain sorts of theoretical name, and for anaphoric pronouns.[16] We will examine his account of the semantics of these two categories of referring expression in the next two chapters. Having stated Raghunātha*'s position in the Śaktivāda, he simply asserts (1927: 62):

> This is not correct. If it were so, then [a hearer's] knowledge of the meaning relation for newly introduced (*ādhunika*) and established (*śakti* = *ājānika*) terms would be causes in the same way. Suppose someone [makes] the stipulation that from the word 'substance' a substance in the sense of a quality-possessor (*guṇavattvādinā*) is to be known. [If Raghunātha* were correct] the hearer [then] knows the meaning via a relation whose qualificandhood is delimited by substancehood. This is not right, because if it were, the [hearer] would think of a substance under the mode substancehood and never under the mode being-a-quality-possessor.

Gadādhara's point is that we have here a mandate which does explicitly state how the referent is to be identified, even though it is not identified in that way by the person making the mandate. Raghunātha*'s theory makes the wrong prediction about the correct way the referent of such a term has to be thought of.

Notes

[1] I here closely follow McGinn (1987: 5–8), whose notation I also adopt.

[2] McGinn (1987: 7) puts it thus: 'Often we want to attribute beliefs about an obect *x* to a subject although we do not know what expressions that subject has in his repertoire for referring to *x*, and which particular ways of thinking of *x* the subject has employed in his thoughts.'

[3] Sudarśanācārya (1892: 42) makes the point very well: 'Even though the property being-in-the-content-of-[a hearer's]-thought [Q] is obtained as the

qualifier in [the qualificand] the pot, it occurs in pothood through a delimitation relation. So pothood has a qualificand-hood conditioned by a qualifier-hood which is resident in Q, and delimited by the relation of delimitation (*ghaṭaviśeṣaṇatāpanneti—ghaṭe viśeṣaṇatāprāptam api bodhaviṣayatvam avacchedakatvasaṃbandhena ghaṭatve vartate iti tādṛṣabodhaviṣayatva-niṣṭhā'vacchedakatvasaṃbandhāvacchinnā yā prakāratā tannirṃupita-viśeṣyatā ghaṭatvasya = ghaṭatve ityarthaḥ*). Gerschheimer (1996: 507) supplies a diagram representing to two different ways in which pothood enters the content of the divine mandate. Note too that Gadādhara, it seems, adopts a convention of using *bodhaviṣayatva* for the qualifier in the divine mandate, and *bodhaviṣayatā* for the content of the hearer's thought. The risk of an equivocation is thereby diminished.

Let '$\sum$' be an arbitrary sentential context, which can combine with the word 'pot' to form a sentence. Then, to a first approximation, the logical form of (1) is either (4a) or (4b):

(4a) ($\forall z$: z is a token of 'pot')(only y: y is a pot)($\forall x$: x is a person)(hears $(x, \sum[z]) \rightarrow B(x, \langle y, P\rangle \,\hat{}\, \ulcorner\sum\urcorner)$).

(4b) ($\forall$: z is a token of 'pot')(only y: y is a pot)($\forall x$: x is a person)(hears $(x, \sum[z]) \rightarrow (\exists X)(B(x, \langle y, X\rangle \,\hat{}\, \ulcorner\sum\urcorner))$).

Both state that pots are what hearers form beliefs about on hearing tokens of the word 'pot'. But (4a) is the reading Gadādhara wants; it states that in the beliefs so formed, the mode under which a pot is presented is P, pothood. Let us see how it matches what he says. He claims that, in (1), the property pothood figures twice over. First, it delimits the qualifier-hood, where the qualifier is the property being-in-the-content-of-hearers-thoughts. Secondly, Gadādhara says that pothood figures as the mode in the content of hearers thoughts about pots. That is, a hearer thinks of an object under the mode pothood. That corresponds, in (4a), to the name of the sense '$\langle y, P\rangle$'.

[4] Strictly, of course, we should have an ordered triple, with a place for the relation between x and P. I am ignoring this extra factor in my discussion. Therefore, for some suitable analysis of the meaning relation $\mathcal{M}_2$, it should be possible to rewrite (4a) in the form:

(5) $\mathcal{M}_2 |$'pot' $\subseteq P \times \{P\}$.

According to Gadādhara, to be the meaning of an utterance of 'pot' is to be the qualificand of a mandate to think of an object under the mode pothood, on hearing 'pot' uttered. So the relation $\mathcal{M}_2(\langle y, Y\rangle, z)$ is defined as ($\forall x$: x is a person)(hears $(x, \sum[z]) \rightarrow B(x, \langle y, Y\rangle \ulcorner\sum\urcorner)$).[5] Substituting this definition into (5) gives (4a).

[5] I have supressed an implicit quantification over sentential contexts.

[6] For notes on Raghunātha and his work, see Ingalls (1951: 9–20) and Frauwallner (1966).

[7] Raghunātha's position seems to have been anticipated by Śaṅkara Miśra (fl. AD 1430). He says (1917: 26) the qualifier in the hearer's knowledge of the meaning relation need not be a meaning relatum, as it is presented by memory (*smṛtyupanītasyāpi śaktigrahaprakāratvād aśakyam api*). Potter and Bhattacharyya (1993: 396) note that Śaṅkara Miśra himself worked outside the mainstream Nyāya tradition, and his commentaries went 'unrecognized by the followers of Gaṅgeśa'.

[8] The idea behind the austere conception is explained thus by McDowell: '[K]nowledge that "Hesperus" stands for Hesperus would suffice, in the context of suitable other knowledge not directly involving the name, for understanding utterances containing "Hesperus"; and similarly with knowledge that "Phosphorus" stands for Phosphorus and utterances containing "Phosphorus". Now, if someone knows that "Hesperus" stands for Hesperus and that "Phosphorus" stands for Phosphorus, it does not follow that he knows either that "Hesperus" stands for Phosphorus or that "Phosphorus" stands for Hesperus' (1977: 164).

[9] *tanmate śaktigraha-viśeṣyatāvacchedakatvasyaiva śābdaprakāratā-niyāmakatvād iti bhāvaḥ* (1934: 119).

[10] Compare Dummett, who describes the austere theory as countenancing the 'possibility that the sense of a word is part of the psychological mechanism by which a speaker attaches a meaning to the word, and not a genuine ingredient of the meaning' (1981: 130).

[11] Harinātha: *upalakṣaṇatvaṃ pada-janya-bodhīya-viṣayatāvaccheda-katvāvacchinna-śaktiviṣayatā-śūnyatvam.* (1929: 91). *Nyāyakośa*, s.v. *upalakṣaṇa: 'upalakṣaṇasya śābdabodhe bhānaṃ nāstīti siddhāntaḥ'*. Compare Viśvabandhu Tarkatṛtha: 'That which is not a content of understanding due to an expression, but helps in cognising the referent of it, is called "an indicator"' (1994: 341).

[12] Note that these clauses are therefore consistent with the clauses for compounds given in §3.2. Note too that Gadādhara stresses the extensionality of indicators: if *p* is an indicator for *r*, and *p* is co-extensive with *q*, then *q* is also an indicator for *r* (see 1927: 40, 41, 71, 105).

[13] The (1927) edition reads '*viṣayatayā*', but most editions and manuscripts have '*viṣayatāvacchedakatayā*'. See Gerschheimer (1996: 265).

[14] In (Raghunātha), A is the *śaktijñāna-viśeṣyatāvacchedaka*; in (Raghunātha*), it is the *īśvarecchīya-viśeṣyatāvacchedaka*, and in (Gadādhara) it is the *padajanyabodhaviṣayatāvacchedaka.*

[15] I therefore believe that, in Dummett's terminology (Dummett 1993, Essay 1), Raghunātha*'s theory is modest, and Gadādhara's full-blooded.

[16] The first claim is in the *Śaktivāda* (172: 62), the second in the *Gādādharī* (1970: 60–1).

Part IV

Special Cases

8

Pāribhāṣikī

The Meaning of Names

While most terms are part of the established, given language, new terms can always be introduced. One way to introduce a new term is by explicit stipulation. Theoretical terms are introduced into Vaiśeṣika proto-physics as names for objects whose existence is inferred from known facts. The name 'space', for example, is introduced as a theoretical term for that substance which grounds spatial relations among objects. Another example is the introduction of new terms in grammatical theory, as names for hypothesized syntactic groupings. A different way to introduce a new term into the language is by ostension, pointing to a perceptible object. In both cases, the problem for the philosopher of language is one of accounting for the relationship between the meaning of the term and the method by which it was introduced. It is unlikely that there will be any univocal solution; different sorts of terms will have different sorts of meaning. Another more general problem, then, is to find principled ways of dividing terms into semantic groups. These problems, and their solution within the theory of meaning we have been developing, are what we shall investigate in this chapter.

8.1 Theoretical Names

Praśastapāda (c. AD 550) was the first major commentator on the *Vaiśeṣika-sūtras*, and it was he who initiated the discussion. He claimed that the usual model for the meaning of a name (*saṃjñā*), according to which a name refers to an object on the basis of that object's possession of a certain property, cannot apply to the names 'time', 'space', and '*ākāśa*'. The reason he gave for this claim was that, since space, time and *ākāśa* are unique, unrepeatable physical entities, the property with which their names would be associated would have to be singly instanced. This, however, contradicts a guiding principle in Vaiśeṣika metaphysics, that a genuine universal property must be plurally instanced (§3.2). He therefore asserts that these terms belong to a new semantic category, which he calls the class of *pāribhāṣikī* or 'theoretical' names:

> In the absence of a genuine universal property, which is due to the uniqueness of *ākāśa*, space, and time, the three names ['ākāśa', 'space' and 'time'] are [to be called] *pāribhāṣikī* [terms].[1]

Praśastapāda himself offered no positive account of the semantics of this new class of expression, nor did he give any clear criterion for deciding which terms belong to it. His examples have at least three unusual properties. First, they are all proper names. Second, the objects to which his terms refer are all homogenous and ubiquitous substances. Third, and perhaps most significantly, the *pāribhāṣikī* terms are theoretical terms, terms introduced into the Vaiśeṣika philosophical discourse via specific stipulations. Following the later authors,[2] let us concentrate on the term 'ākāśa'. The Vaiśeṣikas argue that sounds, as tropes, must subsist in some substance, and they infer that whatever that substance is, it cannot be any substance already known.[3] There has, then, to be some other substance which is, among other things, the substratum of sounds. A name for this substance was now introduced via the following stipulation: ⟨Let the name 'ākāśa' stand for that substance which is the substratum of sounds⟩. Analogous chains of reasoning presage the introduction of the terms 'time' and 'space' as terms of art in Vaiśeṣika theory. The mode of introduction of the term 'ākāśa' is very like the introduction into nineteenth-century physics of the term 'aether', aether having been postulated as the medium for the propagation of electromagnetic radiation. A rather different example is the naming of the planet Neptune, even before it was observed. Leverrier introduced the name 'Neptune' to refer to the planet hypothesized to be the cause of certain discrepancies in the orbits of other planets.[4]

In his *Kiraṇāvalī*, Udayana (1971: 70) introduces an influential threefold division in the types of name. The division is between:

1. *naimittikī* natural kind terms
2. *aupādhikī* synthetic kind terms
3. *pāribhāṣikī* theoretical names

Names in the first category designate objects belonging to a natural kind (*jāti*). In the second case, it is a 'synthetic' kind (*upādhi*), a kind not corresponding to a natural carving up of the world but in some way fabricated or artificial. The usual example is the term 'beast'. As a beast is by definition a thing having a tail, long hair, and certain other beastly properties, the category cuts across natural taxonomies. Terms in the first and second categories refer to objects 'on the basis' of a property, natural or synthetic, a basis being a property which restricts the scope of the term. In the notation of Chapter 2, a property A is the basis of 'A' just in case:

(1) $\mathscr{M} \mid$ 'A' $\subseteq$ /A/,

where /A/ is the extension of A.

Udayana understands the distinction between synthetic kind terms and natural kind terms as being derived from an ontological distinction among the properties on which they are based, but it is not clear why he thinks this will lead to any semantic differences between the two. In view of the fact that the vast majority of synthetic kinds are composite properties (*sakhaṇḍopādhi*), the important difference is presumably between terms with homophonic and terms with non-homophonic meaning clauses (cf. §3.2).[5]

What account does Udayana give of terms in the third group? In an important passage (1971: 70; 1956: 333–6), he says that:

> The three terms, '*ākāsa*', 'time' and 'space', are [terms which] refer directly, without a basis.
>
> (Question:) What is the reason [for saying this]?
>
> (Answer:) It is because of the absence of any universal such as *ākāśa*-hood, etc.
>
> (Question:) And why is that?
>
> (Answer:) It is due to the fact that there is no plurality of particulars, since [*ākāśa*, etc.] are unique [entities]. That is to say, the [Vaiśeṣika] definition of a universal, as that which is eternal, unitary, and occurring in a plurality of particulars, is not satisfied, the obstacle being due to the nature [of *ākāśa*, etc.] itself.
>
> (Opponent:) Even then, [the term '*ākāśa*'] cannot be a *pāribhāṣikī* term, for it is held to be imperceptible. What is said [however] is that '*ākāśa* is that which is sound's substratum'. So the property of being sound's substratum could be a synthetic property.
>
> (Reply:) No! [That is not right] because [the function of] the property of being sound's substratum is to be an indicative syndrome, just as when we say 'This is that Devadatta'. Otherwise, the apposition '*ākāśa* is the substratum of sound' would be impossible.

(Opponent:) The addition of [the abstraction suffices] *-tva* and *-tal* to the word '*ākāśa*' would then [form a] senseless [word].

(Reply:) No. [The term '*ākāśa*-hood'] denotes the own-nature of ākāśa, either metaphorically or as the discrimination [of *ākāśa* from everything else].

Terms in the third group do not refer on the basis of any associated descriptive clause,[6] but *directly*. For Udayana, the meaning clause for 'ākāśa' and other such names is the simple

(2) 'ākāśa' refers to *ākāśa*.

We could write this as:

(3) $\mathcal{M}$ | ' ākāśa' = {*ākāśa*}.

Singular classes like {*ākāśa*} are denoted in Nyāya as the extensions of singular properties, for example the property-of-being-*ākāśa* (*ākāśatva*). Indeed, for any proper name 'a', the Nyāya formal language permits the abstract proper name 'a-hood' (or 'a'). Whether or not this commits them to a doctrine of individual essences or haecceities will depend on how realistically the properties such names denote are construed. Udayana says that *ākāśa*-hood cannot be a natural kind (*jāti*), for a natural kind must be plurally instanced. There are, for Udayana, strong theoretical reasons to suppose that no genuine natural kind can have, as a matter of necessity, just one instance. Perhaps he thinks of the role of a natural kind as determining a relation of 'relevant likeness' between distinct individuals, or, with Raghunātha, as sortal, enabling the counting and measuring of its instances (see below). If genuine natural kinds must have more than one instance, what is the meaning of the abstract term 'ākāśa-hood'? Udayana's suggestion is that this term does not denote anything like the essence of *ākāśa*, but simply the property of being distinct from other substances, $(\lambda x)\ (\forall x)\ (x \neq y \text{ iff } y \neq \bar{a}k\bar{a}\acute{s}a)$.[7]

Given that *ākāśa* is an imperceptible substance, the reference of the name cannot be fixed by an act of ostension. It is fixed instead by the stipulation ⟨Let the term 'ākāśa' stand for that substance which is the substratum of sounds⟩. Should we not then classify 'ākāśa' as a synthetic kind term, since the stipulation links 'ākāśa' with the composite descriptive clause 'the substratum of sound'? The meaning clause would then be:

(4) $\mathcal{M}$ | '*ākāśa*' = /**K**/,

where **K** is the property being-the-substratum-of-sounds. Udayana's intention is that, on this supposition, the relation between 'ākāśa' and being-the-substratum-of-sounds is exactly like the relation between 'beast' and being-a-hairy-animal-with-a-tail.[8]

Udayana's reason for rejecting this proposal is important. He alleges that the proposal entails that the sentence which places the name and the description in apposition, viz.

(L) *ākāśa* is the substratum of sounds

would then be 'impossible'. Vardhamāna explains that the impossibility consists in its saying what has already been said (*paunaruktya*). That is, the predicate in (L) will repeat what has already been said in the subject.[9] (L) would state, tautologously, that the substratum of sounds is the substratum of sounds.

A description gives the meaning of a synthetic kind term. The appositive use of such a term and its defining description results in a sentence which is a tautology, a repetition. An argument against (L)'s being tautologous would be an argument against the conjecture that the stipulation (4) defines 'ākāśa' as a synonym for 'the substratum of sounds'. While no explicit argument is forthcoming from Udayana, it is not difficult to see why Nyāya philosophers of language find the claim that (L) is a tautology difficult to accept. Acording to the epistemological conception of language, the meaning of a sincerely uttered declarative sentence is the proposition it is apt to make known to the hearer (§§4.1, 5.2). A tautology, however, is not knowledge-apt: it can communicate no information. So a tautology can have no literal meaning, if this conception is correct. (L), however, appears to be meaningful, and so, if the appearance is to be believed, it cannot be a tautology. That is, I think, the reason so many Naiyāyikas dismiss the descripivist theory of theoretical names. We will see in this chapter that Gadādhara has a very different solution. He insists that tautologies have no literal meaning, but that we can explain their seeming to be meaningful in terms of their non-literal significance. Tautologies, like any other type of sentence, can be used to convey a proposition which is not their literal meaning, by exploiting the pragmatics of the conversational context.[10] This is the distinction we explained in §1.2, between literal meaning (*śakti*) and derived meaning (*lakṣaṇā*). Gadādhara claim will be that the apparent meaningfulness of (L) is explained by its having a derived but no literal meaning, and hence that there is no argument here against the descriptivist treatment of theoretical names.

Udayana, however, concludes that 'ākāśa' is a directly referring name. He might well be sympathetic with Kripke's claim that (L) is only contingently true (Kripke 1980, esp. pp. 55–8). Kripke's idea is that directly referring names are 'rigid designators', terms which designate the same object in any possible world in which that object exists. A stipulation like (4) serves only to 'fix' the reference of the name. Although the description used to fix the reference is true of the name's referent in the actual world, it does not follow that the object satisfies the description in all possible worlds. So (L) is a contingent truth.[11]

According to Udayana, the account we are considering misconstrues the role of the descriptive clause. This, he says, functions simply an 'indicative syndrome', which he compares with the role of the demonstrative 'that' in 'That is Devadatta'. The demonstrative functions as an heuristic device, indicating to the audience who Devadatta is. Someone can be informed who Devadatta is by being told that Devadatta is *that man*. Likewise, Udayana suggests that someone can be informed which object is *ākāśa* by being told that *ākāśa* is the substratum of sounds. That *ākāśa* is the substratum of sounds is a useful piece of collateral information that learners of the term can appeal to in order to learn the correct meaning of the term, given by clause (2). A consequence is that the sentence (L), like 'a tiger is an animal with black stripes' or 'a cow is an animal with dewlap', is a 'definition' only in that it gives a true description of the substance or kind in question (cf. §§3.2, 6.3). Given that any unique property of *ākāśa* is as good as any other in serving as an indicating syndrome, Udayana cannot follow Kripke further, and regard (L) as being a priori.[12] For Udayana, 'ākāśa' is a genuine proper name of a substance concerning which (L) and other such statements make informative claims. Likewise, Udayana must regard (4) as an extensional truth, the right hand side of which could be replaced with any other co-extensive property, or just the property *ākāśa*-hood itself.

8.2 Proper Names and Direct Reference

Udayana assimilates theoretical names to the class of directly referring names, and thereby to some extent loses Praśastapāda's insight that theoretical names have distinctive semantic properties by virtue of being introduced by descriptive stipulations. In his *Pariśuddhi*, Udayana (1911a: 363) reports a view, later endorsed by Śaṅkara Miśra, that there are *five* distinct kinds of name, in which the insight is preserved. It is a semantic classification, based on the claim that there are five different ways in which names can designate their objects. The five types are:

1. Directly referring names
2. Names linked with an 'indicative syndrome'—the *pāribhāṣikī* terms
3. Names having an etymological meaning
4. Names having as their basis a natural kind
5. Names having as their basis a 'restricted' kind

The last three here are relatively straightforward. Some terms are synonymous with descriptions in virtue of their etymology, such as the verbal noun 'the cook', which is synonymous with 'the person who does the cooking'. Such terms are what Putnam (1975: 141) calls 'one-criterion' words, for their application is completely determined by an explicit criterion. Then there are the nouns like 'earth' or 'cow' which refer to objects belonging to a particular natural kind. Finally, some terms restrict their reference to a special sub-class of a kind. For example, the reference of the term 'milch cow' is limited to a subset of the species of cow, those which can give milk; and the term 'heaven' is said to pick out its reference on the basis of its being an abode of goodness, as restricted by not being an abode of evil. These terms are 'mixed'—partly natural kind term, partly one-criterion term. So the fivefold division roughly corresponds to a distinction between (1) directly referring names, (2) theoretical names, (3) one-criterion terms, (4) natural kind terms, and (5) mixed terms.

Names in the first group directly 'grab by the horns' their referent, without the aid of any descriptive or general feature. Śaṅkara Miśra includes proper names and demonstratives in this class:

> Some names, like 'Devadatta' and 'that', refer directly.... One might wonder how the name 'Devadatta' can be direct, when the property Devadatta-hood is the basis-for-usage. In fact, the name 'Devadatta' is accepted as such when [it is a name of] insentient objects, like a post or a pot. Or else, Devadatta-hood is a property which is located in the body [of Devadatta], and in just one object at any given time. So [the sentence] 'That is Devadatta' delimits [one] from many for someone who does not know [who Devadatta is]. The name is then direct (1917: 260–7).

Śaṅkara Miśra's point seems to be that even if we associate a name with a diachronic criterion of identity, telling us how to identify an object across times, it will not help to distinguish the referent of the name at any given time. It is not clear, however, why he thinks this, since presumably at any *given* time the feature Devadatta-hood, being possessed by at most one individual, would suffice to discriminate that individual from all others present at that time. What about theoretical names like 'ākāśa'? Śaṅkara Miśra only repeats that these are ones for which a syndrome such as 'being the substratum of sounds' serves as an indicator of the referent.[13] The point to note here is that those who endorse the fivefold classification refuse to reduce the semantics of the *pāribhāṣikī* terms to that of ordinary proper names: the former are tied, in one way or another, with a descriptive feature, but the latter refer directly. A distinct account has to be given for the semantics of each of these types of expression.

The same distinction is made by Vardhamāna. Vardhamāna wrote an influential commentary on Udayana, the *Kiraṇāvalī-prakāśa*, in which he sets down for the first time the classic definition of a basis-for-usage for an ordinary nominal. He defines it (1933: 34) as a feature which (i) occurs in all the individuals to which the term can refer, (ii) is itself a meaning relatum of the term, and (iii) regulates the presentation of the term's reference. I examined the significance of the first two clauses in §6.1. What about the last clause in this definition? Vardhamāna uses this to isolate a fourth category of referring expressions, in addition to Udayana's three groups, the members of which he calls 'indicator terms' (*upalakṣaṇavatī*). The descriptive features attached to these terms satisfy only the first and third clauses of the definition: they guide the hearer in identifying the reference of the term, but do not themselves fall under the meaning relation.[14] Vardhamāna significantly claims that 'ākāśa' is an example of an indicator term, saying that 'ākāśa' refers to that which is indicated by the feature being-the-substratum-of-sounds.

The *pāribhāṣikī* terms, as before, refer directly, and include proper names. He makes the following suggestion:

> When a particular perceptually presented object is the object of a stipulation [for a given name], without either a descriptive basis or a heuristic indicator, then such a name refers directly, and is called a *pāribhāṣikī* term. [Ordinary names] like 'Caitra' are examples (1933: 34).

Vardhamāna's claim is that directly referring terms are *ostensively* introduced, while the theoretical 'indicator' terms are introduced by a stipulation in the form of a description of the referent. We can directly refer only to the objects of perception. Vardhamāna is adamant that there is no such thing as a quasi-perceptual acquaintance with *ākāśa*:

> Some people say that the word '*ākāśa*' designates *ākāśa* without any descriptive basis, and that it is desirable to accept that even from words one can have non-qualificative thoughts [about objects] (*padād api nirvikalpakam*). But they [have then to] say that *ākāśa* is visible, and not inferred as the substratum of sounds. [However] *ākāśa* is neither visible nor perceived by any of the external senses, just like the soul. (1911: 336–7)

Vardhamāna's way of drawing the distinction makes good sense in the light of our discussion in Chapter 7. Semantic groupings are based on different explanations of what is involved in understanding. Someone who understands a name knows which object is the referent. If the discriminating knowledge of the referent is diagnostic, then the person knows which object is the referent because she knows that the referent is *N*, for some value of '*N*'. When '*N*' is a perceptual demonstrative, the person knows which object is the reference by being acquainted with it, and in that case her discriminatory knowledge is not description-based but direct. When '*N*' is a description, like 'the substratum of sounds', the person knows which object is the referent because she possesses an item of collateral information sufficient to identify it. Both cases are distinguished from the case in which someone knows which object is the referent by having a practical discriminating knowledge, the knowledge implicated in understanding the natural kind terms like 'cow'. These are distinguished too from the case in which someone knows which object is the referent by knowing an analytical definition—that a beast is a hairy animal with a tail, for example. Such knowledge is implicated in understanding synthetic kind terms. A fourfold division of names, based on four sorts of discriminating knowledge of reference, has much to recommend it.

Let us examine further the idea that proper names refer directly. The origins of this view are in Vyāḍi's theory of meaning (§2.2); among the Nyāya it can be traced back at least to Jayanta (c. AD 850), who remarked that

> Only a particular is meant (*ucyate*) by a word in whose referent there is no repeatable property. Thus in the case of a word like '*Ḍittha*', understood to be a proper name, the meaning is a particular, since we cannot speak of a universal [Ḍitthahood]. We therefore call such a word a substance-word (*dravya-śabda*). [15]

Gadādhara (1927: 65) remarks that this theory is associated with the older Naiyāyikas' slogan 'an object can be presented in a pure, unqualified state even by a word' (*padād api nirvikalpakam*). The same slogan was formulated by Vardhamāna. In its crudest form, this view states that in order to understand a directly referring term, one has a 'bare acquaintance' with its referent, in which one thinks of the referent *under no mode*. The Naiyāyikas who propound this view claim that it is not the names merely of sense-data but names of ordinary objects which refer in this way. Vardhamāna, however, insists that the referent must be presented perceptually, and in doing so conformed with the general opinion in later Nyāya that if there are states of pure, construction-free awareness of things, they must be perceptual states. So the most likely candidates for the direct theory are names and demonstrative pronouns referring to objects in the common perceptual field of speaker and hearer.

It was, I believe, Bhartṛhari (*c.* AD 500) who first set down the classic critique of the theory that proper names directly refer. I quote from the *Mahābhāṣyadīpikā*:

> Even in the case of [the person] Ḍittha, he [scilicet Ḍittha] 'proceeds/continues' (bhavati) from his origin to his death, [and we say] 'This is Ḍittha, this [again] is Ḍittha'. It is the identity in childhood, early youth, maturity, and old age which is [the basis of] the identity judgement (*saṃpratyaya*) 'This [is Ḍittha, this again is Ḍittha]', [and] the [common] 'form' (*ākṛti*) is the meaning of the word ['Ḍittha']. Therefore, there is an [element of] generality here too.[16]

Bhartṛhari is not here questioning the existence of states of 'pure' or 'construction-free' awareness of objects, but is denying rather that such states are either necessary or sufficient for understanding proper names. For one who has mastered the use of a proper name, or at least a proper name for an enduring entity, must have a conception of what it is to encounter the same object at different times, and hence be able to judge '*this* (currently perceived thing) is the same as *that* (thing previously encountered)'. In mentioning the various states of the person Ḍittha—childhood, early youth, maturity, and old age—what Bhartṛhari clearly implies is that one could have a pure awareness of Ḍittha as a child without having the ability to recognize Ḍittha again later. What is involved in having this ability is knowledge of the underlying 'form' (*ākṛti*) of Ḍittha, and it is this 'form', not the object, which for Bhartṛhari is the meaning of the name.

There is a striking similarity between this argument and a well-known critique of the Millian theory of proper names, the doctrine that names are merely labels attached to objects. The argument is that the sense of a proper name is partly constituted by an associated 'criterion of identity' for the object to which it refers, for, as Dummett puts it, 'Merely to know that a name has as its referent an object with which we are confronted, or which is presented to us in some way, at a particular time is not yet to know, in Frege's terminology, "how to recognise the object as the same again", that is, how to determine, when we are later confronted with an object or one is presented to us, whether or not it should be taken to be the same object' (Dummett 1981: 545). Where Dummett differs from Bhartṛhari is in his further claim that grasping the 'criterion of identity' associated with a proper name involves knowing a sortal concept, the concept of a person in the case of names like 'Ḍittha': to judge that this is Ḍittha and this again is Ḍittha is to judge that this is the same *person* as that. Because of this further claim, Dummett is able to reprimand Mill's theory of proper names for presupposing that the world comes to us already sliced up into discrete objects: the correct view, rather, is of reality as 'an amorphous lump', of which 'the proper names we use, and the corresponding sortal terms, determine principles whereby the slicing up is to be effected' (p. 179). It is not that Bhartṛhari would necessarily be hostile to this conception of the relation between metaphysics and semantics, for he notoriously defined a substance as that which a pronoun like 'this' or 'that' is used to refer to.[17] But in saying that the meaning of a proper name is a particularized concept like Ḍitthahood, which in turn is the 'criterion of identity' associated with that name, he overlooks the fact that different proper names can have different meanings but nevertheless be associated with the same criterion of identity.

The Buddhist Kamalaśīla puts forward a different version of the argument. He is commenting on a passage in the *Pramāṇasamuccaya*, where Diṅnāga somewhat cryptically remarks that '[conceptual construction is] the association of name, genus, etc.'. Diṅnāga adds that 'in the case of "arbitrary" names (*yadṛcchā-śabda*), a thing distinguished by a name is expressed by a word [such as] "Ḍittha"; in the case of genus-words (*jāti-śabda*), a thing distinguished by a genus is expressed by a word [such as] "cow", [and so on]' (Hattori, 1968: 25; Hattori's translation). Kamalaśīla claims that we should not take the phrase 'the association of name, genus, etc.' straightforwardly, as specifying a string of different ways to distinguish objects. We should read it rather as: the association of name [with thing] by means of genus, etc. What now becomes of proper names? Kamalaśīla says this:

> Words like 'Ḍittha' are known as 'arbitrary names'. They too take as [their] 'meaning' (*abhideya*) a universal, [one] which inheres in entities which are restricted by boundaries of temporal duration. [This is because] it is impossible for proper names to convey an object which

> is divided into different moments without any common feature, whilst continuing to follow [the object] from birth to the moment of death. Otherwise, when used to denote the portion of an object as delimited by the state of childhood, how could [it] then denote the object having as its condition the state of old age?
>
> Even in the view that [a single enduring object undergoes] transformations, the object at a certain state, with which the relation of denotation is admitted to obtain, could go to another state, and that object is not denoted by the word. Just as the word 'milk' (*kṣīra*), whose meaning is fixed with reference to [fresh] milk (*payas*), does not apply to coagulated milk (*dadhi*), so too [a personal proper name] does not apply to other states of the 'body/person' (*śarīra*) [than the one with respect to which its meaning was fixed]. So [even for proper names] a universal has to be admitted (*Pañjikā* under TS 1226: Śāntarakṣita 1968: 453).

Kamalaśīla here describes the situation from the point of view of Buddhist ontology, which considers ordinary material objects to be 'perduring' entities, that is, entities comprise a series of fleeting temporal stages, but he suggests that the argument can be extended to suit even those who take objects to endure through time. Taking Ḍittha to be an enduring object, present at different times, Kamalaśīla's argument repeats that of Bhartṛhari. If words like 'Ḍittha' were, so to speak, logically proper names, they would be tagged to an object as presented at the time the word was first learned, and could not be used to refer to the same object at different times if its appearance had changed. The example Kamalaśīla given to illustrate his point is very interesting. The word 'milk' is what is sometimes called a 'phased-sortal' term: it applies to a sample of milk when it is fresh, but not when it has coagulated, even though it is the same entity throughout. What Kamalaśīla seems to be saying is that if this theory were true, then it would at best associate a proper name with phased sortal as its criterion of identity. If the name 'Ḍittha' is tagged to the boy Ḍittha, it might be able to be used to refer to Ḍittha while he is still in the stage of boyhood, as long, that is, as he has not changed significantly from the way he was when initially presented, but could not be used to refer to him when he ceases to be a boy by reaching maturity. But, and this is the point of Kamalaśīla's argument, this picture is quite wrong. A proper name can be used to refer to an object at any stage in its life—the criterion of identity associated with a name is not phased but permanent.

Suppose instead, with the Buddhist, that material objects are temporally composite. There is no enduring entity Ḍittha, but only a series of temporally indexed entities, Ḍittha$_{t_1}$, Ḍittha$_{t_2}$, Ḍittha$_{t_3}$, etc. The argument against the theory now reduces to the argument already given against the application of this theory to descriptive nominals. Since there are an arbitrarily large number of Ḍittha-stages, a semantic theory which merely assigns to utterances of 'Ḍittha' clauses of the form ⟨'Ḍittha$_{t_i}$' refers to Ḍittha$_{t_i}$⟩ is either unlearnable or incomplete. Kamalaśīla concludes that the 'meaning' of the proper name is the feature Ḍitthahood, a feature which inheres in each of the temporal stages that comprise Ḍittha. The role of the feature Ḍitthahood is not here a 'criterion of identity', as it was in Bhartṛhari's formulation, for there is no longer any question of an identity through time of a single object. Its function now is to be, as Hattori puts it, the 'generalisation of the innumerable moments that constitute the series of the individual Ḍittha' (1968: 84).

So the meaning of 'Ḍittha' cannot consist entirely in a 'bare' association with its referent; rather, the name is associated with a property Ḍitthahood. On one interpretation, Ḍitthahood is what might be called an 'individual sortal', that is, a uniquely instanced property. Someone who knows this property, or possesses the concept of what it is to be Ḍittha, is able, not only to discriminate Ḍittha from other objects, but to recognize Ḍittha at different times, to judge, in other words, 'This is the same Ḍittha as that'. A second interpretation sees Ḍitthahood as a multiply-instanced universal feature, that which all the different temporal parts constituting the persisting entity Ḍittha have in common. It is the 'particularized genus' to which all the moments of Ḍittha belong. Although there is now no question of an identity judgement, what takes its place is the judgement 'This object and this object are both members of (the particularized genus) Ḍitthahood'.[18]

So much for the earlier criticism of the direct reference theory of proper names. From the Navya-Naiyāyikas' point of view, the central drawback to this theory lies in its commitment to a doctrine of 'pure acquaintance' with the objects referred to. Gadādhara (1927: 65–6) explores this issue in some depth:

> Now it might be thought [as the older Naiyāyikas did] that, even if we accept that the qualifier, just like the object, is a meaning-relatum, we still cannot say that the [hearer has a] thought whose qualifier is being-the-substratum-of-sounds from the word '*ākāśa*', so it is an established tenet that the property of being-the-substratum-of-sounds is not a meaning-relatum of the word '*ākāśa*'. It is to avoid exactly this that the clause 'is itself a meaning-relatum' is included in the definition of a basis-for-use [for we could then agree that words like '*ākāśa*' do not have such a basis].

> We do not follow this line. The old Naiyāyikas, not admitting that being-the-substratum-of-sounds is a meaning-relatum of the word '*ākāśa*', allow for the possibility of a thought which does not have any qualifier at all, arising from the word '*ākāśa*'. They say that 'it might alternatively be granted that even from a word there can arise a non-qualificative awareness'. Here, to be non-qualificative is to lack such a qualifier as is presented by the word. It is not to be lacking any qualifier at all. This is because there must be qualifiers, such as being single, which are presented by the case-inflections. And [this in turn] is because a [hearer's] thought in which there is no relation between *ākāśa* and another meaning-relatum [viz. being single, etc.] cannot occur.
>
> In fact, in that quotation, the word 'non-qualificative' refers to such a non-qualificative memory as is the cause of a hearer's thought whose object is a substratum which is not qualified by something which is presented by the word. Moreover, [Murāri] Miśra, having raised the query that 'non-qualificative memory is impossible, because a [perceptual] experience causes only such a memory as has the same qualifier as itself', described such a memory as having another qualifier [a qualifier which is different from that of the original experience].
>
> Furthermore, since in this view *ākāśa*, not being a universal [or a simple synthetic property], cannot [appear as] a qualifier of another word-meaning by itself, [phrases] such as 'an inhabitant of *ākāśa*' would be incomprehensible. And also the rule that the connection to another word-meaning is delimited by the delimitor of adjuncthood would be impossible to apply. Therefore, since the meaning relation is after all directed towards the qualifier as well as to the object, the possibility that being-the-substratum-of-sounds is a relatum of the word '*ākāśa*', just as cowhood is of the word 'cow', must be considered [afresh].

On behalf of the advocates of the direct reference theory, Gadādhara notes that the doctrine of bare acquaintance has two readings. According to the strongest reading, it states implausibly that someone who understands a directly referring term thinks of the referent as completely unqualified by any feature. There is, however, a weaker reading. This states only that the referent is not thought of as qualified by any feature conventionally tied with the term. In any sentence in which the uninflected nominal stem '*ākāśa*' occurs, there will be other words, nominal affixes, etc. and someone who understands the sentence will think of *ākāśa* as qualified by their denotata. For example, in the sentence '*ākāśa* is a substance', the word 'ākāśa' is construed with the masculine singular affix from the first triplet (that is, nominative). So *ākāśa* will be qualified by singularity, and so on.

Gadādhara points out two problems even with this weaker version of the direct theory. He notes that the direct theory is technically inconsistent with a certain convention in Nyāya. The Nyāya claim that in the specification of the content of a thought, a qualifier of something may itself be unqualified only if it is either a universal or a non-composite synthetic property.[19] *Ākāśa*, however, is neither of these things, and yet becomes the qualifier in a phrase like '... is an inhabitant of *ākāśa*'. What Gadādhara suggests is that there are problems incorporating such clauses into a systematic theory of meaning. The problem hardly seems insuperable, however; Gadādhara, for example, gives no reason why the above principle cannot be reformulated in such a way that allows certain other objects to function as unqualified qualifiers.

Gadādhara has an argument against the whole direct reference approach. The hearer is said to know that 'ākāśa' means *ākāśa*, where *ākāśa* is not singled out by any description. However, in order to acquire such an item of dispositional, memory-based knowledge, the hearer must have been introduced to *ākāśa* in some way, and, since *ākāśa* is imperceptible, this is presumably by means of some description. So the proponent of this view must somehow explain why the mode under which *ākāśa* appears in the hearer's dispositional knowledge of the meaning relation does not regulate the way it appears in the thoughts that constitute understanding an utterance of '*ākāśa*'. We have already seen the importance of such regularities in the causal explanation of understanding. Murāri Miśra, it seems, suggests that in our dispositional or memory-based knowledge of things we do not need to grasp those things under the mode in which we were first presented with them, but that seems dangerously ad hoc. It amounts to the claim that each time someone hears and understands an utterance of a directly referring name, we can give an explanation of their coming to think of its referent, but that there is no single explanation of their ability to think of the referent whenever they hear the name. The only other option is to claim that memory itself presents the object non-qualificatively, but that is not an attractive position.[20]

8.3 Diagnostic Stipulations

Let us return to the idea that, when a name is introduced by stipulation, the stipulative description is a syndrome or indicator of the referent of the term. This idea enjoyed considerable popularity, and, as we saw in the last chapter, a version of the doctrine is attributed to Raghunātha. Raghunātha tries to systematize the discussions of his predecessors:

> The Root's [=Udayana's] own view is that there are just three sorts of name. There are *pāribhāṣikī* words, which are introduced by explicit stipulation. For example, 'Caitra'. There are *aupādhikī* words, whose basis is a synthetic property. For example, '*ākāśa*' [!], 'beast' and 'material element'. And there are *naimittikī* words, whose basis is a natural kind. For example, 'cow'. A basis-for-use (*pravṛtti-nimitta*) is [by definition] the property which delimits the scope (*śakyatāvacchedaka*). An explicit stipulation is not a divine mandate, so [proper names] like 'Caitra' are not so [mandated]. However, the author of the *Bhaṣya* [=Praśastapāda] said that names like '*ākāśa*' are *pāribhāṣikī* words. To respect that, it could be said that an *aupādhikī* word is one whose basis is a multiply instanced synthetic property, while a *pāribhāṣikī* word is one which lacks a multiply instanced basis.
>
> It is desirable to conduct a step by step examination of the notion of the basis-for-use of words. A name (*saṃjña*, denoting expression) is a nominal stem endowed with a distinct mandate (*saṃketa*)—this distinguishes names from verbal roots, nominal and verbal affixes, words ending in a present participle affix, etc. However, words for the Agent, the Patient, and so on, have a distinct mandate.
>
> Words like 'the cook', 'the weaver' and so on do not have their own mandate, and so are not really names at all. However, if we wish to include these as names, then let us say that a *pāribhāṣikī* name is one which either has a mandate but no descriptive basis, or else has a mandate but no multiply instanced descriptive basis, and an *aupādhikī* word is one which does not have a mandate but whose meaning is determined by its etymology. That will exclude words like '*paṅkaja*' [which etymologically means 'mud-born', but conventionally means a lotus]. Finally, we could say that a *naimittikī* word is a name endowed with a basis or a name endowed with a multiply instanced basis .... Here we must take 'basis' to be qualified by being a natural kind, whether higher or lower [in the hierarchy of kinds], and not to be qualified by being a dividing synthetic kind, for that would be very prolix. Moreover, a natural kind, higher or lower, is always multiply instanced. Because of this there can be counting and measuring [of its instances]. So [let us say that] a *ruḍhi* (common noun whose meaning is governed by convention and not etymology) is one which applies to members of a natural kind. Otherwise, [the abilities of] counting and measuring will be lost.
>
> However, it must also be explained how words introduced by explicit stipulations, by writers of grammars and so on, are not *naimittikī* words, even though they belong in the class of names. So [let us say that] a *pāribhāṣikī* word is a name which denotes exactly

> one object, that an *aupādhikī* word is one which denotes more than one object and either must or only do so on the basis of a synthetic kind. Finally, a *naimittikī* is a word which denotes on the basis of a natural kind (1932: 47–8).

Raghunātha attempts to devise a coherent classification of names. He finally defines a *pāribhāṣikī* term simply as an expression which refers to a single object, an *aupādhikī* term as an expression which refers (on different occasions) to a plurality of objects with the help of a synthetic property, and a *naimittikī* term as an expression which refers (on different occasions) to a plurality of objects with the help of a natural kind. He thus sharply isolates the category of 'singular terms', terms which refer to just one thing, and defines them explicitly as such, without giving any account yet of how they refer.

An important feature of Raghunātha's schema is apparent: he seeks to group nouns by non-semantic criteria, such as the number of objects in the name's scope, and the ontology of the name's basis. The reason for this is that he thinks a single semantic model can be applied to every referring expression. In this model, the mode in the hearer's knowledge of the meaning relation regulates the mode in the thought which constitutes understanding of an utterance. After describing his view, in the passage quoted in §7.1, he states:

> This is the truth of the matter .... Some people think that the property being-the-substratum-of-sound is not like this, as [a hearer can also think of *ākāsa*] under the mode being-a-substance-different-from-the-other-eight-recognised-substances, and hence there can be variations in the [mode in] understanding (*vyutpatti*). Although some people think of [*gavaya*] under the mode being-a-*gavaya* and some under the mode being-an-animal-similar-to-a-cow, the meaning is taken to be thing-qualified-by-being-a-*gavaya* for simplicity. Just as this is understood there, so it should be understood here too. Thus, being-the-substratum-of-sound is indeed the delimiting property of the scope [of 'ākāśa'], in just the same way as is cowhood [of 'cow'] (1932:49)

Gadādhara (1927: 67) comments:

> When [Raghunātha, the author of] the *Dīdhiti*, in the '*rūpa*' section of the *Guṇaṭippaṇi*, wrote 'this is the truth of the matter', he implied that, since that there is no difference between being-the-substratum-of-sounds and cowhood, the inclusion of the clause 'being a meaning-relatum' in the *Prākāśa* definition of a basis-for-use is a mistake. And in the *Pratyakṣamaṇidīdhiti*, having conceded that the property limiting of the scope (*śakyatāvacchedaka*) regulates [the appearance of] cowhood as a qualifier, [he further said that] it is a mistake to take

> this delimiting property to be itself within the scope of the meaning relation. However, the problems mentioned above should be taken into consideration here.

When I discussed Raghunātha's theory in the last chapter, I pointed out that the regularity to which he appeals, between the mode under which the referent is presented in a hearer's knowledge of the meaning relation and the mode under which it is presented in the thoughts that constitute their understanding of particular utterances, supports an intra-personal explanation of understanding. For each person, there is an explanation of their thinking of the referent under a particular mode. It seems, however, that we need more; in particular, we need an explanation of why it is that, at least for certain sorts of term, the constraints on understanding are such that anyone who understands the term correctly must discriminate the reference in a particular, conventionally specified, way. Raghunātha now addresses that problem. His response is to deny that it is true that there are any terms for which the conventions do determine how understanders must discriminate the reference. It is not required that someone who understands a natural kind term like 'gavaya' must have the sort of practical ability to identify members of the kind, based on acquaintance with some of its members, which is attributed when we say that a person thinks of the object under the mode *gavaya*-hood. A person who simply knows that *gavaya* are animals similar to cows, and discriminates them on that basis, understands the term just as well. It is, Raghunātha suggests, merely out of deference to consideration of simplicity that we describe the meaning of 'gavaya' with the homophonic clause ⟨'gavaya' denotes things possessing *gavaya*-hood⟩.

Raghunātha's semantic liberalism is more plausible as an account of certain sorts of name than as a hypothesis about the nature of referring terms generally. Let us consider its application to names introduced by descriptive stipulation. The idea is that any hearer knows which object is the referent of 'ākāśa' because they know a uniquely identifying description true of *ākāśa.* Such descriptions are syndromes of *ākāśa*; that is, no two hearers have to know the same description, and, in particular, the description used in the stipulation, 'the substratum of sounds', has no privileged status. It is therefore quite possible for someone to find the sentence (L), '*ākāśa* is the substratum of sounds', non-trivial. For this reason, Gadādhara considers a version of the 'indicator' theory of names, one which allows for the possibility just described (1927: 70–1):

> [Here is a plausible theory.] When a thought about *ākāśa* arises from the word '*ākāśa*', it can even be of *ākāśa* qua substance different

> from [the other] eight substances, and other such modes—there is no fixed rule that [it be of *ākāśa*] qua substratum of sound. This being so, the appositional construction '*ākāśa* is the substratum of sound' cannot be chief (*mukhya*). [But] though *ākāśa* is qualified by each of several properties, the view that the word '*ākāśa*' is ambiguous (*nānāśakti*) is untenable, because a single word bearing a meaning relation to a single locus which is delimited by many properties is nowhere seen. Therefore, [we should say that] the meaning relation of the word '*ākāśa*' is directed towards that which is merely indicated (*upalakṣita*) by the property being-the-substratum-of-sounds. This is a respected older view. For there is no problem in holding that an indicator is the qualifier in thoughts generated by words which do not designate a determinative complex.
>
> It might be thought that if the property being-the-substratum-of-sounds were a mere indicator, then similarly [less specific] properties like being-a-knowable-entity could be the qualifier in thoughts generated by the word '*ākāśa*'. This, however, is not a proper objection to the above account. [Any hearer's] knowledge of the meaning relation causes [a thought about] what is indicated by a property which is not wider in scope [i.e. all such properties must have the same extension].

According to this view, each speaker identifies the referent of 'ākāśa' under a mode or descriptive feature, but the particular mode may vary from person to person. One hearer might identify *ākāśa* under the mode 'the substance different from the other eight substances', another under the mode 'the substratum of sound'. For each person, there is a mode **Y**, such that S knows, of *ākāśa*, under the mode **Y**, that it is the meaning of '*ākāśa*'. The conventions governing 'ākāśa' are such that anyone who understands an utterance of 'ākāśa' must think of *ākāśa* under some mode co-extensive with being-the-substratum-of-sounds.

Gadādhara distinguishes the class of names for which the theory is true, calling them non-designators of what is determined (1927: 72):

> Suppose we think that the word '*ākāśa*' in the sentence '*ākāśa* is the substratum of sound' has its literal meaning and that there is no such thing as a thought which lacks a delimiting mode under which its object is grasped. Then, in order to explain how, from the word '*ākāśa*' taken literally, a thought of *ākāśa* qua substance different from the [other] eight substances is possible, there is no alternative but to admit that names like '*ākāśa*' belong to a [special class] of 'non-designators of the determined' (*viśiṣṭāvācaka*), in the knowledge of the meaning of which the object appears under a certain mode, and even though it is not itself a meaning-relatum, thoughts about the referent have that as their mode. In the case of 'designators of the determined' (*viśiṣṭa-vācaka*) like 'cow', on the other hand, thoughts about the reference

> have as their mode a property which is also a meaning-relatum. Therefore, there cannot arise, from a word such as 'cow', a thought whose mode is not a meaning relatum, such as the property of being the designatum of the word 'cow', unless [it be] through faulty knowledge of meaning or through metonymy.

As an account of what is involved in understanding ordinary proper names, this theory has much to recommend it.[21] But as applied to theoretical names like 'ākāśa', it is implausible. The problem with such an account is this. Both the direct and the syndrome theories are motivated by the thought that the sentence '*ākāśa* is the substratum of sounds' is not a tautology, the predicate merely repeating the subject. Yet neither gives the stipulative description 'the substratum of sounds', *any* distinct semantic role.

8.4 Descriptivism: A Nyāya Theory Defended

Udayana rejected the descriptivist account, that a theoretical name is defined by its introducing description. However, the later philosophers reconsider the merits of subsuming theoretical names into the category of *aupādhikī* terms. The first philosopher explicitly to defend a descriptivist account is Jagadīśa. Jagadīśa does not accept Udayana's claim that there can be referring expressions which pick out their referents unaided by any descriptive feature. Like Raghunātha, he too reconstructs Udayana's classificatory schema to fit his own theory:

> When it is said [by Praśastapāda] that a *pāribhāṣikī* word is a name endowed with an explicit convention, and an *aupādhikī* is one endowed with a basis which is a synthetic kind, like being-the-substratum-of-sound, the intention is that a pāribhāṣikī name is one endowed with a convention delimited by a singly instanced property. That is because it is accepted that an aupādhikī is a name delimited by a multiply instanced synthetic property.
>
> According to our Teacher [Udayana], a *pāribhāṣikī* word is one endowed with a convention which is not delimited [by any descriptive feature], on the ground that the word '*ākāśa*' presents gagana [=*ākāśa*] on its own without any delimiting property. Otherwise, an unacceptable result would follow, that the sentence '*ākāsa* is the substratum of sounds' is a tautology. And [Udayana further notes that] one should not think that, on such a view, the phrase '*ākāśa*-hood' is ill-formed, the affix '-hood' denoting the essential nature of a thing. For the affix '-hood' can mean 'discrimination of the thing from others'.

> That view is not correct. The word '*ākāśa*' cannot present *gagana* by itself, for that is contrary to experience, and would prevent it from being a cause. Neither is it right to say that we understand the word by knowing the meaning relation between the word '*ākāśa*' and the object, with the property being-the-substratum-of-sounds being just a heuristic indicator, and not the property which delimits the scope of reference (*śakyatāvacchedaka*). For that would have the consequence that cowhood would in the same way be prevented from being a property which delimits the reference. Finally, since the meaning of the sentence '*ākāśa* is the substratum of sounds' is that 'the referent of the word "*ākāśa*" is the substratum of sounds', there is no problem about it (1927: 309).

Jagadīśa defends the view that anyone who understands 'ākāśa' does so because they know that *ākāśa* is by definition the substratum of sound. He responds to the criticism that it renders sentence (L), '*ākāśa* is the substratum of sound', tautologous by suggesting that (L) does indeed have a non-vacuous content, the metalinguistic content that the word '*ākāśa*' refers to the substratum of sound.[22] Jagadīśa also notes that Udayana's view is unsatisfactory in its own right, for it is contrary to experience (*anubhavavirodhāt*; counter-intuitive?) to suppose that the word 'ākāśa' presents *ākāśa* by itself, that is, in a pure unqualified form. This move reflects the Naiyāyikas' growing discomfort with the idea that objects can appear as unconceptualized 'givens' in thought.[23] Jagadīśa points out that it will be difficult for Udayana to explain the causal relations in which *ākāśa* is involved, because causal relations are thought to be general relations obtaining between universals, and on Udayana's view the word refers to the pure object. Causal laws do not contain proper names.

Gadādhara himself defends a descriptivist theory of theoretical names. The description 'substratum of sounds' gives the meaning of the name '*ākāśa*', and anyone who understands that name must think of *ākāśa* under the mode substratum-of sounds. The main problem that must be addressed is to explain how it is that the sentence '*ākāśa* is the substratum of sound' seems to have non-trivial content. Jagadīśa, as we have seen, recommends a metalinguistic reading of the sentence, as asserting 'the term "*ākāśa*" refers to the substratum of sound'. Gadādhara has another suggestion. The key idea in Gadādhara's approach is that, as used in (L), the term 'ākāśa' has a non-literal significance (1927: 72, 75–6):

> Given that the construction '*ākāśa* is the substratum of sounds' cannot be taken as literal, it is accepted that there a non-literal relation obtains

> [between the word '*ākāśa*'] and either the property of being a substance different from the [other] eight substances, or else the property of being designated by the word 'ākāśa'.
>
> When the sentence 'No cow is here', or 'No substance is here', which contains a descriptive term, is applied to a particular cow drawing a plough or [a particular substance] gold, the special qualifiers are non-literal. This is because thoughts with such qualifiers cannot be explained by taking the terms literally, since the special qualifiers are not part of the literal meaning of the descriptive terms.
>
> Furthermore, when a word like 'heaven', which designates that which is qualified by the property of having happiness unmixed with unhappiness, or [a word like] 'milch cow', which designates that which is qualified by the property of being a cow capable of giving milk, is intended by the speaker to apply merely to that which is delimited by happiness or that which is delimited by being a cow, then [the meaning] is non-literal. A linguistic comprehension [cannot arise] through literal meaning when part of the basis for use is abandoned.

To give the literal meaning of a term is to specify how anyone who understands the term has to think of the referent. Anyone who understands the term 'cow' must think of its referent as a cow. It is possible, however, for someone to think of the referent in a more specific way, the additional qualifier being possibly implied by the pragmatics of the speech context, but not a qualifier that the hearer must apply in order to satisfy the conventions on the literal use of the term. Someone who asserts that there is no cow here, though literally denying the existence of any cow at all, might intend to convey that some particular sort of cow is absent. The general idea here is familiar to those who defend Russell's theory of descriptions (Neale 1990: 95–102). According to Russell's theory, a sentence like 'The cat is not in the kitchen' literally states that there is a unique cat in the world and it is not in the kitchen. To explain how it is that the sentence is usually construed as asserting that some particular cat is not in the kitchen, it is argued that extra descriptive material is somehow 'supplied' by pragmatic features of the speech context, such as what is conversationally implicated by the speaker. The sentence is taken 'non-literally', as asserting that there is a unique cat belonging to me in the world, and it is not in the kitchen.

Gadādhara's idea is that something similar happens when people find the sentence '*ākāśa* is the substratum of sound' non-trivial. Its literal meaning is, trivially, that the substratum of sound is the substratum of sound. However, when uttered in a particular context, it might carry additional pragmatic implications. Someone who asserts that *ākāśa* is the substratum of sounds, having just been asked whether space is the substratum of sounds, conveys the information that *ākāśa* is not identical to space. Again, if uttered in response to the question 'What is the substratum of sounds?', it may convey the information that the name 'ākāśa' designates the substratum of sounds. Thus the literal triviality of the sentence is consistent with its having a significant 'metaphorical' reading in a particular context.[24, 25]

Notes

[1] *ākāśakāladiśām ekaikatvād aparajātyabhāve sati pāribhāṣikyas tisraḥ sañjñā bhavanti. Praśastapāda* (1927: 308). The term '*pāribhāṣikī*' is usually translated as 'technical term', but in view of the wide range of theories about these terms, such a translation may easily become misleading. It is unclear whether Paśastapāda's use of this term is in any way influenced by the Pāṇinian term '*paribhāṣa*' or 'meta-rule'.

[2] The main later sources for the discussion of the *pāribhāṣikī* terms in the later literature are the commentaries and sub-commentaries on Praśastapāda, especially Udayana's *Kiraṇāvalī*, Vardhamāna's *Kiraṇāvalī-prakāśa*, Raghunātha's *Kiraṇāvalī-prakāśa-dīdhiti*, and Jagadīśa's *Sūkti*, a commentary directly on Praśastapāda. Gadādhara gives a whole chapter to the discussion of these terms in the *Śaktivāda*.

[3] Potter (1977: 90) summarizes the inference: 'Sound cannot be a quality of earth, water, fire, or air, since it is found where those substances are absent. It cannot be a quality of the internal organ, for it is apprehended by an external sense organ. The reasons why sound cannot be a quality of time or space are somewhat more complex ... [t]he Naiyāyika argues first that sound is a specific quality (*viśeṣaguṇa*) like touch, taste, colour, and smell, since it is grasped by one sense organ only. Granting that, he next points out that time and space have no specific qualities.... Finally, selves are not the loci of sounds, since none of the qualities of selves are apprehendable by external sense organs. Therefore, an additional substance must be inferred to be the locus of sound, and that substance is *ākāśa*'. As Potter notes, some later Naiyāyikas, notably Śivāditya and Raghunātha, identify ākāśa with space and time after all (and Raghunātha identifies God with both!).

[4] The example is Kripke's; see Kripke (1980: 79, n.33). Still another sort of example is Evans' 'Julius', introduced as a name for whoever invented the zip (Evans, 1982: 31).

[5] Matilal (1968: 50; 1986: 417–18) examines other criteria sometimes employed to make out this distinction.

[6] Cf. Jagadīśa (1930: 309): *niravacchinna-saṃketa-śālitvam eva pāribhaṣikatvam ... ityācāryamatam.*

[7] Cf. Jagadīśa (1930: 309): *na caivam ākāśatvam ityādiprayogo na syāt praktyarthatāvacchedaka-dharmasyaiva tvatalādyarthatvād iti vācyaṃ vyāvartaka-dharmasyaiva tvatalādinā bhāva-pratyayenābhidhānāt.*

[8] In fact, the formulation (4) will not do, for the reason discussed in §6.1: the description does not have an intensional role. Udayana, however, does not have the theoretical resources available to him to do better. Preceding the clause with a modal operator would have the desired effect, as would making essential use of intentionally individuated properties. One might argue that Udayana used the second of these methods, somewhat in the manner of Bealer (1982).

[9] He says that the mode under which the subject appears (*uddeśyatāvacchedaka*) in (L) will be identical with the mode under which the predicate-object (*vidheyatāvacchedaka*) appears.

[10] For example, if I say to you 'Either you have the book or you don't', I might convey that I am annoyed with your equivocation, even though what I literally state is vacuously true.

[11] One might worry, however, that the counterfactual 'something other than ākāśa could have been the substratum of sound' is true only if there could be different laws of physics holding between the same set of physical objects.

[12] More accurately, what is a priori the claim that *ākāsa* is the substratum of sounds, if anything is. There is very little discussion of the a priori in Nyāya, although the concept is not entirely absent. See Matilal (1982: 128–51; 1986: 76–7). Matilal (1986: 31) writes that 'It is surely a lacuna in the Indian *pramāṇa* theory that it has little to say about the nature of a priori knowledge. We can catch only occasional glimpses of some background notions, that of purportedly necessary truths and a priori arguments.'

[13] *pāribhāṣikī yathākāśam iti iyam eva taṭasthalakṣaṇety ucyate śabdāśrayatvasyopalakṣaṇasya taṭasthatvāt* (1917: 26).

[14] *tacca vācyopasthāpakamātram na tu śaktyantarbhūtam* (1933: 34).

[15] *yeṣām artheṣu sāmānyaṃ na sambhavati taiḥ punaḥ ucyate kevalā vyaktir ... evaṃ ḍitthādiśabdānāṃ saṃjñātvaviditātmanām abhidheyasya sāmānyaśūnyatvād vyaktivācitā ata eva hi dravyaśabda ity ucyate* (Jayanta, 1936: 298).

[16] *ḍitthe' pi yadutpattiprabhṛtyāvināśāt eva tad bhavaty ayaṃ ḍitthoyaṃ ḍittha iti. bālyakaumārayauvanasthāvireṣv abhinnaḥ sa evāyaṃ iti saṃpratyayaḥ sā ākṛtiḥ śabdavācyā. unmugdhe' pi ca saṃpratyayo bhavati ḍitthoyam likhyata iti. tasmāt sāmānyam atrāpy asti* (Bhartṛhari, 1970: 18) .

[17] For a discussion of Bhartṛhari's definition of a substance, and its implications for ontology, see Matilal (1971: ch. 3.5), Matilal (1985b: 381–2), and Deshpande (1992: 33–4).

[18] These two interpretations are carefully distinguished in the *Kāvyaprakāśa: bālavṛddhaśukādyudīriteṣu ḍitthādiśabdeṣu ca, pratikṣaṇaṃ bhidyamāneṣu ḍitthādyartheṣu vā ḍitthatvādyastīti* (Mammaṭa 1917: 37).

[19] The doctrine that there are non-composite synthetic properties (*akhaṇḍopādhi*) is strange. The typical example of a non-composite synthetic property is *ākāśa*-hood. It seems that this was another attempt to reconcile the fact that *ākāśa*-hood cannot be a genuine universal with the fact that it cannot be identical with the property being-the-substratum-of-sounds.

[20] Russell famously claimed that memory is a mode of acquaintance, that 'we are immediately aware of what we remember, in spite of the fact that it appears as past' (1912: 26). Gadādhara, however, wrote a short tract on the question, the *Nirvikalpakasmaraṇavāda*, in which he tries to supply arguments to support his contention that memory cannot present a past object in a qualification-free way. The existence of non-qualificative memory states seems indeed to have been a source of great controversy among later Naiyāyikas.

[21] Cf. Frege (1952: 58): 'In the case of genuinely proper names like "Aristotle", opinions as regards their sense may diverge. As such, e.g. may be suggested: Plato's disciple and the teacher of Alexander the Great. Whoever accepts this sense will interpret the meaning of the statement "Aristotle was born in Stagira", differently from one who interpreted the sense of "Aristotle" as the Stagirite teacher of Alexander the Great. As long as the nominatum remains the same, these fluctuations in sense are tolerable. But they should be avoided in the system of a demonstrative science and should not appear in a perfect language'. Wiggins has something like the indicator theory of names in mind when he remarks that 'The sense of a proper name simply consists in its having been assigned whatever reference it has been assigned: to know the sense of *n* is to know to which entity *n* has been assigned, a single piece of knowledge which may be given in countless different ways by countless different descriptions' (1975: 11). There are resemblances too with cluster theories of names.

[22] A view once endorsed by Frege, but later rejected on the grounds that the sentence does not seem to be about the name 'ākāśā' but about the object *ākāśā* itself. See Salmon (1986: 51–4).

[23] For more on this point, see Matilal (1988).

[24] This move closely resembles Śaṅkara's claim that the essential definition of Brahman ('Brahman is truth, knowledge and infinite') is to be understood non-literally. In an article on this definition, Lipner (1997) persuasively argues that we must read it as both a definition and what he calls an 'oblique predication' (*lakṣaṇā*, non-literal). Śaṅkara does not, it appears, regard the word 'Brahman' as a referring expression at all. He says (Lipner 1997: 304–5):

> It stands to reason that Brahman cannot be plainly expressed (*ucyate*) [even] by such [comprehensive] words as 'being' and 'non-being', for words are ordinarily used to reveal some object and when heard by their hearers conventionally make known their object by reference to a genus, action, attribute or relation .... But Brahman belongs to no genus, whence It cannot be plainly expressed by such words as 'being', nor does It possess attributes by which It may be plainly expressed by words denoting attributes, for It is

> attributeless; nor is It expressible by action-words since It is actionless ... [so] It cannot be plainly expressed by any word, whence scriptural passages [such as] 'Words turn back from It ...'.

This argument leaves open the possibility that 'Brahman' refers directly. Indeed, Śaṅkara's failure here to mention the possibility that 'Brahman' is a proper name (*yādṛcchā-śabda*) is striking, given the similarity between his classification of names and the classifications of Patañjali, Praśastapāda and Diṅnāga (see Matilal 1971: 35–6).

[25] The descriptivist account of theoretical names is defended widely in current literature. Ramsey, and following him Carnap and Lewis, argue that a theory T containing names of theoretical entities should be replaced by a 'Ramsey sentence' R, in which theoretical names are replaced by variables bound externally by existential quantifiers. The Ramsification of the theoretical statement '*ākāśa* is the substratum of sound' would be 'There is something x, such that x is the substratum of sound'. According to Carnap, the empirical content of the theory is given by the Ramsey sentence R, while the conditional 'R → T' is analytic. That is to say, the statement 'If there is anything which is the substratum of sounds then *ākāśa* is the substratum of sounds' is an analytic statement.

9

Sarvanāma

Indexicality and Pronominal Anaphora

9.1 Changing Reference, Constant Meaning

An indexical expression is a term able to refer to different objects in different contexts. Standard examples include demonstratives ('this', 'that'), spatial and temporal indexicals ('here', 'now'), and the first person ('I'). Even the ordinary nominals are analysed as indexicals in Nyāya semantics. The treatment of indexicality within the realist theory of meaning is problematic, for if the meaning of a term is identified with its reference, an indexical expression will be ambiguous. The later Nyāya discussion of the problem therefore focused on the search for an element in the meaning of an indexical expression which, as they put it, 'runs through' (*anugama*) the various referents.[1]

There are two models of the nature of the running element: the 'determiner' (*viśeṣaṇa*) model, and the 'indicator' (*upalakṣaṇa*) model. The determiner model states that the running element in the meaning of an indexical expression is the single mode under which the hearer thinks of any of its referents when she understands a statement containing that expression (technically, it is called the *śābdabodha-viṣayatāvacchedaka*). I have argued that we should think of the theory of modes as an account of a hearer's discriminatory capacities. The idea behind the determiner model is then that an indexical expression is univocal because there is a single account of the hearer's capacity to recognize the reference of any use of that expression. This is Gadādhara's explanation of the running element in the meaning of an ordinary noun. The mandate for a noun 'A' states that one correctly understands an utterance of 'A' only if one thinks of its reference as being-an-A; that is, under the mode **A**. The Fundamental Principle for modes (thinking of *a* as being-$F \rightarrow Fa$) ensures that this mode is also the delimitor of the scope of the noun (the *śakyatāvaccheda*): utterances of 'A' semantically refer only to As. So being-an-A is what all the semantic referents of 'A' have in common.

The indicator model states that the running element in the meaning of an indexical term is a property which the mandate or linguistic rule for the term asserts every referent to have. Someone who understands the expression knows that it refers only to objects having that property. The property, however, need not be implicated in the hearer's capacity to recognize the reference, and so need not be a cognitive mode in the hearer's understanding. The mandate does not itself state how the understander is to identify the reference.[2]

As an example of the two models, consider the first-person pronoun. The linguistic rule for the pronoun is of the form ⟨any utterance of 'I' refers to its utterer⟩, in which a single property being-the-utterer is asserted of any referent. Someone who understands the pronoun knows this rule. The issue which will separate the two models is whether understanding is further conditional on thinking of the referent of any utterance of the term in a certain way. The determiner model would claim that the hearer identifies any referent of 'I' qua being-the-speaker; that is, the property being-the-speaker is the cognitive mode under which the referent is identified. In this model, correctly understanding the statement 'I am Φ' consists in forming the thought that *a*, the speaker, is Φ. One might well feel, however, that this account of what it is to understand utterances in the first person is incorrect. Someone who understands the statement thinks that *a* is Φ, but need not think of *a* as being the speaker, but perhaps as the person standing in front of me, as Jones, or in any other suitably identifying way. If that is the correct account of its meaning, then the first pronoun is an indexical whose common running element, being-the-speaker, is an indicator and not a determiner. Gadādhara's own theory is more complex than either of these, for he introduces individual essences as the modes under which speakers think of themselves in uttering the first person pronoun (§9.4).

Related distinctions are drawn in recent literature on indexicals. Kaplan's celebrated distinction between the 'content' and the 'character' of an indexical expression (Kaplan 1989a: 500–507) is similar without, I think, being identical. Consider again the indexical 'I', and its rule ⟨'I' refers to its utterer⟩. Kaplan calls the associated rule for an indexical the 'character' of the term, which he defines as a function from contexts of utterance to contents. The 'content' is part of what is said by any sentence containing the term. For Kaplan, the content of an utterance of 'I' is just the person referred to on that occasion; so a statement 'I am Φ' does not *state* that the speaker is Φ.

The rule for the first person pronoun has another feature, a feature which will be important too in Gadādhara's discussion of pronouns. Notice that the rule is that an utterance of 'I' refers to *its* utterer; the running element is indexed to a particular utterance. In the Nyāya technical language, such indexing is represented by means of the reflexive pronoun 'own' (*sva*).[3] The running element in the meaning of 'I' is the property being-its-own-utterer (see §9.4).

A similar account is the theory favoured by some authors for descriptive singular terms like 'ākāśa'. Someone who understands the name 'ākāśa' can think of its referent under any mode they like, as long as that mode is co-extensive with the property being-the-substratum-of-sounds. As the mode varies from utterance to utterance, we might describe this as case in which the second member in the meaning pair is itself indexical. There is, furthermore, a running element in all the possible modes, namely, that they are all co-extensive with K. Note, however, that 'ākāśa' is not genuinely indexical, since its reference is not dependent on context.

Let us call indexical terms which are such that the mode itself has to be indexed to the utterance, 'intensional indexicals'. Gadādhara claims that pronouns too are intensional indexicals. Or rather, he claims that third-person pronouns used in a certain anaphoric manner are intensional indexicals.[4] So let us first examine the different uses of pronouns in Sanskrit.

Sanskrit grammar labels a pronoun a 'name for all' (*sarvanāma*). Third-person pronouns in Sanskrit fall into two pairs: *etat* 'this', and *tat* 'that, it'; and again *idam* 'this' and *adaḥ* 'that'. The first member of each pair is usually said to signify what is near at hand, the second what is more remote (*Vivṛtti*, 1929: 160). Gadādhara says that *etat* 'this', *idam* 'this', and *adaḥ* 'that' are deictic pronouns, 'this' referring to a perceptually present object, and *adaḥ* 'that' to something which is out of sight (*parokṣa*) (1927: 179–80). The uses of *tat* 'that, it', however, are more complex and varied. Gadādhara claims that there are three distinct uses of this pronoun, and some of his commentators add a fourth. In the first and by far the most important use, the pronoun is correlated with an antecedent noun, which may occur in the same sentence or in some previous sentence. Gadādhara's example is:

(1) There is a pot here; bring it *ghaṭa ihāsti tam ānaya*,

in which the pronoun is correlated with the preceding noun 'pot'. As noted in §1.1, Sanskrit nouns do not take definite or indefinite articles, and we must consider the individual case when deciding which determiner to supply. I follow Matilal (1985a: 389), Bhatta (1995: 72), and Bhattacharyya (1997: 19) in translating Gadādhara's example with an indefinite.[5] This pronoun is called the *prakrānta-parāmarśaka* pronoun, a pronoun whose construal depends on something previously uttered. In other words, the pronoun is here used anaphorically. It is the semantics of the pronoun as it occurs in sentences like (1) that we will be mainly concerned with in this chapter.

A second recognized use of the pronoun *tat* 'that, it' is as a correlative to the relative pronoun *yat* 'which'. An example of this use would be the construction:

(2)	Bring that which is here	*tam ānaya ya ihāsti.*

The pronoun 'that' in (2) is called the *prakramyamāṇa-parāmarśaka* pronoun, that is, a pronoun whose syntactic construal depends on something else (viz. a relative pronoun) in the currently uttered sentence.

Gadādhara notes that a pronoun is occasionally used when the object signified is well-known or famous. For example:

(3)	That lunar phase is the lovely one	*kalā ca sā kāntimatī,*

where the use of the pronoun suggests that the phase in question is known to everybody (*Ādarśa*, 1892: 163). Speijer, who notes this use, remarks that it resembles the Latin *ille*, and cites as another example, '*tat koṭimatkuntiśamābharaṇaṃ madhonaā*, that (renowned) thunderbolt, Indra's attribute' (1886: 206). This is a deictic use of the pronoun when the reference is known to the audience.

A fourth use, isolated by his commentators[6] but not by Gadādhara himself, is illustrated by the sentence:

(4)	Those eyes now cast around disconsolately.	*te locane pratidiśaṃ vidhure kṣipanti.*

The pronoun is held here to refer back to the person's eyes as they were previously, presumably calm. This is dubbed the *anubhūta-parāmarśaka* pronoun, a pronoun 'which refers to something already perceived'. Lasnik's (Lasnik, 1989: 90–1) sentence: 'Well, he's left', said of someone who has just walked out of the room, and is thus no longer perceptually present might be an English version of this use. This fourth use is again deictic, and perhaps for that reason is not distinguished by Gadādhara from the third.

To summarize, the pronouns, 'this' and 'that' (*adaḥ*) are purely deictic, while the pronoun 'it' (*tat*) has an anaphoric, a correlative and a pair of deictic uses.[7] Gadādhara's discussion centres on the anaphoric use of a pronoun. His account of such constructions represents an important application of his semantic framework.

9.2 Pronouns, Anaphora, and Speakers' Thoughts

Consider the meaning of the pronoun 'it', as it occurs anaphorically in sentences like (1a) and (1b):

(1) a. There is a pot here—bring it.

b. There is a cloth here—bring it.

Gadādhara makes a number of assumptions about the pronoun 'it' here. First, he takes the pronoun in these cases to be an indexical referring expression, referring in (1a) to a certain pot and in (1b) to a certain piece of cloth. If the antecedent noun were itself a referring expression (for example, a proper name or demonstrative), this assumption would be quite uncontroversial. As Neale (1990: 168) notes, the idea can be implemented in a number of different ways; in §9.3, I will consider various possibilities, including Gadādhara's own suggestion. The problem arises when the antecedent is a description, and descriptions are taken to be quantifiers. For then an alternative is to claim that the pronoun functions like a bound variable, taking (1a), for example, as stating that $(\exists x)(x$ is a pot & x is here & x is to-be-brought). The pronoun in 'Every potter loves his pots' is used in this way, and pronouns used like the variables of quantification theory cannot be construed as referring expressions.[8]

Recent work on anaphora, however, has shown that one cannot always take a pronoun whose antecedent is a quantified phrase to be bound by that quantifier. One argument is that the pronoun might not be in the same sentence as its antecedent, as when we say 'There is a pot here. Please go and get it.' If the pronoun were a bound variable, there would be cross-sentential binding, by the quantifier in 'There is a pot here' of the pronoun in the consequent 'Please go and get it'. To permit such cross-sentential binding, however, would entail that we could give the truth-condition only of whole discourses, and not of individual sentences (cf. Heim 1982: 10–11). Another influential argument is given by Evans (1985: 104–47). Consider the sentence:

(2) Smith owns few sheep and Jones beats them.

This sentence intuitively entails that Jones beats all the sheep Smith owns. The bound-variable truth-condition for the sentence, however, is that there are a few sheep which are both owned by Smith and beaten by Jones, a truth-condition consistent with there being sheep owned by Smith but not beaten by Jones. There is indeed a general syntactic criterion for determining which anaphors are bound by their antecedents and which are not (cf. Neale 1990: 173). The criterion is that only a pronoun which is *c-commanded* by a quantifier antecedent Q is interpretable as a variable bound by Q. One noun phrase NP1 c-commands another NP2 if, in the syntactic tree for the sentence, the first branching node dominating NP1 also dominates NP2. In sentences like (2), the antecedent does not c-command the pronoun. It follows too that the pronoun in Gadādhara's (1a) is not bound, even if we take the antecedent (which in Sanskrit is a determinerless NP) to be a quantifier. A simplified syntactic tree diagram for (1a) is given in Figure 9.1.[9]

In this tree, the first branching node dominating the NP 'a pot' does not also dominate the pronoun 'it'. So the pronoun is not c-commanded by its antecedent. Thus, whether or not Gadādhara is right to say that the pronoun in (1a) is a referring expression, it should not be thought of as a case of bound anaphora.

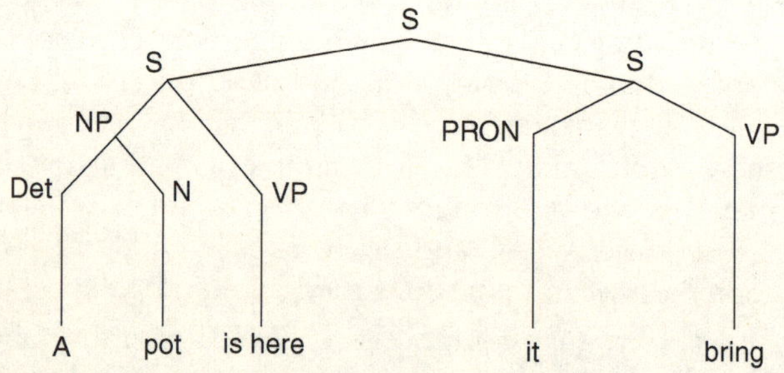

FIGURE 9.1

Gadādhara's next assumption is that the semantic reference of the pronoun is determined by the speaker's thoughts in uttering it. This second feature of Gadādhara's account places his theory within the domain of so-called 'pragmatic' theories of anaphora, of the sort suggested by Lasnik (1976), Kripke (1977), and Lewis (1979), according to which the reference of the pronoun is determined by considerations relating to the salience of a particular object in the given context, rather than by any semantic relationship with its antecedent. Such accounts treat anaphors as deictic pronouns of a special sort. Let O^u be the property being-the-object-thought-of-by-the-speaker (*vatṛbuddhiviṣayatā*), the thought in question being the referential intention governing her utterance *u* of the pronoun 'it'. A first attempt to give the meaning of the pronoun might be to say that an utterance of the pronoun refers to that object about which the speaker is thinking of and intending to refer to in uttering it. This theory of pronominal reference was indeed current among earlier Navya-Naiyāyikas.[10] Gadādhara (1927: 97–101) begins his discussion by criticizing their account:

> Pronouns too, just like the word 'sun-&-moon' (*puṣpavant*), are not ambiguous but have a univocal meaning.
>
> Now a pronoun reveals [such an object as] a pot, a cloth, and so on, as is the object of the speaker's thought, under a specific mode being-a-pot, being-a-cloth, and so on; not under the mode being-an-object-of-the-speaker's-thought (*vaktṛbuddhisthatva*). For the sentence 'There is a pot here—bring it!' induces [in the hearer] the understanding that [he is commanded to perform] an action of bringing whose Patient is a pot. No doubt of the form 'Does the specific action of bringing have as its Patient a pot, or not?' then arises; this is established by everyone's experience. So the property delimiting the scope (*śakyatāvacchedaka*) of a pronoun is not being-an-object-of-the-speaker's-thought but being-a-pot, being-a-cloth, and so on. [The problem] however, is that it is impossible to have a univocal meaning [for the pronoun], when [its reference] is in this way delimited by many different properties, as there are in the case of 'sun-&-moon', for [the hearer] cannot [then] come to understand a particular object as qualified merely by a single property. For this reason, the ambiguity of pronouns is hard to keep in check.
>
> But neither is it acceptable to concede the ambiguity. For then a person who has not learned that the pronoun 'it' produces verbal behaviour concerning what is delimited by a given property, will not know that the meaning of 'it' is what is delimited by that property. Even if previously mentioned, a thing delimited by that property cannot be understood by that person from the word 'it'.

The problem in giving the meaning of the anaphoric pronoun, as with any indexical expression, is one of avoiding the threat of ambiguity. The problem is compounded here, if, as Gadādhara claims, the anaphoric pronoun is an intensional indexical. Gadādhara draws an analogy between the pronoun and the word '*puṣpavant*', a word which means both the sun and the moon. '*Puṣpavant*' is not ambiguous term; when used, it refers simultaneously and plurally to both the sun and the moon. It is a term which is not ambiguous even though two different modes are implicated in its meaning—hence the analogy with the pronoun.

Someone who understands (1a) takes 'it' to be referring to a particular as determined by being-a-pot: if one heard the command and then wondered what sort of object one was being asked to bring, one would not have understood the sentence correctly. Likewise, in (1b), it is understood as referring to a particular as determined by being-a-cloth. Matilal significantly links this with the explanation of the hearer's actions. He says (1985: 389) that 'There are strong reasons for believing that in the sentence ["There is a chair, bring it"], the word "it" presents the chair, the object, as having a necessary connection with chairhood. For nobody would claim here that the hearer who understands the sentence could bring a non-chair, something else that may be qualified by being in the thought of the speaker, and still be said to behave correctly. For successful behaviour, the hearer must be aware, from the utterance of "it", of the actual chair qualified by chairhood.' In order to understand the sentence, the hearer must identify the reference of the pronoun, and to do this she must work out to which object the speaker intends to refer. But she will have no chance whatsoever of identifying the speaker's intended reference unless she knows what type of object the speaker is thinking about, and herself singles out the object as being of the same type.[11] When the speaker intends to refer to an object, she intends to refer to it in a certain way. The speaker's choice of antecedent reveals to the audience which way the object is intended to be referred to, for it is generally true that speakers choose their antecedent descriptions with the aim of manifesting the way they intend the referent to be identified. It would thus seem that the speaker will choose such an antecedent clause as not only singles out the intended referent, but manifests the way it is to be identified.[12]

The linguistic rule for the anaphoric pronoun must therefore prescribe the cognitive mode under which the reference is to be thought of, and, moreover do so in such a way that the mode varies from utterance to utterance. It would be as wrong to say that the reference of every utterance is determined by the same property, viz. being-thought-of-by-the-speaker, as the analogous claim appeared to be for the first person pronoun 'I'. So this first attempt cannot be right, for it places no constraint at all on the mode under which hearers identify the reference.

Perhaps then we can do better if we formulate the meaning of the pronoun as follows. On hearing the sentence (1a) for the first time, the hearer comes to learn that the pronoun can refer to pots (things determined by pothood). Likewise, on hearing (1b), for the first time, the hearer comes to learn that the pronoun can refer to cloth (things determined by clothhood). Each time one hears the pronoun used in such a context, the hearer expands the scope of things to which it is believed to refer. The problem for this is that we are able to understand the pronoun even when we hear it used anaphorically on a particular antecedent for the first time. Someone who knows the meaning of the anaphoric pronoun can understand an assertion of 'There is a lamp here—bring it', even though she has never heard the pronoun used anaphorically with 'lamp' before. One cannot, of course, avoid this objection by taking the union to be infinite, without rendering the meaning of the pronoun unlearnable. These are just the 'infinity' and 'discrepancy' arguments of §2.2, applied now to intensional indexicals.

Neither is it any better to take the property being-the-object-thought-of-by-the-speaker-of-*u* to be a running element of the determiner type. Gadādhara insists, however, that hearers do not identify the reference of the pronouns as that object which is thought about by the speaker, but as a pot, as a cloth, and so on. Now, if we want the mode element itself to be indexical, we might perhaps take it to be determined by the speaker's intentions. In particular, suppose we let M^u be the *mode* in the speaker's governing intention to refer to some object in uttering *u*. The utterer of (1a.) thinks of an object under the mode pothood; the utterer of (1b.) thinks of an object under the mode clothhood; and so on. Let us denote the second-order property being-the-mode-in-the-speaker's-thought (*vaktṛ-buddhi-viṣayatāvacchedakatva*) as $\underline{M}^u$. This is a property whose extension is a first-order property like pothood. Perhaps then we can formulate the meaning clause for the anaphoric pronoun as asserting that the meaning of an utterance of 'it' is such an object as possesses the mode thought of by the speaker. Gadādhara considers such a proposal next:

> [In reply to this last point] the following might be said. The qualifying properties being-a-pot and so on have in common (*anugamaka*) the fact that they are objects of the speaker's thought. Furthermore, the hearer's knowledge of meaning has the form 'The meaning of the word "it" is that which has the qualifier thought of by the speaker' (*buddhistha-prakāravāṃs tatpadaśakyaḥ*). And that item of knowledge takes for its content each and every [such] property via a 'generic perception' (*sāmānya-pratyāsatti*) [of every instance of the universal] being-a-qualifier-thought-of-by-the-speaker. Thus, it is not impossible [for the hearer to] understand a property not previously [learned as a qualifier of 'it'].
>
> Even if one does not concede [the theory that there is] 'generic perception' [of all the instances when cognizing a universal], [one must concede that] an object not previously encountered can be understood

> [on hearing a word] if it is the locus of such a qualifier as is the cognitive mode (*viśeṣyatāvacchedaka*) in the knowledge of the meaning of the term, even though it is not [itself] in the content of the knowledge of meaning. Likewise, it is not impossible for a property not previously encountered to be understood [on hearing the word 'it'] if it is the locus of such a common feature (*anugata-rūpa*) as is the delimitor of the property of being a cognitive mode (*dharmitāvacchedakatāvacchedaka*) in the knowledge of the meaning of the term, without it being in the content of the knowledge of meaning. This is because there is no rule that an object in the content of the hearer's comprehension of a sentence (*śābdajñāna*) must also be in the content of the hearer's knowledge of meaning (*śaktidhī*).

The doctrine of 'generic perception' is rather strange. It is advanced as a solution to the problem of our knowledge of universal correlations 'all *F* are *G*'. It might seem that, in order to know a universal correlation, one has to know, of every individual *F*, that it is *G*, and hence be acquainted with every *F*. Some Naiyāyikas proposed, as a solution, that it is possible to perceive every instance of a universal property if one is acquainted with the universal itself. This is the doctrine of 'generic perception'. If one accepts this doctrine, then one can reply to the objection that (4) above, construed as a potentially infinite union, would be unknowable. One could claim to be acquainted with every possible mode, even ones with which one has not previously heard as an antecedent of the pronoun, on the ground that each is an instance of the property $\underline{M}^{u}$.

A rather better idea is that the above meaning rule does not contain a specific reference to every mode. Rather, it should be read as quantifying over modes, as asserting that for every utterance of 'it', there is some qualifying mode in the speaker's thought, and the utterance of 'it' means an object under that mode. The hearer's knowledge of the meaning will not then be list-like, and indeed will not mention specific modes at all.

Gadādhara, however, thinks that the property $\underline{M}^{u}$ will then still have to be a mode in the hearer's understanding:

> [This reply is wrong], for the property being-a-qualifier-thought-of-by-the-speaker cannot be the common element in the delimitors of the scope [of the term 'it'] (*śakyatāvacchedakānugamaka*) without also being the delimitor of the property of being a delimitor of the scope (*śakyatāvacchedakatāvacchedaka*). But if it is the delimitor of that, then there would follow the unacceptable consequence that it too will appear systematically in the hearer's comprehension, as a qualifier of the property like being-a-pot, which is the delimitor of the scope. [This is unacceptable] because the property being-a-pot is a qualifier by itself in the hearer's comprehension.

Gadādhara now introduces the idea which will inform his final account, namely that the property $\underline{M}^u$ is an *indicator* and not a determiner of the specific modes. He goes to some lengths to show that the claim must be understood in the right way. We cannot simply *say* that $\underline{M}^u$ is an indicator, for then we could equally well say that the first-order modes are indicators as well:

> If it is as an indicator (*upalakṣaṇa*) that [the property being-a-qualifier-thought-of-by-the-speaker] is the common element in the delimitors of the scope, then even the common element in the referents will be an indicator as well. But then how is it that the meaning is a thing-as-determined (*viśiṣṭa*)?
>
> [In reply to this point] the following might be considered. In order to block the unacceptable position that the word 'substance' is properly understood [by a hearer whose thought of an object] has as its qualifier the property being-a-pot, we agreed that the meaning [of the word 'substance'] is thing-as-qualified [by the property being-a-substance]. Since we have already done that, there is no problem in having the common element [for the word 'it'] as the property being-a-qualifier-thought-of-by-the-speaker, taken to be an indicator.
>
> [This is wrong:] Suppose we let the various qualifiers which are in the content of [the hearer's] knowledge of the meaning [of 'it'] have as their common element the property being-a-qualifier-thought-of-by-the-speaker. Then the [conclusion that] pronouns are ambiguous really is irrepressible. This is because the unity of what is delimited follows, directly or indirectly, only from that delimitor which is unitary; and the property being-a-qualifier-thought-of-by-the-speaker is not such. If the meaning [of 'it'] is unitary on account of [that] unitary indicator, then the property being-a-qualifier-thought-of-by-the-speaker, being an indicator, could give a common element even to the delimitors of the scope of the reference of an [ambiguous] word like 'Hari'. [In that way,] all ambiguity is eliminated.
>
> Therefore, it is not right [to say] that the hearer's knowledge of meaning, in the form 'The meaning of the word "it" is that which has the qualifier thought of by the speaker,' is what leads to a hearer's comprehension, which is a memory whose qualifier is the property being-a-pot by itself. From an item of knowledge like 'the thing connected to the elephant-driver is a thing of a generic type', there can be no memory whose qualifier is the type elephanthood by itself. For when one knows a relation [between *a* and *b*], and the qualifier [*b*] appears by itself, then a cognition of the relatum [*a*] triggers a memory in which the qualifier [*b*] appears by itself. Just as, when one knows a relation [between an *F* and a *G*], each relatum appearing in a given way, then a cognition of one relatum in its way [*F*] triggers a memory

> of the other relatum appearing in its way [*G*]. As it would contradict this, the desired position [above], that a cognition of one relatum having as its qualifier a qualified property leads to a memory whose qualifier is an unqualified property, is impossible. There would otherwise be the unacceptable consequence that there could be no rule as to when a memory has its qualifier delimited by another property and when the qualifier appears by itself.
>
> There is indeed no escape even for those who do not accept [the theory of] 'generic perception'. [For them] there can be no presentation of a previously unencountered property, by itself, when this is not in the content of the [hearer's] knowledge of meaning. Nor can a cognition having as its qualifier a property as qualified by the property being-the-cognitive-mode-in-the-speaker's-thought be allowed to cause a cognition whose qualifier is a property by itself, for that too would violate the same-qualifier rule.

Gadādhara's point is that, as knowledge of meaning figures in the causal explanation of the hearer's understanding of utterances, the meaning relation must have a specific form. If the norms on understanding are such that understanding an utterance involving a given term requires the understander to think of its reference under a specific mode, then the referent must appear under that mode in the understander's tacit knowledge of its meaning. We have already decided what is involved in properly understanding utterances of the anaphoric pronoun. So the remaining problem is to specify the meaning rule in such a way that having knowledge of such a meaning rule causally explains understanding. Gadādhara finally states his own position:

> Here is my view. When the properties which are the delimitors of the scope (*śākyatāvacchedaka*), like being-a-pot, being-a-cloth, and so on, appear in the divine mandate [for 'it'] as qualified by the indicator property being-the—mode-in-the-speaker's-thought, they appear there as the modes in the hearer's thought caused by the word 'it'. The mandate has the form ⟨From the word 'it', that which is delimited by such a property as is the mode in the speaker's thought is to be understood⟩, or else ⟨the word 'it' makes understood that which is delimited by such a property as is the cognitive mode in the speaker's thought⟩. Although the content of this mandate resides in the uncollected (*ananugata*) properties being-a-pot, being-a-cloth, and so on, the meaning [of 'it'] is unitary because those properties are delimited by the property being-the—mode-in-the-thought-of-the-speaker-who-uttered [the word]. In just the same way, while the content of the mandate for the word 'pot' or 'cloth' resides in the many individual pots, the meaning of the word 'pot' is unitary because those objects are delimited by the common property being-a-pot. Again,

while the content of the mandate for the word 'beast' resides in the many individual tails and so on, the meaning of the word 'beast' is unitary because they are delimited by the common property being-a-tail.

This is the difference [between the two cases]. The properties being-a-pot, being-a-tail, and so on are said to be 'qualifying features' (*viśeṣaṇa*), because they appear as modes in the hearer's thought produced by the word ['pot', etc.]. However, the mandate [for 'it'] does not make the property being-the—mode-in-the-thought-of-the-speaker appear as a mode in the hearer's thought produced by the word 'it', but merely as being co-located with such modes. So it is called an indicator.

While the content of the mandate for the ambiguous word 'Hari' resides in the uncollected properties being-Hari, being-a-lion, and so on, the meaning of the word 'Hari' is not unitary because those properties are not delimited by any common property. In the divine mandate, the properties being-Hari and so on appear as modes in the hearer's thought produced by the word 'Hari', without appearing as qualified by any indicator property. So the ambiguity [of such words] is not lost.

I suggest that we formulate Gadādhara's proposal for the meaning clause for the anaphoric pronoun as follows. An utterance u of the pronoun 'it' means an object under such a mode as is the mode under which the speaker thinks of the object which is the intended reference of her utterance of 'it'. In other words, the meaning of an utterance of the anaphoric pronoun is an ordered pair $\langle x, y \rangle$ such that $x \in y$ and $y \in \underline{M}^u$. Notice that the property $\underline{M}^u$ is an indicator of the mode under which the hearer identifies the referent, but is not itself a mode. So the problem with the earlier account does not arise. Notice too that the meaning rule states only that the referent is an object which possesses the speaker's identifying mode, and not that the referent is itself the speaker's intended referent. I will consider this surprising feature of Gadādhara's proposal below.

Gadādhara's theory of anaphora is that the anaphoric pronoun is an intensional indexical, the intensional element of which is 'indicated' by the description 'being the mode under which the speaker intends to refer to the object'. He is careful to formulate his view with precision, for he notes that there is a pitfall which must be avoided. We have the following criterion of synonymy: two expressions are synonymous iff they have the same constant meaning element. If, however, we allow such features as 'the mode in the speaker's referential intention' to be constant meaning elements, then this criterion appears to collapse. Take an ordinary ambiguous noun like 'Hari', which can mean either a lion or the lord Viṣṇu, and which is judged by the usual criterion to be ambiguous because it has two distinct constant meaning elements, being-a-lion and being-Viṣṇu. Now even such disparate properties can be collected under the general rubric 'the mode in the speaker's referential intention', for whenever the speaker uses the expression 'Hari', she intends it to mean one or the other of its two meanings. So it seems that if this feature is allowed to be the constant meaning element of an expression, then even paradigmatically ambiguous expressions like cease to be analysable as ambiguous.

Gadādhara's reply to this is that, although it is true that waterhood and Viṣṇuhood fall under the general rubric 'the qualifying feature in the speaker's referential intention', this is not a normative truth; that is to say, it is not true in virtue of the linguistic rules which govern the use or interpretation of the word 'Hari'. The linguistic rules governing the pronoun *explicitly* introduce this rubric as the constant determinant of the pronoun's token-reflexive mode. However, in the rule or rules for the ambiguous word 'Hari', no such invariant feature is mentioned. The meaning of 'Hari' is:

(3) $\mathcal{M}_2 \mid$ 'Hari' $\subseteq L \times \{L\} \cup V \times \{V\}$

where L = being-a-lion and V = being-Viṣṇu, and these modes are not collected under a single description.

Gadādhara is in effect emphasizing that there are two quite distinct ways in which consideration of speakers' intentions can enter a theory of meaning. They can enter either as criteria for disambiguation, that is, for deciding which of a plurality of meanings is the one intended. Alternatively, they can enter as criteria for fixing semantic value, if there are expressions whose semantic value is a function of the speaker's intended reference. The pitfall considered above depends on confusing these two quite separate roles.

9.3 The Pragmatic Theory of Anaphora

The pragmatic theory of anaphora claims (i) that anaphors are referring expressions, and (ii) that the reference of an anaphor is an object made salient in the conversational context by the speaker's utterance of the antecedent phrase. In a typical case, the speaker uses a referring expression (proper name, demonstrative) to refer to an object she has in mind. Consider the following sentence:

(1) Venus is a planet; it orbits the Sun.

The pragmatic account claims that the planet Venus has been raised to conversational salience by the speaker's utterance, and thereby becomes a target for a quasi-deictic use of the later utterance of the pronoun 'it'. The distinction between properly deictic and anaphoric uses of the pronoun is merely in the sorts of contextual feature on which the hearer must depend in ascertaining the reference of the pronoun. A deictic pronoun will often be accompanied by an act of pointing, from which the hearer is able to ascertain that a certain object in the perceptual environment is the object to which the speaker intends to refer, and hence which is the semantic referent of the pronoun. An anaphoric pronoun will be uttered in the context of an antecedent sentence, and the utterance of this sentence will perform an analogous evidential function. A leading motivation of the pragmatic theory, and I think Gadādhara's motivation as well, is to give a unitary explanation of deictic and anaphoric uses of the pronoun. The pragmatic theory stands in contrast to the account of anaphora which explains the reference of the pronoun by appeal to a 'coreference rule' specifying that the pronoun has the same reference as its antecedent.

A feature of the pragmatic theory is that an object can be raised to conversational salience even if the speaker does not refer to it by name, but only indefinitely describes it. The idea is developed in a well-known passage by Lewis (1979, [1983: 243]):

> I may say 'A cat is on the lawn' under circumstances in which it is apparent to all parties to the conversation that there is some one particular cat that is responsible for the truth of what I say, and for my saying it. Perhaps I am looking out of the window, and you rightly presume that I said what I did because I saw a cat; and further (since I spoke in the singular) that I saw only one. What I said was an existential quantification; hence, strictly speaking, it involves no reference to any particular cat. Nevertheless it raises the salience of the cat that made me say it. Hence this newly-most-salient cat may be denoted by brief definite descriptions, or by pronouns, in subsequent dialogue: 'No, it's on the sidewalk.' ... Thus although indefinite descriptions—that is, idioms of existential quantification—are not themselves referring expressions, they may raise the salience of particular individuals in such a way as to pave the way for referring expressions that follow.

We might likewise paraphrase Gadādhara's account of (2):

(2) There is a pot here—bring it.

Some one particular pot is brought to conversational salience by the speaker's utterance 'There is a pot here', and this pot is denoted by the subsequent pronoun in 'bring it'. Recall, however, that for Gadādhara, it is the speaker's thought that is criterial in determining the reference of the pronoun. We must therefore consider the relation between conversational salience and the speaker's beliefs and intentions.

One view is that an object is raised to conversational salience just in case it is the object the speaker has in mind. The speaker has in mind and intends to refer to some one particular object, and it is that object which their subsequent utterance of the pronoun refers to. Kripke (1979), for example, suggests that we should appeal to the distinction between the semantic reference of an expression, its reference as fixed by the linguistic rules, and the speaker's reference, that is, the object which the speaker has in mind, and intends to talk about, when she utters the expression in question. Kripke argues that, even if an indefinite description does not refer semantically, it may be used to make a speaker's reference to a particular pot, and we can then say that the semantic reference of the anaphoric pronoun is the speaker's reference of the antecedent noun.

Such a view invites the natural objection (cf. Neale 1990: 178) that there are cases of unbound anaphora in which the speaker has no particular object in mind, and does not use the antecedent description referentially. Neale's example is:

(3) An insurance agent is coming to see me today. I'm sure s/he just wants to sell me a policy.

The speaker is not using the description to express an object-directed thought about some one particular insurance agent, but believes that whichever agent it is who is coming wants to sell a policy. Neale claims that the existence of such examples shows that 'although the salience-based suggestion seems to work for some cases—specifically, those in which the antecedent description is used referentially—it cannot be the whole story.'

I remarked earlier that Gadādhara does *not* say that the reference of the pronoun is an object about which the speaker is thinking. What he says is that the reference is such an object as qualified by the mode in the speaker's thought. Perhaps we can now understand his reason for saying this. For Gadādhara's formulation covers both the case where the speaker has in mind a particular object, and the case where he is thinking about an object by description. In the latter case, the mode in the speaker's thought is still said to be being-a-pot, even if he utters 'There is a pot here—bring it' with no particular pot in mind (cf. §6.2). The claim is that the content of speaker's thoughts determines only that the conversationally salient object is a pot, but other considerations determine which pot is the most salient one. Note that it is conventionally implicated by (2) and (3) that the speaker believes that there is just one object of the type described by the speaker in the salient conversational context. If there is indeed just one object of the relevant sort, then that object will be raised to conversational salience by the speaker's utterance, even though it does not feature in the content of an object-directed thought.

It seems to me that Lewis's formulation allows for such a possibility. Lewis says that there is 'some one particular cat that is responsible for the truth of what I say, and for my saying it.' Singular propositions can be the truth-makers of existential assertions. Likewise, beliefs whose content is purely existential can 'embody' information from particular objects if the object is appropriately causally related to the belief (cf. Evans 1982: 127–8). The speaker's belief that a cat is on the lawn might be produced by their observing fresh scratch marks on the tree trunk, or by their being told that such is the case by someone who has seen the cat. In a loose sense, it is 'about' that cat, in that it embodies information from the particular cat. In their subsequent utterance 'Catch it', the pronoun refers to the particular cat made salient by being the cat about which the speaker's belief carries information.

A related objection to the pragmatic approach is formulated by Geach (1972: 11) as follows. For the sake of clarity, let us modify our example from the imperative (2) to the declarative (4):

(4) There is a pot here—it is blue.

Suppose now that there are two pots in the relevant place, one blue and one red. Geach observes that, 'We might find ourselves trying to determine the truth value of [4] by asking wh[ich pot] a man would have in mind when he uttered or wrote down th[is] sentence' (1972: 11). Geach, however, thinks that 'such psychologizing is really not necessary', since, he says, the truth conditions for (4) are independent of what its utterer had in mind. The general point is that there are cases of anaphora in which the contribution of the pronoun is determined entirely by 'sentence-internal' semantic rules and not by pragmatic considerations. Particularly striking are cases involving definite description antecedents which are semantically complete. Neale (1990: 180) calls such cases 'descriptive anaphora'. His example is:

(5) The inventor of the wheel was a genius. I suspect s/he ate fish on a daily basis.

The speaker does not know who invented the wheel, and does not even have a thought 'about' them based on a causal or informational link. The speaker merely reasons that whoever invented the wheel must have eaten fish regularly. Here is an example from an Indian text. In the *Tarkasaṃgraha*, Annambhaṭṭa says that:

(6) The substratum of sounds is [known as] *ākāśa.* It is unitary, all-pervasive, and eternal.[13]

As we saw in the previous chapter, the description 'the substratum of sounds' is used in the stipulation introducing the theoretical name 'ākāśa'. That the substance which is the possessor of sounds is unitary, all-pervasive, and eternal is known by reflection on its defining properties, and not by acquaintance with the substance *ākāśa* itself. Once again, the speaker's thought is purely descriptive, embodying no information from the object to which the pronoun purports to refer.

There are two main accounts of descriptive anaphora, the most detailed expositions of which are given by Evans (1985) and Neale (1990). Evans says of that the pronoun in sentences like (5) and (6) that 'they are not genuine singular terms in the sense in which ordinary proper names and demonstrative expressions are; rather they are *singular terms whose reference is fixed by description*' (1985: 104, my italics). The description in question is that which is embedded in the antecedent clause, and this leads Evans to reformulate his view as that these pronouns 'refer to the object or objects which verify the antecedent clause' (1985: 222). He calls pronouns whose reference is fixed by a description in the antecedent, 'E-type' pronouns, to distinguish them from deictic and bound uses. To illustrate his idea, consider again the pronoun in (6). The specification of the reference of the pronoun 'it' will take the form (cf. 1985: 124–5):

For any *x*, the denotation of 'it' in the second clause of (6) is *x* iff *x* is the only substratum of sounds.

The other approach rejects the claim that descriptive anaphors refer at all. Instead, the claim is that the pronoun *goes proxy for a definite description* extracted from the antecedent clause, and that definite descriptions are to be given a quantificational analysis. Neale calls such pronouns, 'D-type' pronouns, and proposes the following generalization for cases like (5) and (6) (in which the antecedent is 'maximal'):

If x is a pronoun that is anaphoric on, but not c-commanded by, a maximal quantifier '[*Dx*: *Fx*]' that occurs in an antecedent clause '[*Dx*: *Fx*](*Gx*)', then x is interpreted as '[the *x*: *Fx*]' (1990: 183).

The idea is that the pronoun in (6) goes proxy for the description 'the substratum of sounds'. So (6) is to be paraphrased as:

(7) The substratum of sounds is [known as] *ākāśa*. The substratum of sounds is unitary, all-pervasive, and eternal.

Let us try to formulate an account like Gadādhara's along parallel lines. Call pronouns for which his account is true 'G-type' pronouns. G-type pronouns are quasi-deictic referring expressions, and they have a sense as well as a reference. The sense is a mode by which the reference is discriminated. Generally, then, a G-type pronoun is interpreted as a complex quasi-deictic 'that *F*', where the matrix '*F*'? of the pronoun is a noun recovered from the antecedent clause, for example 'pot' or 'cloth'.

Gadādhara assumes that the utterance of the antecedent is non-defeasible evidence of the mode in speaker's thought, for he says that someone who hears (2) cannot then be in any doubt as to whether the mode in the speaker's thought is pothood or not. This is nothing but the principle that someone who sincerely and comprehendingly says that *p*, thereby expresses a thought that *p*. Slips of the tongue are possible, however, and it seems that it is the uttered antecedent clause itself rather than the speaker's thought, which is then criterial in determining the matrix of the complex quasi-deictic. If a speaker who utters (2) does so by mistake, intending really to refer to a cup, it seems more natural to take the pronoun as going proxy for 'that pot' than 'that cup'.

We may formulate a principle for the interpretation of G-type pronouns as follows:

If x is a pronoun that is anaphoric on, but not c-commanded by, a quantifier '[*Dx*: *Fx*]' that occurs in an antecedent clause '[*Dx*: *Fx*](*Gx*)', then x is interpreted as the complex quasi-deictic 'that *F*'.

A complex quasi-deictic 'that *F*' refers to the most salient *F* in the conversational context. Notice that such deictics differ from ordinary (perceptual) deictics in that their reference is to what is conversationally salient, rather than what is perceptually salient.[14] As we have seen, an object can be conversationally salient even if it is neither present in the context of communication, nor the object in a speaker's object-directed thought. (2) is to be interpreted as:

(8) There is a pot here; bring that pot.

This account shares features with both the D- and the E-type approaches. It agrees with Evans in treating unbound anaphoric pronouns as referring expressions, but it takes the antecedent clause as not merely fixing the reference of the pronoun, but as giving the meaning. The importance of giving such pronouns a sense as well as a reference is seen in the following consideration. Suppose there were no constraint on the mode under which a hearer thinks of the reference of the pronoun. In particular, imagine a hearer who understands (4) by forming the belief that:

(9) There is a pot here; that substance is blue.

Clearly, such a hearer has not heard the pronoun as anaphoric on its antecedent description. This hearer, unlike someone who understands (4) correctly, is not in a position to infer that the pot is blue. Nothing ensures that the object to which the demonstrative 'that substance' refers is the object which verifies the antecedent clause. Someone who correctly understood (4) will form the belief that:

(10) There is a pot here; that pot is blue.

Knowledge of (10) does place the hearer in a position to infer that the pot is blue, for such a hearer understands the pronoun as anaphoric.

We see here the connection between Gadādhara's account and the epistemological conception of language, the coneption which sees the possibility of testimony as informing the theory of meaning. Someone who understands an utterance of (4), sincerely and truly spoken by a credible speaker, is in a position to know that the pot here is blue. This puts a constraint on the sense of the pronoun, the mode under which anyone who understands it must think of its referent. If the pronoun in (4) is referential, then it must have the same sense as 'that pot', if an utterance of (4) is to be epistemically apt in the right way. The epistemology of anaphora is what drives Gadādhara's analysis of anaphors as intensional indexicals.

It is clear that the pronoun is not treated as what Geach has called a 'pronoun of laziness', a pronoun which replaces its antecedent and 'ha[s] no point beyond variety, perhaps elegance, of expression' (1980: 151). He suggests that the pronoun 'he' in 'Smith broke the bank at Monte Carlo, and he has recently died a pauper' is a pronoun of laziness, because it is eliminable without any alteration of meaning by replacing it with its antecedent, 'Smith'. While each use of such a pronoun inherits the descriptive content, if any, of its antecedent, it is clear that pronouns with indefinite descriptions as antecedents cannot be construed as pronouns of laziness, for (4) would then be paraphrased incorrectly as 'There is a pot here; a pot is blue'.

In giving pronouns a descriptive content, Gadādhara's approach shares a feature with the D-type approach. What would he say of the purely descriptive cases like (6)? This would be paraphrased as:

(11) The substratum of sounds is [known as] ākāśa. That substratum of sounds is unitary, all-pervasive and eternal.

The problem is that we cannot regard the phrase 'that substratum of sounds' as genuinely deictic, given that the matrix in this phrase is complete, and indeed that the pronoun refers to whatever verifies that matrix. Recall, however, Gadādhara's theory of theoretical or descriptive names: a theoretical name is a referring expression with a uniquely satisfied descriptive sense. The pronoun here is synonymous with such a name; so, in (6), the pronoun goes proxy for the name 'ākāśa'. We must therefore emend the formulation of Gadādhara's theory of anaphora slightly. An anaphoric pronoun goes proxy either for a complex quasi-deictic 'that *F*', or for a descriptive name synonymous with 'the* *F*', where in either case the matrix '*F*' is a noun recovered from the antecedent clause.[15]

Scott Soames (1988, 1989a, 1989b) has written on the importance of treating anaphoric pronouns as having intensional as well as extensional content. He considers the possibility that attributing to pronouns a sense as well as a reference can account even for pronouns which are c-commanded by their antecedents. His argument (1989b: 198–200) is based on the behaviour of pronouns within propositional attitudes contexts, such contexts being sensitive to the intensions as well as the extensions of the embedded sentences. Consider:

(12) Mary says, and believes, that John loves his mother.

Soames points out that:

> If *his* is a directly referential term referring to John, then ... it is sufficient for Mary to assert and believe this proposition that she sincerely and comprehendingly asserts 'John loves his [pointing to John] mother' in a context in which *his* is a demonstrative referring to John. Note, there is no requirement in these truth-conditions that Mary may realize that the referent of the demonstrative is the person whose love she is reporting .... This conflicts with our ordinary understanding of at least one anaphoric interpretation of (12). That understanding is one in which Mary is characterized as asserting and believing a proposition

> that attributes to John the property of loving one's own mother (1989: 199, my numbering).

Soames conjectures that an anaphoric pronoun c-commanded by an antecedent singular term is not a directly referential term, but has the same semantic content or sense[16] as the singular term which c-commands it. Now:

> (12) is true iff Mary asserts and believes the proposition (13) expressed by the anaphoric interpretation of 'John loves his mother'.
>
> (13) John loves John's mother.
>
> ... We may imagine the proponent of the anti-direct reference analysis as maintaining that in order to believe and assert (13), one must recognize the purported lover as the person whose mother is said to be loved. In short, the proposal is to appeal to fine-grained semantic content, over and above reference, to ensure that 'John loves his mother' characterized John as an own-mother-lover (1989: 200, my numbering).

The idea, then, is that noticing that pronouns have a sense as well as a reference gives us a way to answer Evans' (1985: 216) criticism of the pragmatic account, that assimilating the anaphoric uses of pronouns to the deictic uses, leaves us with no hope of a unified account of the assimilated group and the c-commanded uses.

There are, however, problematic cases for this proposal, to do with the behaviour of pronouns embedded within speech reports. Soames, indeed, does not think that the intensional account will work, because of examples like (14):

(14) Mary told John that he wasn't John.

This is true if Mary addresses John (not realizing that the addressee is John) with the remark 'You aren't John'. The intensional account of the anaphoric pronoun here, however, would require her to assert and believe the proposition that John is not John. It seems that, when so embedded, pronouns do not behave in their customary manner; indeed the pronoun in (14) should not be construed as having an intension at all.

What such examples show is that we need a principled way to distinguish between the two cases. In fact, Gadādhara discusses the behaviour of pronouns *within speech reports* in some detail, in the context of his examination of the meaning of the first person pronoun. Indeed, he even offers a criterion to distinguish between the two sorts of anaphora which these examples illustrate. Let us see what he has to say.

9.4 Quotation and Reference

The first person distinguishes all three grades of meaning isolated by Gadādhara: reference (*śakya*), mode (*śakyatāvacchedaka*), and constant or running element (*anugama*). The reference of the word 'I' is a person. Each time I utter the pronoun, it refers to the same person, myself. The reference is indexical: for each person it is true that when they utter the pronoun it refers to them. What then serves as the distinguishing property of the reference, the mode under which I identify myself when I use the word 'I', or by which you identify me when you hear me use the word? Gadādhara claims that each person has a uniquely identifying property (*tadvyaktitva*), the property of being Caitra or the property of being Maitra, and it is in virtue of a person's possessing this property that they identify themselves as the reference of their utterance of the word 'I'.

Difficult questions arise in connection with this notion of a uniquely identifying individual property. It is natural to suppose that each of us, when we single ourselves out in thought, do so in a way quite distinct from the way in which we individuate other objects or are individuated by others. Each person, as Frege (1967: 25–6) puts it, 'is presented to himself in a particular and primitive way, in which he is presented to no-one else'. However, if my uniquely identifying property is something to which only I have access, how do others understand my use of the first person pronoun? If a hearer is to understand Caitra's assertion 'I am going out', she must, according to Gadādhara, think of Caitra under his uniquely identifying mode Caitra-hood. Yet the property Caitra-hood is surely a property to which Caitra alone has access. Frege noted the same difficulty with his doctrine of private senses: 'Lauben may want to communicate with others. He cannot communicate a thought which he alone can grasp. Therefore, if he now says "I have been wounded", he must use the "I" in a sense which can be grasped by others, perhaps in the sense of "he who is speaking to you at this moment" ...'. Frege, in the Nyāya terminology, suggests here taking the running element of the pronoun to be a determiner of the mode under which hearers think of the reference.[17]

We have not in fact as yet isolated the constant or running element in the meaning of the first person pronoun. Clearly, the reference is not constant. Neither is its mode, if it has one, for that is here a property which uniquely identifies the reference. Nevertheless, the first person pronoun is not ambiguous, since someone who has learnt the meaning of the first person is able to understand each and every utterance of it, no matter who has made that utterance. It must therefore be possible to identify a common element in the meaning. Gadādhara's main concern is to give a plausible account of what this might be. The most natural hypothesis is that any utterance of the word 'I' is governed by a rule of the form ⟨'I' refers to its utterer⟩, so that the common property (*anugama*) is the property being-its-utterer.

The view which results is summed up by Gadādhara as follows (1927: 112):

> The meaning of the first and second person pronouns is not merely a person, but one who is an Agent of uttering or hearing. It is not in general right to say that the mode is by definition such a property as Caitrahood which is indicated by a running element in the [simple] form of being-the-utterer or being-the-audience .... The meaning of the first person pronoun is that object which is delimited by such a property [viz. Catirahood] as is indicated by the property being-the-Agent-of-that-very-utterance (*sva-uccāraṇa-kartṛtā*).

The distinctions between reference, mode, and invariant element are clearly drawn here. Gadādhara emphasizes that the rule must be of the form ⟨'I' refers to *its* utterer⟩ and not merely ⟨'I' refers to *an* utterer⟩. The rule must be self-reflexive, for if it were not, then *my* utterance of 'I' could refer to anybody who happens to utter the word 'I'.

According to Gadādhara, then, the meaning of an utterance of 'I' is an ordered pair, the first member of which is the speaker, and the second member of which is the individual essence of the speaker. How ought we to formulate this in our notation? We have that S^u is the property being-the-speaker-of-utterance-*u*-of-'I'. The extension S^u of this property is a class having the speaker of that utterance as its sole member. We need a device for generating a name of the individual essence of the utterer. The device employed by the Naiyāyikas is a new abstraction suffix: *tad-vyaktitva* 'being that very object'. The individual essence of the speaker is the property of being that very object which is the speaker.[18]

Gadādhara finds such an account problematic for a reason which is of great philosophical interest. His worry concerns the role of the pronoun when it occurs within a direct report of someone else's speech, that is, within Sanskrit *iti* constructions. For clearly, when a sentence containing the first person pronoun is quoted by somebody, its reference is to the person who first made the utterance, and not to the person now uttering it. Gadādhara makes the point with a nice example (1927: 118):

> Now if the meaning of the first person pronoun is its utterer, and the meaning of the second person pronoun is its hearer, then on hearing

> the sage's utterance 'The lord killed the demon, saying "When I kill you, the gods will roar then and there",' one would not understand that the lord is the Agent [of the killing] and the demon is the Patient, for the lord is not the speaker and the demon is not the hearer. Instead, wrongly construing the sentence, one would think that the sage is the Agent and [his audience] Suratha is the Patient, for it is the sage who utters the sentence and it is Suratha who hears it.

The problem arises because Sanskrit syntax does not display pronominal substitution within speech reports. In order to report someone's speech in English, one must transform the pronouns in such a way as to preserve the original reference. To report Caitra who has said 'I am going out', we must say in English 'Caitra said that *he* is going out'. Thus, in English, pronouns are always evaluated with respect to their own context of utterance. The *iti* particle, however, is quotational,[19] so pronouns embedded within an *iti* clause ought to take the values they had with respect to the context in which they were originally uttered. That, however, is in tension with the claim that when the first person pronoun is uttered, it refers to its utterer. The problem, then, is to explain how it is that a report of the form 'Caitra said "I am going out" ' means the same as 'Caitra said he is going out', and does not state that Caitra said that I, the speaker, am going out.

Gadādhara offers two distinct solutions to the problem, both of which are of considerable merit. I will call them the 'paratactic' and the 'anaphoric' solutions. Let me consider each in turn.

The paratactic solution. What is it to report another's speech? On the paratactic proposal, it is to produce another token of the originally uttered sentence, and to ascribe the content of that token to the reportee. A speech report is a statement of the form: S said '*p*'. The paratactic construal takes this to have two semantically independent components—an utterance of '*p*', followed by an attribution of that utterance to S. In contemporary philosophy of language, Donald Davidson has done the most to promote the role of paratax in speech reports (cf. Davidson 1968 [1984: 93–108]). Sanskrit grammar, however, *naturally* lends itself to such an interpretation. For the quotation particle *iti* is a demonstrative adverb, meaning 'so' or 'thus'. It is natural then to regard the quoted utterance as being demonstrated by the quotation particle. Following the grammarians, Gadādhara uses the term 'repeating utterance' (*anuvāda*) to denote the quoted utterance: it is an utterance which repeats or retokens the original utterance of the reportee. In reporting someone's speech, we reproduce the utterance, and then, demonstratively pointing to it, attribute it to the reportee. Gadādhara's example above would be construed as:

(1) When I kill you, the gods will then and there roar. So-said the lord.

The problem now is clear. If the utterance above is evaluated with respect to the reporter's context of utterance, then the pronouns have their referents fixed with respect to the reporter's context, rather than the reportee's.

Gadādhara's first solution is to insist that, when a pronoun occurs as embedded in a *repeating* utterance, its reference must be fixed with respect to the context of the original utterance. He labels such occurrences 'dependent' (*paratantra*), and says (1927: 119):

> The explanation is that the [above] rule covering the use of the first person pronoun is [applicable only to] an independent utterance, that is an utterance not depending on another person's self-referential utterance. In the above example, the sage's utterance is not of such a sort, since it depends on the lord's utterance as the route to denoting its referent. So the sage is not denoted by the first person pronoun.
>
> The qualification that an independent utterance not be another's *self-referential* utterance is introduced because even a statement like 'I am going out' may depend upon [another] utterance, perhaps the question 'Who is going out?'.

The usual rule, that ⟨'I' refers to its utterer⟩ applies directly only if the utterance is an independent one, that is, it is not an utterance whose function is to reproduce another's utterance and hence quote it. When the utterance is quotational, the reference of the pronoun is the utterer of the original utterance. The new rule is:

A token of 'I' embedded in an utterance *u* refers to the speaker

(i) of *u*, if *u* is not a repeating utterance, and
(ii) of *u*´, the repeated utterance, if *u* is a repeating utterance.

This entails that the original utterance is a self-ascription, something Gadādhara explicitly stipulates as necessary. According to the paratactic solution, then, the logical form of an indexical speech report 'S said "I am Φ" ' is that S produced some past utterance to the effect that S is Φ. More formally:

(2) 'S said "I am Φ"' is true iff $\exists t\, \exists u$ [S uttered *u* at *t* & *u* is true iff S is Φ].

Substantially the same theory is cited by Rāmarudrī, while commenting on the *Dinakarī* (in Viśvanātha 1988: 580–1):

> *Dinakarī*: In like manner, the mode (*śakyatāvacchedaka*) of the word 'I' is a property like Caitra-hood, Caitra being the utterer of the independent utterance at the time of utterance. To amplify: we said 'independent' because, in the verse 'On account of my words with you, the king ...', it is not the case that the poet is the person conveyed by the word 'my'.[20]
>
> *Rāmarudrī*: *In like manner* ... '*śakyatāvacchedaka*' is supplied from the previous line. *Independent* .... The intended meaning here is that the property Caitra-hood is collocated with the property of being the Agent of the independent utterance. It is to be understood that the utterance is of the intended word 'I' qua designator whose meaning is of such a sort. An utterance is independent if it is not subservient to another utterance. More fully, 'another' utterance is one which is a repetition (*anuvāda*). *It is not the case that the poet is the person conveyed* .... The intended meaning is that the poet is not the person conveyed by the word 'I' because, although the poet is the utterer of the word 'I' embedded in the verse, [his utterance] is a repetition of another person's utterance.[21]

The idea behind this solution can be generalized. The claim is that it is possible to isolate situations in which an indexical statement must be evaluated, not with respect to its own context of utterance, but with respect to some other circumstance. For Gadādhara, the relevant situation is that the utterance is a paratactic repetition of some earlier utterance, a fact which is marked syntactically by the use of quotation marks or the *iti* particle. The same analysis can be applied to examples involving temporal, spatial, and other indexicals. Consider for example, the statement 'The Prime Minister will say the pound has been devalued'. Here, the 'has been' might refer either to times before the time of this report, or to times before the PM himself speaks. I might for example be asked on Monday what the PM will say in his speech on Friday, and know that the Chancellor intends to devalue the pound on Wednesday.

The anaphoric solution. Although the paratactic solution has much to recommend it, and is I think worthy of further elaboration,[22] Gadādhara himself believes that it is problematic. It obviously presupposes that there exists a previous utterance now being repeated, but Gadādhara suggests that this will not always be the case. He points out that quotation is used not only to report others' speech but also to report others' beliefs, and these need not have been explicitly articulated. Seeing a proud-looking person, we might say '"I am a pandit"—that's what he believes'. In belief attribution, the quoted, dependent utterance need not be a repetition of any earlier utterance. Gadādhara therefore introduces a new definition of dependence in the light of such cases. He says (127: 120):

> In fact, an independent utterance is an utterance containing the pronoun which does not depend on an intention to convey the meaning of the statement containing the pronoun, when that statement is the grammatical object of another statement.
>
> In the case of a repeated utterance there is not such independence, because the repeated statement, which contains the pronoun, is used to denote its meaning as the grammatical object of another statement, namely 'The lord said "..."'.
>
> The meaning of the first person pronoun in dependent cases is the Agent of the other sentence, whose Patient is the meaning of the sentence containing the pronoun.

Gadādhara's second proposal is to regard any belief or speech report as being a single sentence whose grammatical object is a second sentence. When that second sentence contains a first person pronoun, the rule is that it refers anaphorically to the Agent of the main sentence. So in the sentence 'The lord said "when I kill you the gods will roar" ', the pronoun 'I' and the name 'the lord' corefer. Likewise, in the sentence ' "I am a pandit"—that's what he believes', the pronoun 'I' corefers with 'he', the Agent of the main sentence. The new rule is:

> A token of 'I' in a statement *u* refers to
>
> (i) the utterer of *u*, if *u* is not the grammatical object of a speech or attitude report, or
>
> (ii) to the Agent of the report, if it is.

This is the most explicit statement of an anaphoric co-reference rule I have yet come across in Gadādhara or any other Nyāya philosopher of language. What the anaphoric solution states is that the logical form of an indexical speech report 'S said "I am Φ"' is that S said of S that he is Φ. More formally:

(3) 'S said "I am Φ"' is true iff $\exists x\,[x$ said that x is Φ & $x = \mathrm{S}]$.

There is no quantification over past utterances here, and so the analysis is applicable to intentional reports other than saying; for example believing, wishing, and desiring.

Gadādhara's new criterion is that dependent occurrences of the pronoun 'I', that is, occurrences within the *iti*-clause of a speech or attitude report, corefer with the noun denoting the Agent of the report. If we use an underscore to indicate coreference, we can write the analysis of the sentence (4) as (5):

(4) Mary said that she is happy.

(5) *Mary said*: 'I am happy'.

A very similar criterion can be used to solve the puzzle at the end of the last section. That puzzle concerned the sentence:

(6) Mary told John that he is not John.

The pronoun 'he' (or the spoken pronoun 'you') cannot inherit the intension of its antecedent, the name 'John', for then Mary would be represented as uttering a tautology. Note, however, that its occurrence is dependent, in Gadādhara's new sense. We can formulate a new coreference rule for 'you' analogous to the rule for 'I': a dependent occurrence of the pronoun 'you' corefers with the noun encoding the Target in the report. Thus (7) is:

(7) Mary told *John*: '*You* are not John'.

Belief reports involving self-attribution, reports of the form 'The man believes himself to be a pandit', are sometimes labelled '*de se*' belief reports, to distinguish them from *de re* and *de dicto* reports. Castañeda, one of the first to consider the special features of *de se* reports, forcefully argued against the anaphoric analysis (Castañeda 1966). Castañeda pointed out that it is possible for someone, Caitra say, to believe that Caitra is bald, without believing that he himself is bald. Caitra might, for example, see his reflection in a mirror but not realize that the reflection is his. Analogously, Caitra might be told and believe that the oldest man in the room is bald, but fails to realize that he himself is that man. Believing that some uniquely identified person has some property need not entail believing that you yourself have that property, even if it is you who are so identified: you must further recognize that you are the uniquely identified person. As we have seen, Gadādhara has two separate accounts of anaphora for the two separate sorts of cases. In one case, an anaphoric pronoun is a complex quasi-deictic with both sense and reference. In the other case, a co-reference rule fixes the reference of the anaphoric pronoun. *De se* belief reports would be analysed as involving the complex deictic sort of anaphor, and not the co-reference-rule-governed sort of anaphor.

We have seen in this section that Gadādhara introduces two important semantic hypotheses. One is that it is possible for indexical utterances to be evaluated with respect to non-actual contexts. The other is that ordinary indexical terms can function anaphorically when they are within the grammatical object of a propositional attitude verb. They reveal Gadādhara to be a philosopher wrestling with problems which are at the very heart of modern concerns in linguistics and the philosophy of language.

Notes

[1] Note the *Nyāyakośa*, s.v. *anugama*: 'the running element = the basis-for-usage. For example, cowhood is the running element of all cows' (*anugama* = *anugata-pravṛttinimittam, yathā sarveśāṃ ghaṭānām anugamo ghaṭatvam*).

[2] Thus Harinātha: 'To be an indicator is to be a property [mentioned in the meaning rule] which does not appear in that part of the content of the meaning rule which specifies the type of mode in thoughts produced by hearing the word' *upalakṣaṇatvaṃ pada-janya-bodhīya-viṣayatāvacchedakatvāvacchinna-śaktiviṣayatā-śunyatvam.* (1929: 91)

[3] See also Bhattacharyya (1996: 54–6). Bhattacharyya emphasizes the use of the relative pronoun as a bound variable rather than as an index.

[4] For other discussions of Gadādhara's account of pronominal reference, see Matilal (1985a), Visvabandhu (1992), and Bhattacharyya (1997). I would like to acknowledge a particular debt to Sibajiban Bhattacharyya, with whom I read portions of the *Śaktivāda* dealing with anaphora, along with its *Ādarśa.*

[5] Certain arguments from the recent literature on anaphors depend crucially on a consideration of their behaviour with indefinite rather than definite antecedents; I will consider them below.

[6] Cf. *Ādarśa* (1892: 162): *tatpadaṃ prakramyamāṇa-prakrānta-prasiddhānubhūtārtha-parāmarśaka-bedhāc caturdhā bhavati. See also Mañjūṣā* (1929: 159).

[7] Pāṇini (*Pāṇini-sūtra* 2.4.32–3) notes a difference in stress when a pronoun is used deictically and when it is used in anaphora (*anvādeśe*). Cf. Speijer (1886: 204).

[8] See Geach (1980) for the classic defence of this claim.

[9] I take it that there is an implied sentential connective in this sentence.

[10] Cf. Gaṅgeśa (1901: 617), and Jayadeva's *Āloka* thereon.

[11] Compare Evans: 'If [the hearer] understands the remark, he will know which object is meant; and in the normal course of events (i.e. without assistance from others, etc.), he will know which object is meant only if he thinks of it in the particular way intended by the speaker' (1982: 315–16).

[12] The idea of a complex speaker-demonstration is employed by Taylor (1980: 192) in constructing truth-theories for indexical languages. He notes that 'in many cases, a speaker apparently demonstrates his object as an *F*, supplementing any indicative gestures with a specification of some feature *F* the object possesses'.

[13] *śabdaguṇakam ākāśaṃ tat ca ekaṃ vibhu nityaṃ ca.* Annambhaṭṭa (1983: X).

[14] As Evans (1982: 128) notes, such demonstatives differ from usual demonstratives in that 'the object of the thought will be individuated by reference to its role in the operations of the informational system'. Treating the pronoun as a demonstrative of this sort does not entail that the hearer is able to individuate its reference independently of its being the source of the information currently encoded in one's existential beliefs.

[15] This formulation takes Gadādhara even closer to the D-type account. Neale (1990: 200) indeed is tempted by the idea that 'unbound pronouns that are anaphoric on definite descriptions used referentially can receive either D-type or referential interpretations.'

[16] He comments that 'By "senses" I mean whatever names (and indexicals relative to contexts) contribute to propositions. No restrictions are placed on what senses might be—purely conceptual contents, conceptual contents plus referents, linguistic expressions plus referents, etc. (1989: 200, n.7)'. In Gadādhara's theory, a sense is a mode plus referent.

[17] For further discussion of both problems, see Forbes (1989: 20–1). Forbes suggests that it is sufficient for communication that the hearer can employ a sense whose reference is the speaker's private sense. The idea of private individual essences is also discussed by Chisholm (1981).

[18] For Jagadīśa's notion of a *tadvyaktitva* 'individual property of x', see *Nyāya-kośa* s.v. *tadvyaktitva*, Mañjūṣā (1929: 122). Notice here Peacocke's useful distinction between token- and type- senses: anyone who thinks 'I am Φ' thinks of himself in the same type of way, a type which is tokened differently in each person (cf. Peacocke 1981, 1983: 108). The *tadvyaktitva* functor is the nearest we get to the idea of a sense-type in Nyāya. Notice too that the behaviour of this functor, to form a name the individual essence of the object which is in fact the F, resembles Kaplan's 'Dthat', which forms a demonstrative of the object which is in fact the *F* (Kaplan 1979). Jagadīśa suggests that the individual essence of a thing *a* is the property being-identical-to-*a* and that this is nothing but the thing *a* itself (*tadvyaktitvañ ca tādātmyena saiva vyaktiḥ*; cf. Matilal 1985a: 387). If he is right, then individual essences cannot be the senses of proper names, as they would not satisfy Frege's Constraint (I owe the point to Dirk Boeckx).

[19] The use of *oratio obliqua* is rare in Sanskrit, though it exists in the 'accusative with participle' construction (as in 'He saw me coming'). Cf. Speijer (1886: 379–88). This is also the nearest one gets in Sanskrit to constructions like 'He said that I was coming', in which the embedded pronoun has 'wide-scope'. We must, however, distinguish between two grades of quotation: *strict* quotation,

in which the quoted statement is mentioned, and *weak* quotation, in which is it is used (cf. Geach 1972: 166–74). Weak quotation is heard in constructions like 'Quine said that truth is "a device for disquotation" ', or 'The Lord said "let there be light" ' (if this were strictly quotational, the Lord would have had to have said it in English). As Geach notes, usual arguments for preferring *oratio obliqua* to *oratio recta* in the analysis of speech reports falsely assume quotation to be strict. Likewise, *iti*-constructions are only weakly quotational.

[20] *evam ahampadasya tatkālīna-svatantroccārayitṛ-caitratvādi / svatantryoktyā ca vācyas tvayā madvacanāt sa rājetyādau na matpadāt kaver bodha ityāstāṃ vistaraḥ //*

[21] evam asmatpadasyeti // *prāguktena śakyatāvacchedam ityanenānveti* // svatantreti // *svatantroccāraṇakartṛtva-samānādhikaraṇa-caitratvādikam ityarthaḥ / uccāraṇam caitādṛśārtha-vācakatvenābhimatasyāsmacchabdasyaiveti dhyeyam / uccāraṇe svatantratvaṃ cānyoccāraṇānadhīnatvaṃ / anyoccāraṇān anuvādakatvam iti yāvat //* na kaver bodha iti / / *padyasthāsmacchabdasya uccāraṇakartṛtve 'pi kave parakīyoccāraṇānuvādakatvāt taduccaritāsmacchabdān na kaver bodha iti bhāvaḥ /*

[22] In another paper 'Indexicals and Indirect Discourse' (unpublished), I try to show that Gadādhara's version of the *paratactic* solution can cope with an objection raised against the paratactic analysis by Higginbotham (1986) and Segal (1989), that it cannot explain the ambiguity in sentences like 'S said that she is Φ', which can be heard either as a self-attribution or as a statement about a third-party. Gadādhara's *anaphoric* solution, of course, has no trouble accounting for the ambiguity.

Bibliography

Abercrombie, J. (1830). *Inquiries concerning the Intellectual Powers and the Investigation of Truth.* Edinburgh: Waugh and Innes.

Annaṃbhaṭṭa (1983). *Tarkasaṃgrahadīpikā on Tarkasaṃgraha,* edited and translated by G. Bhattacharya. Calcutta: Progressive Publishers.

Audi, R. (1998). *Epistemology.* London: Routledge.

Bach, K. (1987). *Thought and Reference.* Oxford: Clarendon Press.

Bealer, G. (1982). *Quality and Concept.* Oxford: Clarendon Press.

Bhartṛhari (1963). *Vākyapadīya. Kāṇḍa* III.1, with Helārāja's commentary. Edited by K.A. Subramania Iyer. Poona: Deccan College.

_____ (1970). *Mahābhāṣya-dīpikā.* Edited by K.V. Abhyankar and V.P. Limaye. Pune: Bhandarkar Oriental Research Institute.

Bhatta, V.P. (1990). *Vyutpattivāda* (Theory of the Analysis of Sentence Meaning). Delhi: Eastern Book Linkers.

_____ (1994). *Gadādhara's Śaktivāda* (Theory of Expressive Power of Words). Introduction, translation, Notes, and Sanskrit Text. Vol. 1 [Vol. 2: 1995]. Delhi: Eastern Book Linkers.

Bhattacharya, D.C. (1951). *Bāṅgalīr Sarasvat Avadān, pratham bhāg, Baṅge Navyanyāyacarccā.* Calcutta: Sahitya Parisat.

Bhattacharya, K. (1979). 'Les arguments de Jagadīśa pour éstablir la parole comme moyen de connaissance vrai (*pramāṇa*)'. *Journal Asiatique,* 267: 155–89.

_____ (1980). 'Nāgārjuna's Arguments against Motion: Their Grammatical Basis,' in G. Bhattacharya et al. (eds), *A Corpus of Indian Studies: Essays in Honour of Professor Gaurinath Sastri.* Calcutta: Sanskrit Pustak Bhandar.

_____ (1980b). 'The Grammatical Basis of Nāgārjuna's Arguments: Some Further Considerations,' *Indologica Taurinensia,* 8–9: 35–43.

Bhattacharya, K. (1985). 'Nāgārjuna's Arguments against Motion', *Journal of the International Association of Buddhist Studies,* 8: 7–15.

_____ (1995). 'Back to Nāgārjuna and Grammar', *The Adyar Library Bulletin,* 59: 178–89.

Bhattacharyya, S. (1987). *Doubt, Belief and Knowledge.* New Delhi: Indian Council of Philosophical Research.

Bhattacharyya, S. (1990). *Gadādhara's Theory of Objectivity, Containing the text of Gadādhara's Viṣayatāvāda with an English Translation and Explanatory Notes, Parts I & II.* New Delhi: Indian Council of Philosophical Research.

_____ (1996). *Gaṅgeśa's Theory of Indeterminate Perception (Nirvikaplakavāda).* Part I. New Delhi: Indian Council of Philosophical Research.

_____ (1997). 'Gadādhara's Theory of Meaning of Pronouns', in P. Bilimoria and J.N. Mohanty (eds), *Relativism, Suffering and Beyond: Essays in Memory of Bimal K. Matilal.* New Delhi: Oxford University Press.

Bilimoria, P. (1988). *Śabdapramāṇa: Word and Knowledge.* Studies in Classical India 10. Dordrecht: Kluwer Academic Publishers.

Blake, B.J. (1994). *Case.* Cambridge: Cambridge University Press.

Bloomfield, L. (1933). *Language*, London: George Allen & Unwin.

Boghossian, P.A. (1989). 'The Rule-Following Considerations', *Mind*, 98: 507–49.

Boer, S.T. and Lycan, W.G. (1986). *Knowing Who.* Cambridge, Mass.: The M.I.T. Press.

Brough, J. (1953). 'Some Indian Theories of Meaning', *Transactions of the Philological Society*, 161–76.

Brown, J. (1998), 'Natural Kind Terms and Recognitional Capacities', *Mind*, 107: 275–304.

Burge, T. (1974). 'Truth and Singular Terms', *Nous*, 8: 309–25.

Cardona, G. (1967). '*Anvaya* and *Vyatireka* in Indian Grammar'. *Adyar Library Bulletin*, 31–2 (V. Raghavan Felicitation Volume): 313–52.

_____ (1974). 'Pāṇini's *Kārakas*: Agency, Animation and Identity', *Journal of Indian Philosophy*, 2: 231–306.

_____ (1975). 'Paraphrase and Sentence Analysis: Some Indian Views', *Journal of Indian Philosophy*, 3: 259–81.

Carnap, R. (1947). *Meaning and Necessity.* Chicago: Chicago University Press.

Castañeda, H-N. (1966). '"He": A Study in the Logic of Self-Consciousness', *Ratio*, 8.2: 130–57.

Chakrabarti, A. (1985). 'Plato's Indian Barbers: Classical Approches to the Problem of Singular Existence Denials', in B.K. Matilal and J.L. Shaw (eds), *Analytical Philosophy in Comparative Perspective*, Holland: D. Reidel.

_____ (1986). 'Understanding Falsehoods: A Note on the Navya-Nyāya Concept of *Yogyatā*', *The Journal of the Asiatic Society*, 28, pp. 10–20.

_____ (1994). 'Telling as Letting Know', in B.K. Matilal and A. Chakrabarti (eds), *Knowing from Words: Western and Indian Philosophical Analysis of Understanding and Testimony.* Dodrecht: Kluwer.

_____ (1997), 'Why Nyāya Remains Realist: Second Round', *Journal of the Indian Council of Philosophical Research*, 14, pp. 165–7.

Chakrabarti, K. (1975). 'The Nyāya-Vaiśeṣika Theory of Universals'. *Journal of Indian Philosophy*, 3, pp. 363–82.

Chakravarti, P.C. (1930). *The Philosophy of Sanskrit Grammar.* Calcutta: Calcutta University Press.

Chastain, C. (1975). 'Reference and Context', in K. Gunderson (ed.), *Minnesota Studies in the Philosophy of Science,* Vol. 7. Minneapolis: Minnesota University Press.

Chisholm, R.M. (1981). *The First Person: An Essay on Reference and Intentionality.* New York: Harvester Press.

Chomsky, N. (1986). *Knowledge of Language.* New York: Praeger.

_____ (1988), *Language and Problems of Knowledge: The Mangua Lectures,* Cambridge, Mass.: The MIT Press.

_____ (1995). 'Language and Nature', *Mind,* 104, pp. 1–62.

Coady, C.A.D. (1992). *Testimony: A Philosophical Study.* Oxford: Clarendon Press.

Coulson, M. (1976). *Sanskrit: An Introduction to the Classical Language.* Oxford: Hodder and Stoughton (Teach Yourself Books).

Coward, H.G. and K.K. Raja (1990). *The Philosophy of the Grammarians.* Encylopedia of Indian Philosophies, Vol. V. Delhi: Motilal Banarsidass.

Coward, H. (2003). 'Review of Ganeri', Philosophy East and West. University of Hawaii Press.

Davidson, D. (1980). *Essays on Actions and Events.* Oxford: Clarendon Press.

Davidson, D. (1983). 'Communication and Convention', *Journal of the Indian Council of Philosophical Research,* 1, pp. 13–25.

_____ (1984). *Inquires into Truth and Interpretation.* Oxford: Clarendon Press.

Davies, M. (1982). 'Individuation and the Semantics of Demonstratives'. *Journal of Philosophical Logic,* Vol. 11, pp. 287–310.

_____ (1987). 'Tacit Knowledge and Semantic Theory: Can a Five per cent Difference Matter', *Mind,* 96, pp. 441–62.

Derrett, J.D.M. (1956). 'An Indian Contribution to the Study of Property', *Bulletin of the School Oriental and African Studies,* XVIII (3), pp. 475–98.

_____ (1963). 'The Discussion of Marriage by Gadādhara: A Preliminary Investigation', *The Adyar Library Bulletin,* XXVII (1), pp. 171–99.

Deshpande, M.M. (1992). *The Meaning of Nouns: Semantic Theory in Classical and Medieval India (Nāmārtha-nirnaya of Kauṇḍa-bhaṭṭa).* Studies of Classical India, Vol. 13. Dordrecht: Kluwer Academic Publishers.

Donnellan, K. (1966). 'Reference and Definite Descriptions', *Philosophical Review,* 75, pp. 284–304.

Dummett, M. (1978), *Truth and Other Enigmas.* London: Duckworth.

_____ (1981). *Frege: Philosophy of Language* (2nd edn). London: Duckworth.

_____ (1991). *The Logical Basis of Metaphysics.* London: Duckworth.

Dummett, M. (1993). *The Seas of Language.* Oxford: Clarendon Press.

Evans, G. (1982). *The Varieties of Reference.* Edited by J. McDowell. Oxford: Clarendon Press.

——— (1985). *Collected Papers.* Oxford: Clarendon Press.

Fodor, J. (1988). *Psychosemantics.* Cambridge: MIT Press.

Forbes, G. (1987). 'Indexicals and Intensionality: A Fregean Perspective'. *The Philosophical Review,* 9, pp. 3–31.

——— (1990). 'The Indispensability of Sinn', *The Philosophical Review,* 49, pp. 535–63.

Frauwallner, E. (1966). 'Raghunātha Śiromaṇi', *Wiener Zeitschrift für die Kunde Sud-Asiens und Archiv für Indische Philosophic,* 10, pp. 86–207; 11: 140–208; 14: 161–208.

Frege, G. (1952). 'On Sense and Meaning', in P. Geach and M. Black (eds), *Translations from the Philosophical Writings of Gottlob Frege.* Oxford: Basil Blackwell.

——— (1967). 'The Thought: A Logical Inquiry', in P. Strawson (ed.), *Philosophical Logic.* Oxford: Oxford University Press.

Fricker, E. (1994), 'Against gullibility', in Matilal and Chakrabarti (eds), *Knowing from Words: Western and Indian Philosophical Analysis of Understanding and Testimony.* Dodrecht: Kluwer, pp. 125–61.

Gadādhara Bhaṭṭācārya (1892). *Śaktivāda, with Sudarśanācārya's Ādarśa.* Edited by Pt. Sudarśanācārya. Calcutta: Own Press.

——— (1927). *Śaktivāda,* with Kṛṣṇa Bhaṭṭa's *Mañjūṣā,* Mādhava Bhaṭṭācārya's *Vivṛtti* and Sāhitya Darśanācārya's *Vinodini.* Edited by G.D. Sastri. Benares: Kashi Sanskrit Series no. 57.

——— (1929). *Śaktivāda,* with Harinātha Tarkasiddhānta's *Vivṛtti.* Edited by G.D. Sastri. Benares: Kashi Sanskrit Series no. 77.

——— (1933). *Nirvikalpakasmaraṇavāda,* in B. Misra and Dh. Sastri (eds), *Vādavāridhi.* Benares: Chowkhamba Sanskrit Series nos. 421, 446.

——— (1970). *Gādādharī. A Commentary on Dīdhiti the Commentary by Raghunātha Śiromaṇi on the Tattvacintāmaṇi of Gaṅgeśa Udāphāya (anumāna-khaṇḍa).* Edited by V.P. Dvivedi, V. Bhattacharya, R. Sastri, and Dh. Sastri.—2nd edn. Revised by K. Jha and S. Vangiya. Varanasi: Chowkhamba Sanskrit Series.

——— (1990). *Viṣayatāvāda. Test, Translation and Power.* In S. Bhattacharyya, ed. (1990, Part II, ICPR Translation of Indian Philosophical Classics). New Delhi: Indian Council of Philosophical Research, Motilal Banarsidass Publishers.

Gadamer, H.G. (1975). *Truth and Method.* London: Sheed and Ward.

Ganeri, J. (1994). 'Review of Deshpande: The Meaning of Nouns', *Mind,* 103, pp. 83–6.

——— (1995). 'Vyāḍi and the Realist Theory of Meaning', *Journal of Indian Philosophy,* 23, pp. 403–28.

Ganeri, J. (1996a). 'The Hindu Syllogism: 19th century Perceptions of Indian Logical Thought', *Philosophy East and West*, 46.1, pp. 1–16.

_____ (1996b). 'Numbers as Properties of Objects: Frege and the Nyāya', *Studies in Humanities and Social Sciences, Vol. 3: Epistemology, Logic and Ontology after Matilal.* Shimla: Indian Institute of Advanced Studies, 3.2, pp. 111–21.

_____ (1999). 'Dharmakīrti Semantics for the Quantifier Only', in Shoryu Katsura, ed., *Dharmakīrti's Thought and Its Impact on Indian and Tibetan Philosophy.* Wien: Verlag der Österreichischen Akademie Der Wissenschaften, pp. 101–16.

_____ (2001a). 'Objectivity and Proof in a Classical Indian Theory of Number', *Synthese*, 129.3, pp. 413–37.

_____ (2001b). *Philosophy in Classical India: The Proper Work of Reason.* London: Routledge Press.

Ganeri, J. (forthcoming). *The Concealed Art of the Soul: Truth, Concealment and Self in Indian Thought.*

Gaṇgeśa Upādhyāya (1897). *Tattvacintāmaṇi (Pratyakṣakhaṇḍa)*, with Mathuranātha Tarkavāgīśa's *Rahasyam.* Edited by K. Tarkavagisa. Calcutta: Bibliotheca Indica.

_____ (1901). *Tattvacintāmaṇi (Śabdakhaṇḍa)*, with Mathuranātha Tarkavāgīśa's *Rahasyam* and Jayadeva Miśra's *Āloka.* Edited by K. Tarkavagisa. Calcutta: Bibliotheca Indica.

Gautama Akṣapāda (1936). *Nyāyasūtra*, with Vātsyāyana's *Bhāṣya*, Uddyotakara's *Vārttika*, Vācaspati Miśra's *Tātparyaṭīkā*, and Viśvanātha's *Vṛtti.* Edited by T. Nyayatarkatirtha and A. Tarkatirtha. Calcutta: Calcutta Sanskrit Series nos. 18–19.

_____ (1967). *Nyāyadarśana*, with Vātsyāyana's *Bhāṣya*, Uddyotakara's *Vārttika*, Vācaspati Miśra's *Tātparyaṭīkā*, and Udayana's *Nyāyavārtikka-tātparya-pariśuddhi.* Vol. 1, Chapter 1. Edited by A. Thakur. Mithila: Mithila Institute Series.

Geach, P.T. (1972). *Logic Matters.* Oxford: Basil Blackwell.

_____ (1980). *Reference and Generality: An Examination of Some Medieval and Modern Theories* (3rd edn). Ithaca: Cornell University Press.

Gerschheimer, G. (1987). 'La nature de la *śakti* (relation primaire mot-objet): À propos d'une branche dissidente des Navya-Naiyāyika'. *Bulletin d'Etudes Indiennes*, 5, pp. 109–58.

_____ (1996). *La Théorie de la Signification chez Gadādhara. Le Sāmānyakāṇḍa du Śaktivādavicāra.* Publications de l'Institut de Civilisation Indienne, Collége de France. Fasc. 65V, 2 vols. Paris.

Gettier, E. (1963). 'Is Justified Belief Knowledge?', *Analysis*, 23, pp. 121–3.

Gilbert, M. (1983). 'Agreements, Conventions and Language'. *Synthese*, 54, pp. 375–408.

Gillon, B. and R. Hayes (1982). 'The Role of the Particle Eva in (logical) Quantification in Sanskrit', *Wiener Zeitschrift für die Kunde Sšdasiens*, 26, pp. 195–203.

Gillon, B. (1997). 'Negative Facts and Knowledge of Negative Facts', in P. Bilimoria and J.N. Mohanty (eds), *Relativism, Suffering and Beyond: Essays in Memory of Bimal K. Matilal*. New Delhi: Oxford University Press.

Goldman, A. (1976). 'Discrimination and Perceptual Knowledge', *Journal of Philosophy*, 73, pp. 771–91.

Goldman, A. (1986). *Epistemology and Cognition*. Cambridge. Mass.: Harvard University Press.

Goodman, N. (1954). *Fact, Fiction and Forecast*. London: Athlone Press.

Grice, P. (1989). *Studies in the Way of Words*. Cambridge, Mass.: Harvard University Press.

Guha, D.C. (1968). *Navya-Nyāya System of Logic*. Varanasi: Bharatiya Vidya Prakasan.

Hattori, M. (1968). *Diṅnāga, on Perception*. Cambridge, Mass.: Harvard University Press.

Hayes, R. (1988). *Diṅnāga on the Interpretation of Signs*. Studies of Classical India, Vol. 9. Dordrecht: Kluwer Academic Publishers.

Heck, R.G. Jnr (1995). 'The Sense of Communication', *Mind*, 104, pp. 79–106.

Heim, I. (1982). 'The Semantics of Definite and Indefinite Noun Phrases', Ph.D. dissertation, University of Massachusetts, Amherst.

Herzberger, R. (1986). *Bhartṛhari and the Buddhists*. Studies of Classical India, Vol. 8. Dordrecht: Kluwer Academic Publishers.

Higginbotham, J. (1986). 'Linguistic Theory and Davidson's Program in Semantics,' in E. LePore (ed.), *Truth and Interpretation, Perspectives on the Philosophy of Donald Davidson*. Oxford: Basil Blackwell.

Hiriyanna, M. (1938). 'Vyāḍi and Vājapyāyana', *Indian Historical Quarterly*, 14, pp. 261–6.

Houben, J. (1995). *Bhartṛhari's Philosophy of Language*. Groningen: Egbert Forster.

Hume, D. (1975). *Enquiries Concerning Human Understanding and Concerning the Principles of Morals* (3rd edn). Edited by L.A. Selby-Bigge, notes by P.H. Nidditch. Oxford: Clarendon Press.

Ingalls, D.H.H. (1951). *Materials for the Study of Navya-Nyāya Logic*. Harvard: Harvard University Press.

Jagadīśa Tarkālaṅkāra (1930). *Sukti*, in Praśastapāda (1930).

——— (1934). *Śabdaśaktiprakāśikā*, with Kṛṣṇakānta's *Kṛṣṇakānti* and Rāmabhadra's *Prabodhini*. Edited by Dh. Sastri. Benares: Kashi Sanskrit Series 109.

Jayanta Bhaṭṭa (1936). *Nyāyamañjarī.* Edited by S.N. Sukla. Benares: Kashi Sanskrit Series 106.

Jayatilleke, K.N. (1963). *Early Buddhist Theory of Knowledge.* London: George Allen and Unwin.

Jhalakīkar, Bhīmācārya (1874). *Nyāyakośa or Dictionary of Technical Terms of Indian Philosophy.* Revised and re-edited by Vāsudev Śāstri Abhyankar. Bombay Sanskrit and Prakrit Series, 49. Pune: Bhandarkar Oriental Research Institute, 1976 (4th edition).

Kahrs, E. (1998). *Indian Semantic Analysis: The 'Nirvacana'Tradition.* Cambridge: Cambridge University Press.

_____ (2001). 'Review of Ganeri', *Times Literary Supplement.*

Kajiyama Yuichi (1973). 'Three Kinds of Affirmation and Two Kinds of Negation in Buddhist Philosophy'. *Wiener Zeitschrift für die Kunde Ssdasiens,* 17, pp. 161–75.

Kaplan, D. (1979). 'Dthat', in P. French et al. (eds), *Contemporary Perspectives in the Philosophy of Language.* Minneapolis: University of Minnesota Press.

_____ (1989a). 'Demonstratives: An Essay on the Semantics, Logic, Metaphysics and Epistemology of Demonstratives and Other Indexicals', in J. Almog, J. Perry, and H. Wettstein (eds), *Themes from Kaplan.* Oxford: Clarendon Press.

_____ (1989b). 'Afterthoughts', in J. Almog, J. Perry, and H. Wettstein (eds), *Themes from Kaplan.* Oxford: Clarendon Press.

_____ (1990). 'Words', *Proceedings of the Aristotelian Society,* Supp. Vol. LXIV, pp. 93–119.

Katsura, S. (1991). 'Diṅnāga and Dharmakīrti on *apoha*', in E. Steinkellner (ed.), *Studies in the Buddhist Epistemological Tradition.* Vienna: Institut für Tibetologie und Buddhismuskunde.

Kiparsky, P. and J.F. Staal (1969). 'Syntactic and Semantic Relations in Pāṇini', *Foundations of Language,* 5, pp. 83–117. Reprinted in J.F. Staal (1988).

_____ (1982). *Some Theoretical Problems in Pāṇini's Grammar.* Poona: University of Poona.

Kripke, S. (1977). 'Speaker's Reference and Semantic Reference', in P.S. French *et al.* (eds), *Contemporary Perspectives in the Philosophy of Language.* Minneapolis: University of Minnesota Press, 6–27.

_____ (1980). *Naming and Necessity.* Cambridge: Harvard University Press.

_____ (1982). *Wittgenstein on Rules and Private Language.* Oxford: Basil Blackwell.

Kumārila Bhaṭṭa (1903). *Tantravārttika.* Edited by G. Sastri. Benares: Benares Sanskrit Series.

Lasnik, H. (1976). 'Remarks on Coreference', *Linguistic Analysis,* 2, pp. 1–22.

Leibniz, G. (1902). *Discourse on Metaphysics,* Chicago: Open Court.

Lewis, D. (1975). 'Languages and Language', in K. Gunderson (ed.), *Minnesota Studies in the Philosophy of Science*, Vol. VII. University of Minnesota Press, 3–35. Reprinted in Lewis (1983).

_____ (1979). 'Scorekeeping in a Language Game'. *Journal of Philosophical Logic*, 8, pp. 339–59. Reprinted in Lewis (1983).

_____ (1983). *Philosophical Papers*, Vol. 1. Oxford: Clarendon Press.

_____ (1986). 'Causal Explanation', in *Philosophical Papers*, Vol. 2. Oxford: Clarendon Press.

Lipner, J. J. (1986). *The Face of Truth: A Study of Meaning and Metaphysics in the Vedāntic Theology of Rāmānuja*. London: MacMillan.

_____ (1997). 'Śaṅkara on Satyaṃ Jñānam Ānantaṃ Brahma', in P. Bilimoria and J.N. Mohanty (eds), *Relativism, Suffering and Beyond: Essays in Memory of Bimal K. Matilal*. New Delhi: Oxford University Press.

Lipton, P. (1990). 'Contrastive Explanation', in D. Knowles (ed.), *Explanation and its Limits*. Cambridge: Cambridge University Press.

Mammaṭa (1917). *Kāvyaprakāśa*, with V.R. Jhalakīkara's *Bālabodhinī*. Edited by N.D. Banhatti. Bombay: Government Central Press.

Matilal, B.K. (1968). *The Navyanyāya Doctrine of Negation*. Cambridge, Mass.: Harvard University Press.

_____ (1971). *Epistemology, Logic and Grammar in Indian Philosophical Analysis*. The Hague: Mouton. Reprinted 2005. New Delhi: Oxford University Press.

Matilal, B.K. (1982a). *Logical and Ethical Issues in Religious Belief*. Calcutta: University of Calcutta Press. Reprinted 2004, New Delhi: Chronicle Books.

_____ (1982b). 'Some Comments of Patañjali under 1.2.64', in S.D. Joshi and S.D. Laddu (eds), *Proceedings of the International Seminar on the Aṣṭādhyāyī of Pāṇini*. Pune, 1982, pp. 119–26. Reprinted in Matilal (2002).

_____ (1985a). 'Awareness and Meaning in Navya-Nyāya', in B.K. Matilal and J.L. Shaw (1985), pp. 373–91. Reprinted in Matilal (2002).

_____ (1985b). *Logic, Language and Reality: An Introduction to Indian Philosophical Studies*. Delhi: Motilal Banarsidass.

Matilal, B.K. (1986). *Perception: An Essay on Classical Indian Theories of Knowledge*. Oxford: Clarendon Press. 2nd edn, 1991.

_____ (1990). *The Word and the World: India's Contribution to the Study of Language*. New Delhi: Oxford University Press.

_____ (1991a). 'Some Issues in Nyāya Realism', address to the Radhakrishnan Centenary Conference Realism and Non-Realism, All Souls College, Oxford. Published in Matilal (2002).

_____ (1991b). 'Knowledge, Truth and *Pramātva*', in Daya Krishna and K.L. Sharma (eds), *The Philosophy of J.N. Mohanty*. Delhi: Motilal Banarsidass. Reprinted in Matilal (2002).

Matilal, B.K. (1995). 'A Realist Theory of Perception', in P.K. Sen and R.R. Verma (eds), *The Philosophy of P.F. Strawson.* New Delhi: Indian Council of Philosophical Research. Reprinted in Matilal (2002).

_____ (1998). *The Character of Logic in India.* Edited by J. Ganeri and H. Tiwari. New York: State University of New York Press. 2nd edition: New Delhi: Oxford University Press (2001).

_____ (2002). *Mind, Language and World: Collected Essays,* Volume 1. Edited by J. Ganeri. New Delhi: Oxford University Press.

Matilal, B.K. and R.D. Evans (eds) (1986). *Buddhist Logic and Epistemology.* Studies in Classical India 7. Dordrecht: Kluwer Academic Publishers.

Matilal, B.K. and J.L. Shaw (eds) (1985). *Analytical Philosophy in Comparative Perspective.* Dordrecht: Reidel.

Matilal, B.K. and A. Chakrabarti (eds) (1994). *Knowing from Words.* Dordrecht: Kluwer.

McCullock, G. (1989). *The Game of the Name.* Oxford: Clarendon Press.

McDowell, J. (1977). 'On the Sense and Reference of a Proper Name'. *Mind,* 86, pp. 159–85.

McDowell, J. (1980). 'Meaning, Communication and Knowledge', in Z. van Straaten (ed.), *Philosophical Subjects: Essays presented to P.F. Strawson.* Oxford: Clarendon Press.

_____ (1984). 'De Re Senses', In C. Wright (ed.), *Frege: Tradition and Influence.* Oxford: Basil Blackwell.

Mill, J.S. (1869). *A System of Logic.* New York: Harper.

Mishra, U. (1966). *History of Indian Philosophy.* Volume II. Allahabad: Tirabhukti Publications.

Mohanty, J.N. (1966). *Gaṅgeśa's Theory of Truth, Containing the Text of Gaṅgeśa's Prāmāṇya(jñapti)vāda.* Second revised edition (1989). Delhi: Motilal Banarsidass.

Mohanty, J.N. (1992). *Reason and Tradition in Indian Thought: An Essay on the Nature of Indian Philosophical Thinking.* Oxford: Clarendon Press.

Mukhopadhyay, P.K. (1992). *The Nyāya Theory of Linguistic Performance: A New Interpretation of Tattvacintāmaṇi.* Calcutta: K.P. Bagchi & Co.

Müller, M. (1853). 'Indian Logic', appendix to W. Thomson (1953), *An Outline of the Necessary Laws of Thought* (3rd edn). London: Longmans, Green and Co.

Nāgārjuna (1986). *The Dialectical Method of Nāgārjuna (Vigraha-vyāvartanī).* Translated by K. Bhattacharya, edited by E.H. Johnston and A. Kunst. Delhi: Motilal Banarsidass.

Neale, S. (1990). *Descriptions.* Cambridge, Mass.: MIT Press.

Patañjali (1962). *Mahābhāṣya,* with Kaiyata's *Pradīpa* and Nāgeśa's *Uddyota.* Edited by Vedavrata Acarya (4 Vols). Rohtak: Gurukul Jhajjara.

Patañjali (1968). *Mahābhāṣya, Paspaśāhnika.* Edited & Translated by S.D. Joshi and J.H.F. Roodbergen. Poona: Centre of Advanced Studies in Sanskrit.

Peacocke, C. (1981). 'Demonstrative Thought and Psychological Explanation', *Synthese*, 49, pp. 187–217.

_____ (1983). *Sense and Content.* Oxford: Oxford University Press.

_____ (1986). *Thoughts: An Essay on Content.* Oxford: Basil Blackwell.

Phaṇibhūṣaṇa Tarkavāgīśa (1940). *Nyāyaparicaya. Jatiya Siksaparisad Granthavali*, no. 5. Calcutta. Translated into Hindi by K. Jha (1968). Varanasi: Chowkhamba Vidya Bhavan.

Phillips, S. (1995). *Classical Indian Metaphysics: Refutations of Realism and the Emergence of 'New Logic'.* La Salle: Open Court.

_____ (2003). 'Review of Ganeri', *Mind.*

Pietroski, P.M. (1998), 'Actions, Adjuncts, and Agency', *Mind*, 107, pp. 73–111.

Plantinga, A. (1993). *Warrant and Proper Function.* Oxford: Oxford University Press.

Potter, K. (1977). *Encyclopedia of Indian Philosophies*, ii: *The Tradition of Nyāya-Vaiśeṣika up to Gaṅgeśa.* Delhi: Motilal Banarsidass.

Potter, K. and S. Bhattacharyya (1993), *Encyclopedia of Indian Philosophies.* Volume 6: *Indian Philosophical Analysis: Nyāya-Vaiśeṣika from Gaṅgeśa to Raghunātha Śiromaṇi.* Delhi: Motilal Banarsidass.

Potter, K. and S. Bhattacharyya (1995). *Encyclopedia of Indian Philosophies.* Volume 1: Bibliography (2 sections, revised). Delhi: Motilal Banarsidass.

Praśastapāda (1927). *Praśastapādabhāṣya*, with Jagadīśa's *Sukti*, Padmanābha Miśra's *Setu* and Vyomaśivācārya's *Vyomavatī.* Edited by G. Kaviraja and Dh. Shastri. Benares: Chowkhamba Sanskrit Series 374.

_____ (1971). *Praśastapādabhāṣya*, with Udayana's *Kiraṇāvalī.* Edited by J.S. Jetly. Baroda: Gaekwad Oriental Series 154.

Putnam, H. (1975). *Mind, Language and Reality: Philosophical Papers*, Vol. 2. Cambridge: Cambridge University Press.

Quine, W.V.O. (1960). *Word and Object.* Cambridge, Mass.: M.I.T. Press.

_____ (1970). 'Methodological Reflections on Current Linguistic Theory', *Synthèse*, 21, pp. 386–98.

_____ (1980), 'The Variable and its Place in Reference', in Z. Van Straaten (ed.), *Philosophical Subjects: Essays Presented to P.F. Strawson.* Oxford: Clarendon Press, pp. 164–73.

Raghunātha Śiromaṇi (1932). *Kiraṇāvalīprakāśadīdhiti.* Edited by B.N. Sastri. Benares: Princess of Wales Saraswati Bhavana Texts no. 38.

_____ (1951). *Pratyakṣamaṇidīdhiti (prāmāṇyavāda)*, with Gadādhara's *Ṭippaṇī.* Edited by R.N. Sukla. Banares: Sarada Library.

_____ (1979). *Ākhyātavāda*, with Rāmabhadra's *Ākhyātavādavyākhyā.* Edited by P.K. Sen. Calcutta: Sanskrit Pustak Bhandar.

Raja, K.K. (1963). *Indian Theories of Meaning.* Madras: The Adyar Library.

Ramachandran, M. (1993). 'A Strawsonian Objection to Russell's Theory of Descriptions', *Analysis*, 53.4.

Rāṛhī, K. (1891). *Navadvīpa-mahimā*. Calcutta.

Reid, T. (1983). *Inquiry and Essays*, (eds) R.E. Beanblossom and K. Lehrer. Indianapolis: Hackett.

Richard, M. (1988). 'Direct Reference and Ascriptions of Belief', in N. Salmon and S. Soames (eds), *Propositions and Attitudes*. Oxford: Oxford University Press.

_____ (1990). *Propositional Attitudes: An Essay on Thoughts and How We Ascribe Them*. Cambridge: Cambridge University Press.

Ruben, D-H. (1993). 'Introduction' to D-H Ruben (ed.), *Explanation*. Oxford: Oxford University Press.

Russell, B. (1905). 'On Denoting', *Mind*, 14, pp. 479–93.

Russell, B. (1912). *The Problems of Philosophy*. Oxford: Oxford University Press.

_____ (1956). 'The Philosophy of Logical Atomism', in R. Marsh (ed.), *Logic and Knowledge*. New York: Capricorn Books.

Saha, S. (1991). *Meaning, Truth and Predication: A Reconstruction of Nyāya Semantics*. Jadavpur Studies in Philosophy, 2nd Series. Calcutta: K.P. Bagchi & Co.

Sainsbury, M. (1979). *Russell*. London: Routledge and Kegan Paul.

Salmon, N. (1986). *Frege's Puzzle*. Cambridge, Mass.: M.I.T. Press.

_____ (1988). 'Reflexivity', in N. Salmon and S. Soames (eds), *Propositions and Attitudes*. Oxford: Oxford University Press.

Śaṅkara Miśra (1917). *Praśastapādabhāṣyaṭīkāsaṃgraha*, including Śaṅkara Miśra's *Kaṇāḍarahasyam*. Edited by V.P. Dvivedin. Benares: Chowkhamba Sanskrit Series 231 and 255.

Śāntarakṣita (1937), The *Tattvasaṃgraha of Shāntarakṣita, with the Commentary of Kamalashīla*, tranlated by G. Jha. Baroda: Gaekwad Oriental Series, no. 80.

_____ (1968). *Tattvasaṃgraha*, with Kamalaśīla's *Pañjikā*. Edited by S.D. Shastri. Varanasi: Bauddha Bharati.

Sartwell, C. (1991). 'Knowledge is Merely True Belief', *American Philosophical Quarterly*, 28, pp. 157–65.

_____ (1992). 'Why Knowledge is Merely True Belief', *Journal of Philosophy* 89, pp. 167–80.

Scharf, P. (1990). 'The Denotation of Generic Terms in Ancient Indian Grammar, Nyāya and Mīmāṃsā'. Philadelphia: University of Pennsylvania Ph.D. Dissertation.

Scharfe, H. (1961). *Die Logik im Mahābhāṣya*. Deutsche Akademie der Wissenschaften zu Berlin Institut für Orientforschung, Veröffentlichung nr. 50. Berlin: Akademie-Verlag.

Schayer, S. (1933). 'Studien zur Indischen Logik II', in M. Mejor (ed.), *On Philosophizing of the Hindus: Selected Papers of Stanislaw Schayer.* Warsaw: Polish Scientific Publishers (1988). English translation by Joerg Tuske (unpublished).

Schiffer, S. (1978). 'The Basis of Reference', *Erkenntis*, 13, pp. 171–206.

_____ (1987). *Remnants of Meaning.* Cambridge, Mass.: MIT Press.

Segal, G. (1989). 'A Preference for Sense and Reference', *Journal of Philosophy*, 86, pp. 73–89.

Shaw, J.L. (1974). 'Empty Terms: The Nyāya and the Buddhists', *Journal of Indian Philosophy*, 2, pp. 332–43.

Siderits, M. (1991). *Indian Philosophy of Language.* Dordrecht: Kluwer Academic Publishers.

Soames, S. (1988). 'Substitutivity', in J. Thomson (ed.), *On Being and Saying: Essays for Richard Cartwright.* Cambridge, Mass.: MIT Press.

_____ (1989a). 'Review of G. Evans, Collected Papers', *Journal of Philosophy*, 89, pp. 141–56.

_____ (1989b). 'Pronouns and Propositional Attitudes', *Proceedings of the Aristotelian Society*, 1989–90.

Sosa, E. (1991). *Knowledge in Perspective: Collected Essays in Epistemology.* Cambridge: Cambridge University Press.

Speijer, J.S. (1886). *Sanskrit Syntax.* Leiden: E.J. Brill.

Staal, F. (1965). 'Reification, Quotation and Nominalization', in A-T. Tymieniecka (ed.), *Contributions to Logic and Methodology in Honor of J.M. Bocheński.* Amsterdam: North-Holland.

_____ (1966). 'Indian Semantics 1', *Journal of the American Oriental Society*, 86, pp. 304–11.

_____ (1988). *Universals: Studies in Indian Logic and Linguistics.* Chicago: The University of Chicago Press.

_____ (1995a). 'Indian Theories of Meaning', in E.F.K. Koerner and R.E. Asher (eds), *Concise History of the Language Sciences: From the Sumerians to the Cognitivists.* Oxford: Pergamon, pp. 66–71.

_____ (1995b). 'The Sanskrit of Science', *Journal of Indian Philosophy*, 23, pp. 73–127.

Strawson, P. (1950). 'On Referring', *Mind*, 59, pp. 320–44.

_____ (1952). *Introduction to Logical Theory.* London: Methuen.

_____ (1959). *Individuals: An Essay in Descriptive Metaphysics.* London: Methuen.

_____ (1971). 'Meaning and Truth', in *Logico-Linguistic Papers.* London: Methuen.

_____ (1980). 'Reply to McDowell', in Z. van Straaten (ed.), *Philosophical Subjects: Essays Presented to P.F. Strawson.* Oxford: Clarendon Press.

Tachikawa, M. (1981). *The Structure of the World in Udayana's Realism.* Studies of Classical India, Vol. 4. Dordrecht: Kluwer Academic Publishers.

Taylor, B. (1980). 'Truth-Theory for Indexical Languages', in M. Platts (ed.), *Reference, Truth and Reality.* London: Routledge and Kegan Paul.

Tiwari, H. (Forthcoming). *From Form to Universal.* University of Oxford, D.Phil. Thesis, 1993. Delhi: Permanent Black.

Udayana (1911a). *Nyāyavārttika-tātparya-pariśuddhi*, with Vardhamāna's *Nyāya-nibandha-prakāśa.* Edited by V.P. Dvivedin and L.S. Dravida. Calcutta: Bibliotheca Indica, no. 192.

_____ (1911b). *Kiraṇāvalī*, with Vardhamāna's *Prakāśa* and Rucidatta Miśra's *Vivṛtti.* Edited by S. Sarvabhauma (Fasc. I–III) and N.C. Vedantatirtha (Fasc. IV, 1956). Calcutta: Bibliotheque Indica 190. Reprinted in 1989 by the Asiatic Society, Calcutta.

_____ (1967). *Nyāyavārtikka-tātparya-pariśuddhi*, in Gautama (1967).

_____ (1971). *Kiraṇāvalī*, in Praśastapāda (1971).

_____ (1986). *Ātmatattvaviveka*, with the commentaries of Śaṅkara Miśra, Bhagīratha Thakkura, and Raghunātha Śiromaṇi. Edited by V.P. Dvivedin and L.S. Dravida. Calcutta: Bibliotheca Indica, no. 170 (first published 1907–39).

Vardhamāna Upādhyāya (1911). *Kiraṇāvalī-prakāśa.* Edited by S. Sarvabhauma and N.C. Vedantatirtha. Calcutta: Bibliotheque Indica, p. 190.

_____ (1933 edn). *Kiraṇāvalī-prakāśa.* Ed. G. Kaviraja. Benares: Princess of Wales Saraswati Bhavana Texts no. 45.

Varma, S. (1926). 'Analysis of Meaning in Indian Semantics', *Journal of the Department of Letters*, 13, pp. 1–38.

Vattanky, J. (1995). *Nyāya Philosophy of Language.* Delhi: Sri Satguru Publications.

Vidyabhusana, S.C. (1920). *A History of Indian Logic.* Reprinted 1971. Delhi: Motilal Banarsidass.

Viśvabandhu Tarkatīrtha (1992). 'The Nyāya on the Meaning of Some Words', *Journal of Indian Philosophy*, 20.1, pp. 41–88.

_____ (1994). 'Proper Names and Individuals', in B.K. Matilal, and A. Chakrabarti (eds), *Knowing from Words: Western and Indian Philosophical Analysis of Understanding and Testimony.* Dodrecht: Kluwer. Translated from Bengali by B.K. Matilal.

Viśvanātha Tarkapañcānanda. (1988 edn). *Kārikāvalī and Muktāvalī*, with *Prabhā, Mañjūṣā, Dinakarī, Rāmarudrī* and *Gaṅgārāmī.* Edited by C.R. Shastri. Delhi: Chaukhamba Sanskrit Pratishthan.

Wiggins, D. (1975). 'Identity, Designation, Essentialism and Physicalism', *Philosophia*, v, pp. 1–30.

_____ (1993). 'Putnam's Doctrine of Natural Kind Words and Frege's Doctrines of Sense, Reference and Extension: Can They Cohere?', in A.W. Moore (ed.), *Meaning and Reference.* Oxford: Oxford University Press.

Williams, B. (1978). *Descartes: The Project of Pure Enquiry.* Harmondsworth: Penguin Books.

Wright, C. (1986). 'Theories of Meaning and Speakers' Knowledge', in *Realism, Meaning and Truth.* Oxford: Blackwell, pp. 204–38.

Wujastyk, D. (1993). *Meta rules of Pāṇinian Grammar: The Vyāḍīya-paribhāṣā-vṛtti.* Groningen: Egbert Forsten.

Index